dollars TO donuts

dollars to donuts

COMFORT FOOD & KITCHEN WISDOM FROM ROUTE 66'S LANDMARK ROCK CAFE

DAWN WELCH WITH RAQUEL PELZEL

PHOTOGRAPHS BY JOSEPH DE LEO

RODALE

I dedicate this book to my husband,

who loves me unconditionally and has stuck by my side

through the best and worst of times.

Rodale books may be purchased for business or promotional use
or for special sales. For information, please write to:

Special Markets Department, Rodale Inc., 733 Third Avenue, New York, NY 10017

Printed in the United States of America

Rodale Inc. makes every effort to use acid-free ⊗, recycled paper ♻.

Photographs by Joseph De Leo

Book design by GREYLING & CO.

Library of Congress Cataloging-in-Publication Data
Welch, Dawn.
    Dollars to donuts : comfort food and kitchen wisdom from Route 66's landmark Rock Cafe
/ Dawn Welch with Raquel Pelzel.
        p.   cm.
    Includes index.
    ISBN-13 978-1-60529-571-8 pbk.
    ISBN-10 1-60529-571-X pbk.
  1. Cookery, American. 2. Low budget cookery. 3. Rock Cafe (Stroud, Okla.)
I. Pelzel, Raquel. II. Title.
    TX715.W438 2009
    641.5—dc22   2009030849

Distributed to the trade by Macmillan

2 4 6 8 10 9 7 5 3 1 paperback

We inspire and enable people to improve their lives and the world around them
For more of our products visit **rodalestore.com** or call 800-848-4735

contents

preface: the rock and me

I grew up in the somewhat small town of Yukon, Oklahoma. As far back as I can remember, I had big dreams of working on a cruise ship and seeing the world. Soon after graduating from high school, I packed my bags and headed to Miami (where I didn't know a soul) and miraculously within one day landed a job working for a cruise ship line. I traveled for 4 years, visiting places near and far, from exotic Caribbean islands to fancy European cities, all the while experiencing a huge range of food and flavors as I dug in to dishes at every port of call.

During a trip home to visit my mom, fate intervened in the form of an inheritance from my grandmother, who left me 25 acres of Oklahoma property and a darn good reason to reconsider my nomadic existence. When I was given the opportunity to buy the Rock Cafe, a historic 25-seat restaurant on Route 66 in Stroud (just 1 hour west of my hometown), the chance was just too good to pass up. I thought, why not give it a go?

Considered by many to be a national treasure, the Rock was built by Roy Rieves, who began his passion project with an investment of $100 in 1936. Working mostly alone, he hand-built the Rock from the ground up, using giant sandstone rocks excavated during the construction of Route 66 as the façade for the restaurant's walls. The restaurant officially opened on July 4, 1939. Though Roy owned the restaurant, he didn't have any interest in running it himself, so he hired a number of local folks to manage and operate the Cafe. Over the years, it became a Greyhound bus depot, the spot where GIs would head off to battle during World War II, and the first place they stopped for a bite when they returned home.

Needless to say, a lot of history went down within those four walls before I got involved in the early 1990s (for more historical information about Stroud and the Rock, see page viii). I took over from owner Ed Smalley, who bought the Rock for sentimental reasons—not only did he work at the Rock when he was a boy, but he also left for war from the Cafe and fell in love with and married a Rock Cafe waitress. Ed couldn't bear to see the Rock torn down or mishandled, so he bought it and sat on it for a decade, opening it up for special occasions and Route 66 events.

Then I came along. When I took over the restaurant in 1993, I reopened it for 7-days-a-week service. That took a lot of gumption on my part, as I didn't know the first thing about cooking or running a restaurant, but my hard work and trial-by-error approach paid off. Lucky for me, my customers (not to mention my family) have always let me experiment on them with new dishes. It wasn't long before the locals and tourists were back. Although throughout the years I've made some changes from the original menu—we no longer smoke our barbecue, and we've added quiche and spaetzle to the menu—I like to think we've never strayed too far from the philosophy of good food, good service, and good prices.

Little did I know that running a restaurant on the Mother Road would introduce me to world-famous stars, which is exactly what happened when John Lasseter from Pixar wandered into the Rock while doing research for the animated film *Cars*. After chatting a while and hearing my life story, he decided to base the character of Sally Carrera on me! What a hoot.

Glitz and glamour aside, the Rock is really more than just a restaurant. It's a town hall, a community center, and a human refueling station all in one. Whether you're a superstar musician rolling through town on a tour bus (and we've had plenty of them), a tourist far away from home, one of a troop of 300 bikers crisscrossing the country, or just good friends from town, when you walk through the Rock's door, you're family. And I hope it's always like that.

You Can't Stop the Rock

To understand the spirit of the Rock, you've got to understand the spirit of Stroud. The town's story dips back to the turn of the 19th century, when the land was divided into two territories: Indian to the east (home to Sac and Fox tribes) and Oklahoma to the west. Realizing that cowboys and cattlemen needed a place to unwind, entrepreneur James Stroud opened a small establishment where he could sell whiskey and libations to the rabble-rousing bunch. Stroud founded the town in 1892, more saloons opened, and the town soon gained a reputation as a wild, hell-raising outpost. Soon after Oklahoma gained statehood in 1907, the town went dry and commercial enterprises turned from liquor and saloons to agriculture and oil.

In the late 1920s, big change would once again come to Stroud. It was known as Route 66, and it ran straight through town. Soon after it was finished, more than 200,000 down-and-out folks used it to escape the Great Depression, trading the Dust Bowl of the plains for opportunities in California. Of the thousands upon thousands who fled the heartland and came through Stroud, one man, Roy Rieves, decided to stay and to build a restaurant just on the outskirts of town. Of course it was none other than the Rock Cafe.

In 1936, Roy pulled together his retirement savings and used it to buy $6\frac{1}{2}$ business lots. He paid $5 for giant sandstone rocks excavated during the construction of 66, and over the course of 3 years nearly single-handedly built a restaurant using those rocks as the façade for the outer walls. He named the restaurant after the rocks, hired Thelma Holloway to run and manage it, and opened the doors on July 4, 1939.

Soon the Rock was selected to be a Greyhound bus stop, and during World War II, many GIs kissed their loved ones good-bye before heading off to fight the good fight. When they came back, a burger at the Rock was their first taste of home. In 1959, Mamie Mayfield took over, moved into the house next door, and decided to keep the restaurant open 24 hours a day. She ran the Rock for 25 years, and became a vital connection not just for townspeople and tourists, but also for the many truckers who would pull into the parking lot in the early-morning hours knowing that Mamie would collect messages from their wives and loved ones and pin them to a wall for them to see. In a time before voice mail and CBs, the Rock truly kept families linked.

Route 66 kept business strong for years, but Stroud soon found its fortune turned by another transportation route, the Turner Turnpike that connected Oklahoma City and Tulsa. The town was completely bypassed by the new highway, and the Rock's business dwindled. Mamie closed the restaurant in 1983. Along came Ed Smalley, who had loads of sentimental reasons for buying the Rock—he worked there as a kid, left for war from the Cafe, and even met his wife, a waitress, there. He couldn't stand the thought of the Rock falling into disrepair or, even worse, being torn down. Ed bought the Cafe and opened it for special occasions only. Then, in 1993, when I was in Oklahoma settling my grandmother's estate, I heard he was looking to sell, and, well, the rest is history!

introduction
getting it done, having fun, and saving money too!

Do you ever feel like a short-order cook in your own kitchen? Juggling pots and pans on the stove top while trying to keep an eye on the kids, answer the phone, set the table, and entertain a drop-in neighbor? Welcome to my life!

When I'm not multitasking breakfast, lunch, and dinner for my husband, Fred; my 15-year-old, Alexis; and my 8-year-old, Paul, I can usually be found at my restaurant, the Rock Cafe, a small family joint with a big reputation on Route 66 in Stroud, Oklahoma (population 2,500). I've owned the Rock for more than 15 years, and while we've seen our share of challenges—including a devastating fire that put us out of business for more than a year—I wouldn't be opening the doors every day at the crack of dawn to my family of regulars, day-trippers, and tourists if I didn't truly love it. The people, the action, and the challenge of keeping it fresh positively keep my engine revved.

You can only imagine what a devastating blow it was when the restaurant I worked so hard for nearly burned to the ground on May 20, 2008. All that remained were the Cafe's giant stone walls, which had been built from the rocks excavated to make way for Route 66 so many decades ago. I made a pledge to rebuild—not just for me and my family, but for all the people who consider the Rock their home away from home. One year and 9 days later, we once again threw open the doors, serving more than 1,000 people over the course of that opening weekend. It felt good to be back in the kitchen—and can you believe, the one thing from the kitchen I was able to salvage from the fire and lock into place for the reopening was the original 4-foot Wolf grill from the 1930s? I was ecstatic, and our regulars were over the moon, knowing that they could once again count on my chicken-fried steak, fried pickles, and peach crisp to satisfy their cravings for good home cooking. In fact, the governor proclaimed July 9 to be Rock Cafe Day forevermore—what an honor!

That year away from the Cafe really got me thinking. Whenever customers and friends told me how much they missed my cooking, part of me wanted to ask, "Why don't you just make it yourself, at home?" After all, the food we cooked up at the Rock was really just good home cooking, if not in the literal sense, certainly from a philosophical point of view. We didn't use a lot of fancy, hard-to-find ingredients, and the cooking equipment we relied on at the Cafe was not so far removed from what you'd have at home: just a flat grill, an oven, broiler, gas stove top, and a deep fryer. Moreover, to keep our prices modest (and yes, make a living—the restaurant is first and foremost the family business), we were extremely cost-conscious, avoiding waste whenever possible, using inexpensive ingredients, and giving leftovers a makeover to become entirely new meals later in the week. Pretty darn close, in fact, to the way I thought about food, costs, and efficiencies in my home kitchen.

That's how I got the idea for this cookbook. In *Dollars to Donuts,* besides a slew of my favorite recipes from home and the Rock, I'm sharing lots of kitchen know-how that I've picked up throughout 15 years of making comfort food favorites on a grand scale—ideas that I used to make cooking for my family simpler and more efficient and at the same time more varied and exciting. *Dollars to Donuts* is about cooking, for sure, but it's also about getting the most bang for your buck, feeding your family while having fun, and using time-saving strategies to maximize every minute you spend in the kitchen—and get you out of there quicker!

I take what I learn at the restaurant and apply it to my home cooking, so that my family's kitchen becomes my personal restaurant laboratory. When I make a discovery at home, you can count on seeing it on the Rock's menu! Keeping a playful can-do attitude in the kitchen makes recruiting helping hands all the more easy—now, I can't get my two kids to stay out of the kitchen when I'm cooking. They help out with the peeling, chopping, and sautéing, and in turn, I get to spend time with them, hear about their day, and share some food tips with them, too.

Gifting the kids with the craft of cooking gives me peace of mind that they'll know how to fend for themselves once they leave the nest. I'm passing all of the recipes in *Dollars to Donuts* not just to you, but to them, too. Many of these recipes were handed down to me by my mom, grandma, and even by customers, and I regard them as a legacy of sorts. This is the food we all hold close to our hearts, the comforting slow-roasted meat dishes, the hearty stews, the satisfying sandwiches—it's the stuff we grew up on, whether cooked by our moms and grandmas, aunts, neighbors, friends, or neighborhood bistro. This is why people love the Rock. They can count on it, lean on it, and know that there will always be something on the menu that brings them home. Food is for sharing, after all. It's a common thread that connects us no matter where we're from or what our food budget is.

Even though it's harder than ever to make ends meet, when you're clever and resourceful in the kitchen, it's not all that difficult to cook great meals for your family without sacrificing the foods you all love. By following my tried-and-true cooking and saving strategies and mixing and matching recipes to create a food plan that fits your family's preferences and budget, I promise you that you'll eat better, even if you're feeling the pinch. My mom always said to "get what you want with what you've got." It's a simple philosophy that I follow, and dollars to donuts, I know it'll work for you, too.

Dishing up the same-old same-old stretch-it-on-a-shoestring ground beef and pasta dishes is no fun, and honestly, there's just no way I could survive without a thick and juicy steak every once in a while! My family digs into lots of special meals, such as paella with shrimp and clams, and even strip steak dinners, and I still manage to keep my food costs in check. I've learned how to incorporate these "special occasion" foods into our weekly menus without blowing my budget, and in this book, through my recipes for real-deal meals, secrets, tips, and tricks for saving money and time, you will, too.

I love how my life and the Rock's have come together as one,

and how I can easily jump from being a mom packing lunches and watching track meets to being a restaurant owner, grill cook, and host. I open the Cafe's doors at 6:00 a.m., I cook breakfast for the regulars, I pick my kids up from school, I go to the Friday night games. *Dollars to Donuts* is not about just clipping coupons and getting any old dinner on the table, or hitting some arbitrary cost-per-serving target that puts taste and enjoyment a distant second behind economy. It's a philosophy of cooking and living where you can get it done and still have fun, all without breaking the bank. It's how to get the biggest bang for your buck so you can spend less time fretting and more time enjoying what really matters in life—friends, family, and of course, great food!

Strategize, Economize, Organize

I'm not a professionally trained chef—far from it! I learned on the job, and had fun doing it, and my attitude is that there's absolutely no reason why cooking at home can't be as much fun (or more) as eating out. It just takes a little bit of planning and forethought. The guidelines in *Dollars to Donuts* are rules I live by. I always use what I have, buy what's on sale, cook and shop in bulk, and have go-to standbys in the freezer. I love experimenting with new flavors and ideas.

Over the years I've challenged myself to come up with a system for cooking and grocery shopping that feels more like a game than a chore. Use one or all of the strategies in *Dollars to Donuts,* and you'll always be two steps ahead, whether you're cooking for yourself, your family, or an army.

SHOP. Start by shaking up your shopping routine, hitting different types of stores for different needs. Sometimes I'll hit the warehouse store to stock up on roasts and big cuts of meat, or a giganto bag of rice. Other times I'm at my local mom-and-pop taking advantage of weekly specials or snapping up cheap, seasonal produce at the local farmstand. It's a lot less boring than pushing my cart down the same old aisles week after week, and it guarantees that what ends up on my table is a lot more varied, too.

COOK. Step 2 is to reevaluate your approach to cooking. When you open yourself up to new flavors, ingredients, techniques, and preparations, you'll save money on grocery bills while still eating everything you want. I give in to my cravings, from a meaty slab of barbecued ribs to Pad Thai. I just do it with my menu plan in mind (see page 264 for a sample 2-week menu maker). So instead of denying myself a nice, thick strip steak, I'll plan for it by cushioning the price of a steak dinner with other, less-expensive meals during the week.

ORGANIZE. Step 3 is getting organized and staying organized. I have some simple solutions for that—they're so easy that you'll wonder why you never thought of them yourself. By putting your kitchen and supermarket to work for you, you can downsize your weekly food expenses without changing what you eat.

Think First, Cook Second

The easiest way to spend less on food is to think before you cook. I approach the grocery store with one major goal: to feed my family while beating the supermarket at their money game. Here's how:

1. Hit the pantry before you rev your engine.

It's amazing how much I save just by taking a quick peek in my pantry and fridge before heading to the store. Building meals around what you already have and what should be cooked or eaten before its pull date makes sense and saves money. Don't forget to check your freezer, too; frozen foods don't last indefinitely and should be used and rotated regularly.

2. Shop in bulk.

When I see a good deal, or better yet, a sale, you can bet that I'm going to stock up! Warehouse stores offer great deals on bulk-packed items, as do regular grocery stores and even natural food and health food stores. The latter have fantastic prices on items such as grains and beans, so shop 'em all.

3. Cook big.

I often cook a pork shoulder or roast a turkey for dinner and then freeze the leftovers for another day. From big batches of sauces to a meatball mixture that becomes burgers, kebabs, and meatloaf, cooking in bulk saves money and time.

4. Have some switch-hitters in your lineup.

Knowing when you can use a substitute and having a mental list of alternatives makes good common sense. It allows you to take advantage of deals and sales, or to opt out of buying an item on your shopping list if it turns out to be overpriced. (See the opposite page for a list of common substitutes.) And keep in mind that it is often possible to simply omit an ingredient if you can't find it or it is simply too costly.

5. Learn to love your leftovers.

I am constantly reinventing my leftovers and turning them into snacks, lunches, or completely new dishes altogether. Leftover roasted vegetables, rice, meat, beans, and even soup can be rehashed in countless ways to create new meals from what you already have in the fridge.

6. Don't cut out, cut back.

There are few things I enjoy more than a thick, juicy steak. Instead of shelling out big bucks on a pricey porterhouse, I turn to cheaper cuts, such as flank steak, which is incredibly flavorful and satisfying. I also stretch a pound of steak to feed many people by serving it wrapped in lettuce leaves or tortillas, or as an open-faced sandwich. If nothing else will do except for a big, juicy steak (page 120), then I'll budget it in, and plan less-luxe meals for the rest of the week.

7. Try new things.

Opening up your world to new recipes and flavors increases the options you have for dinner while making your kitchen a more exciting place to be. When you make cooking fun, it becomes an activity the whole family will enjoy from start to finish.

The Big O: Organization

No matter what you do for a living or how many people you cook for, we all have the same problem—there just aren't enough hours in the day to get it all done. That's why organization is absolutely critical. I usually plan out a week's worth of menus and synchronize the family's busy schedules with what I plan to cook for dinner. I keep shopping lists with the essentials already typed in, so all I have to do is check off what I need. If you follow the tips and suggestions throughout this book (look for the boxes marked D2D), you can get organized, too.

Using Dollars to Donuts

Just as every day at the restaurant brings a new challenge, so does every dinnertime at my house. That's why I've organized this book around some of my favorite cooking strategies, refined over the years to help keep the chaos at bay and to reduce the stress around mealtimes. Have a little extra time and want to get a jump on next week's (or next month's) meals? Go to the Big Bang Relay, and cook up a big ham or some roast chickens to transform into two, three, even four more meals down the line. Staring at a package of pork chops and feeling stumped? Check out Say Good-Bye to the Same Old for plenty of inspiration for giving new life to old favorites. Unexpected guests? The Doorbell Dash will give you some easy ideas for channeling your inner hostess with the mostest. From low-stress desserts that look like a million to fun ways to get the flavors of pricey restaurants onto your table for a fraction of the cost, you'll find a bunch of recipes that solve just about any cooking dilemma you're facing with style and, of course, smarts.

Be sure to look throughout the book for my D2D tips, with hints and advice gleaned from my experiences as the head cook (and occasional bottle washer) at my cafe as well as on-the-job training as a mom. They'll help you make better choices at the market, save time and money on weekly meals, and help you get in and out of the kitchen with a smile on your face.

To help you stay organized, you'll find a pantry start-up list on page 151 with everything you need to get your pantry going (photocopy this page and use it as a grocery list for when you run low on pantry items!). There are also meal planners that offer ideas on how to assemble 2 weeks' worth of menus that won't break the bank, and a sample shopping list to help you shop with an eye toward saving money and time. And because I know you're a smart cookie like me and want to watch the bottom line, every recipe indicates the cost per serving, so you can fit the meal to your budget.

I have a crazy life just like you, and I wouldn't trade it for the world. These tips and tricks work for me, and dollars to donuts, they'll work for you, too.

Be Armed with Options

It's smart to have substitutions in mind when you're shopping for meat in case your market is fresh out of something you need, or has it priced at more than what you're willing to pay. Here are some common ones. Photocopy it and keep it in your wallet so it's always handy.

INSTEAD OF	TRY
Filet mignon	Sirloin steak
Sirloin steak	Flank steak (or London broil)
Lamb chops	Pork chops
Pork cutlets	Pork chops (or buy a whole pork loin and cut it yourself into cutlets)
Boneless, skinless chicken breasts	Bone-in chicken breasts, bone-in or boneless thighs, legs (or buy a whole chicken and cut it up yourself), or turkey breast
Chicken cutlets	Boneless turkey breast (cut it up yourself into cutlets)
Chicken parts for broth	Necks, backbones, wings, and turkey wings
Halibut	Cod or salmon
Cod	Haddock, hake, scrod, tilapia
Flounder or snapper	Tilapia or catfish
Salmon	Arctic char, tuna steaks
Large or jumbo shrimp	Medium shrimp, clams, mussels, or monkfish
Lobster or crab	Shrimp or monkfish

How We Got Our Prices

We used consumer price averages from the Department of Labor along with average supermarket prices from across the country to come up with the ingredient costs for each recipe. Your store might offer some items for less or more, but overall, your per recipe cost should come out about the same as ours. We did not use bulk warehouse prices for any ingredients, so if you shop at a big box store, prepare to save even more!

A Note About the Icons in This Book

Many of the recipes in the pages that follow feature one or more icons in a box at the top of the page.

 Indicates a recipe that can be made ahead of time

 Appears by recipes that are especially kid-friendly

 Points out recipes that are super quick and easy to make

 Is for recipes that are good candidates for freezing

the big bang relay

Cooking and shopping in bulk saves money, period, end of story. That's why when I see a deal on a pork shoulder or family packs of ground beef, I pounce, knowing that the $10 or $15 I'm investing today is going to give me three or four meals down the pike.

Cooking big today, whether it's a slow-roasted pork shoulder or a baked ham, means I've already cooked (and paid for) my main-dish protein for another day. When I serve up Chicken and Dumplings (page 6) or Chicken Udon Soup (page 11)—both of which are the delectable spin-offs of an original roast chicken meal—I get the rush of feeling I've gotten something for nothing. Having some cooked meat or a prepped dish stashed away in the freezer is really like finding a hidden treasure.

These main courses offer up brand-new meals to serve

later in the week or stash in the freezer. Cook the Big Bang on day 1, then relay the leftovers into a whole series of main-dish spin-offs. Having an extra freezer in the house comes in handy for this kind of cooking, not just for stashing the leftovers, but also for stocking up when good deals hit your markets on turkeys or roasts (see page 137 for more information on buying a chest or standing freezer). This brings us back to the "free meals a day" concept. Whether you're storing an uncooked roast, portioned cooked meat, or a completely prepped dish, you will already have covered the bulk of that meal's cost. Just add a few veggies, herbs, or sides and you have a real meal deal.

THE BIG BANG	THE RELAY
Rosemary and Thyme Roasted Chickens	Chicken and Dumplings Almond Chicken Salad Cheesy Baked Chicken Enchiladas Chicken Udon Soup
Baked Honey-Glazed Ham	Chef's Pasta Salad Ham and Provolone Melts Ham and Black Bean Soup
Roast Pork Shoulder	Pulled Pork Sandwiches Pork, Currant, and Pine Nut Ragout over Fettuccine Roast Pork, Beans, and Bangers
Meatball Evolution	Spicy Glazed Meatloaf Mozzarella-Stuffed Burgers Middle Eastern Kebabs
Not-Just-For-Thanksgiving Turkey	Turkey Pot Pie with Cheddar Streusel Turkey Tortilla Soup Turkey and Sausage Strata

Rosemary & Thyme Roasted Chickens

THE
BIG
BANG

SERVES 8

$15.75/
$1.95

I love fresh herbs and use them liberally both at home and at the Rock, where they grow in great clumps all around the Cafe. After the building burned down in 2008, I was in shock; the day after, I stood staring at the burning wreckage for hours. What brought me around was the sight of neighbors and friends digging up the herb plants and taking them home to their own gardens for safekeeping until the restaurant could be rebuilt. Now that we've reopened, I once again have a thriving supply of herbs growing around the Cafe to use in dishes such as this fragrant, simple roast chicken. They're the basis of so many great family meals that I usually roast a couple of chickens at the beginning of every week, serving one and saving the other.

MAKE THE SALT RUB. Pulse the salt, garlic, rosemary, pepper, thyme, and oregano together in a food processor, or chop together on a cutting board until the salt is flecked with green bits and it is very fragrant; set aside.

SEASON THE CHICKENS. Heat the oven to 375°F. Pat the birds dry, inside and out, with paper towels. Tuck the wings behind the birds (it should look as if they were putting their hands behind their heads). Divide the onion, rosemary sprigs, and thyme sprigs between the 2 birds and tuck them into the cavities. Slide 1 tablespoon of butter (if using) under the skin of each breast. Tie the legs together with kitchen string, then season each bird with 2 tablespoons of the herbed salt.

ROAST AND CARVE THE CHICKENS. Grease a roasting rack with some canola oil. Place the chickens breast-side down on the rack in a roasting pan, or over a foil-lined, rimmed baking sheet. Roast for 30 minutes, then turn the chickens breast-side up, add 1 cup of water to the roasting pan (or ½ cup if using a rimmed baking sheet), and roast until an instant-read thermometer inserted into the thickest part of the thigh joint reads 170°F, about 1¼ to 1½ hours. Remove the pan

SALT RUB

- ¼ cup kosher salt
- 2 garlic cloves, finely minced or pressed through a garlic press
- 1 tablespoon finely chopped fresh rosemary
- 2 teaspoons freshly ground black pepper
- 1 teaspoon finely chopped fresh thyme
- ½ teaspoon dried oregano (or 1 teaspoon fresh oregano)

CHICKENS

- 2 whole chickens (3–4 pounds each)
- 1 large yellow onion, quartered
- 6 sprigs fresh rosemary
- 4 sprigs fresh thyme
- 4 tablespoons unsalted butter (optional)
  Canola oil

(continues...)

from the oven and let the chickens rest for 5 minutes before carving and serving. If you're saving 1 chicken to use in the recipes on pages 6 through 11, then let the chicken cool completely before removing the meat from the bone. Place the meat in quart-size, resealable bags and refrigerate for up to 3 days or freeze for up to 3 months.

MAKE IT A MEAL
+ Pilaf with Almonds and Golden Raisins (page 153)

Fresh or Dried Herbs?

In the summer and autumn, I have fresh herbs in abundance because they're growing on my windowsill and in my garden. With a quick snip-snip, their fresh flavor is mine for the taking. In the winter, I use mostly dried herbs. There's no shame in it—just halve the quantity called for in the recipe (so if a recipe calls for 1 teaspoon of fresh thyme, use ½ teaspoon of dried) and make sure to go through your dried herbs every fall. Weed out the old herbs and replace them with a new crop—of dried herbs, that is. Of course, you can dry your own fresh herbs, too. Just gather a bunch (still on the stem), tie them together with twine at their base, and hang them upside down in a dark, cool spot until they're dry. Crumble the leaves off of the sprigs and store them in bottles or airtight containers.

SERVES 6

$7.80/
$3.95

Chicken & Dumplings

I'm not one to get sucked into marketing lingo—I look for the best deal and use that to make my shopping decision. Sometimes, though, those marketing geniuses come up with a great idea—take baby carrots. Okay, sure, they're not really "baby" carrots; most often they're big whoppers that are trimmed down to mini size by machine. That aside, they're already peeled, cleaned, and cut. What a time-saver! It often doesn't cost me more than maybe a 20-cent difference to go for the cute little guys. I've got to say that sometimes the time I save in the kitchen is just as valuable (or more!) as money. I like my dumplings on the hearty side; if you're a fan of fluffy dumplings, add the extra teaspoon of baking powder.

CHICKEN

- 2 tablespoons unsalted butter
- ½ pound baby carrots
- 1 yellow onion, finely chopped
- 3 celery stalks, ends trimmed and thinly sliced
- 2 garlic cloves, thinly sliced
- ½ teaspoon salt
- ½ teaspoon freshly ground black pepper
- 3 cups chicken broth, homemade (page 36) or store-bought
- 1 bay leaf
  About 2 cups bite-size pieces roasted chicken

DUMPLINGS

- 2 cups all-purpose flour
- 1–2 teaspoons baking powder
- ½ teaspoon salt
- 1 large egg
- ½ cup whole or low-fat milk
- ¼ cup low-sodium chicken broth

SIMMER THE VEGETABLES. Melt the butter in a large pot or Dutch oven over medium-high heat. Add the carrots, onion, celery, garlic, salt, and pepper, and cook until soft and just starting to brown, 5 to 8 minutes, stirring often. Pour in the chicken broth, add the bay leaf, bring to a boil, and then reduce the heat to medium-low and simmer until the carrots are nearly tender, about 10 minutes.

MAKE THE DUMPLINGS. While the vegetables cook, make the dumplings. Whisk the flour, baking powder (1 teaspoon if you like firm dumplings, 2 teaspoons if you like them fluffy), and salt together in a medium bowl. Whisk the egg, milk, and chicken broth together in a small bowl or liquid measuring cup. Slowly pour the liquid into the flour mixture, stirring with a large spoon to combine, until no dry spots remain and the dough forms a ball.

COOK THE CHICKEN AND DUMPLINGS. Stir the chicken into the vegetables. Spoon about twelve 2" mounds of the dumpling mixture on top of the chicken and bring back to a boil. Cover, reduce the heat to medium-low, and cook until the dumplings are firm, 10 to 12 minutes. Remove the bay leaf. Ladle into bowls and serve immediately.

Almond Chicken Salad with Honey-Mustard Dressing

I like the twang of flavor that olives add to this salad. I use mild, canned, sliced black olives, but if you're a real olive connoisseur, then go for the fancy oil-cured ones (they're pricier, but if you love olives, they're probably worth it to you).

PREPARE THE CHICKEN. Heat the olive oil in a large skillet over medium-high heat. Add the chicken, salt, and pepper and cook until the chicken is warmed through, 2 to 4 minutes. Turn off the heat, stir in the honey, and set aside.

ASSEMBLE THE SALAD. Place the lettuces, tomato, and olives in a large bowl and toss together to combine. Add the dressing and gently toss again. Scatter the chicken, croutons, Parmesan, and almonds on top and serve. You can also plate the salad individually, in which case just divide the dressed salad among 4 plates and top each with some of the chicken, croutons, Parmesan, and almonds.

- 1 tablespoon olive oil
- About 3 cups shredded cooked chicken (page 3)
- ¾ teaspoon salt
- ¼ teaspoon freshly ground black pepper
- 1 tablespoon honey
- 1 head Bibb, Boston, or butterleaf lettuce, leaves separated and roughly chopped
- 1 head romaine lettuce, leaves separated and roughly chopped
- 1 ripe tomato, cored, halved, and finely diced
- ¼ cup finely chopped pitted black olives (preferably cured olives)
- ⅔ cup honey-mustard dressing, homemade (page 180) or store-bought
- ¼ cup croutons
- ¼ cup finely grated Parmesan cheese
- 3 tablespoons sliced almonds

D2D

I remove rubber bands and twist-ties from leafy greens such as lettuce or spinach before bagging them in the market. The ties and rubber bands often bruise and tear the outer leaves, causing them to wilt and rot quickly. By getting rid of the tie, you'll be able to use all of the greens without wasting any leaves.

Cheesy Baked Chicken Enchiladas

I never, ever order enchiladas in restaurants anymore, and neither will you once you've tried making them yourself. First, they're super simple. Second, they're really inexpensive. Third, they taste like a happy explosion of fresh, bright flavors that leave you feeling good, not heavy, after eating. For a quick take on this recipe, make quesadillas with the shredded chicken and cheese and serve with the sauce on the side for dipping.

About 2¼ cups shredded cooked chicken (page 3)

1 small red or white onion, finely chopped

1 jalapeño chile pepper, seeded and ribbed for a milder flavor, finely chopped (optional)

1 cup finely chopped fresh cilantro

3 cups No-Cook Garden Vegetable Sauce (page 58) or your favorite salsa

1 tablespoon fresh lime juice

½ teaspoon salt

¼ teaspoon freshly ground black pepper

8 (8") flour or whole-wheat tortillas

2 cups (8 ounces) grated Cheddar and/or Monterey Jack cheese

Sour cream, for serving

MAKE THE FILLING. Heat the oven to 400°F. Place the chicken in a large bowl and gently mix with the onion, jalapeño (if using), all but 2 tablespoons of the cilantro, ½ cup of the vegetable sauce, the lime juice, salt, and pepper.

ROLL AND BAKE THE ENCHILADAS. Evenly spread ½ cup of the vegetable sauce over the bottom of a 13" x 9" baking dish. Place the tortillas on your work surface and divide the filling among them, arranging it in a strip down the center of each tortilla. Roll the tortillas around the filling and place the filled tortillas seam-side down in the baking dish. Cover with the remaining 2 cups of sauce. Sprinkle evenly with the cheese. Bake the enchiladas until the sauce is golden brown and bubbling, 20 to 30 minutes. Sprinkle with the remaining cilantro and serve hot with sour cream on the side.

 D2D

Ask your deli counter person if they sell cheese ends. These are the heels of the giant cheese logs they get for slicing, and they are often sold for considerably less than sliced cheese. You can slice them when you get home, or grate them and freeze for another time.

 D2D

In this recipe, and in the recipes on pages 6, 7, and 11, you can use a rotisserie chicken in place of leftover roasted chicken.

Chicken Udon Soup

This take on chicken soup is just as satisfying as traditional chicken soup, with a nice twist from the addition of Asian flavorings and ingredients. At the Rock, we get visitors from all corners of the world. Japanese diners go crazy when they see homemade udon soup on a restaurant menu right smack-dab in the middle of Oklahoma, but the locals are pretty sweet on it, too.

COOK THE NOODLES. Bring a large pot of salted water to a boil. Add the udon noodles and boil according to the package instructions. Drain well and divide among 4 soup bowls.

MAKE THE BROTH AND SERVE. While the pasta cooks, place a medium saucepan over medium-high heat. Add the oil and garlic and cook until fragrant, about 30 seconds. Pour in the chicken broth and add the chicken, mushrooms, soy sauce, and pepper, and bring to a boil. Lower the heat to medium and simmer the soup until the chicken is heated through, about 5 minutes. Pour the soup over the noodles and sprinkle with the scallions and the bean sprouts. Serve hot.

1 package (14 ounces) udon noodles (substitute spaghetti or bucatini in a pinch)

1 tablespoon toasted sesame oil

4 garlic cloves, finely minced or pressed through a garlic press

6 cups chicken broth, homemade (page 36) or store-bought

About 2 cups shredded cooked chicken

About 1 cup sliced fresh shiitake mushrooms, stems removed

¼ cup soy sauce

¼ teaspoon white or freshly ground black pepper

3 scallions, white and green parts, trimmed and sliced thinly on the diagonal

1 cup bean sprouts

MAKE IT A MEAL
Stretch 1 leftover bowl of soup into a meal for 4 by adding a few cups of stir-fried vegetables (tossed with garlic, ginger, and soy sauce for flavor) and more boiled noodles.

Baked Honey-Glazed Ham

THE
BIG
BANG

SERVES 8
$19.00/
$2.40

Ham is a crowd-pleaser, delicious, and a great value, so why save it for holidays? I like to bake one for a midweek dinner and use the leftovers for all kinds of dishes to serve throughout the weekend. Keep your eyes peeled for ham on sale, buy a few, and freeze them—they'll keep for up to a year. I prefer bone-in hams with a little bit of fat still on them, but this recipe will work with any kind of large, cooked ham.

SCORE AND BAKE THE HAM. Heat the oven to 325°F. Place the ham on a cutting board fat-side up and make ¼"-deep diagonal cuts in 2" intervals to create a diamond pattern. Grease a roasting rack with a little oil and place the ham on the rack, fat-side up. Set the rack into a roasting pan and bake until the internal temperature of the ham registers 110°F on an instant-read thermometer, about 2 to 2½ hours.

GLAZE THE HAM. While the ham is baking, whisk together the honey, brown sugar, mustard, and fruit juice in a small bowl. Remove the ham from the oven and increase the temperature to 425°F. Stud the center of each diamond with a clove. Brush the entire ham with the glaze, pour ¾ cup of water into the bottom of the roasting pan, and place the pan back in the oven until its temperature reaches 125°F, about 15 minutes longer. Remove the pan from the oven, and transfer the ham to a cutting board. Tent the ham with foil and let it rest until its temperature reaches 135°F to 140°F, 20 to 30 minutes.

1   bone-in ham (7–9 pounds), fully cooked

    Canola oil

¾   cup honey

¾   cup light brown sugar

2   teaspoons dry mustard

1   tablespoon fruit juice, such as apple, cranberry, orange, or pomegranate

10–12   whole cloves

MAKE IT A MEAL
+ Spoon-Tender Green Beans with Bacon (page 196)

D2D
The best time to buy whole, cooked hams is either before or after the holidays—you are virtually guaranteed that they'll be on sale.

Chef's Pasta Salad

My kids always hang out with me in the kitchen, peeling and chopping vegetables and stirring roux. This pasta salad is one of their favorite recipes to make. It's perfect for young cooks because it's simple, totally delicious, and can be varied to their hearts' content just by adding whatever is in the fridge. Toss the pasta salad with the dressing, then give them free rein to raid the fridge and finish off the salad with whatever they think would be tasty additions.

SALAD

- 8 ounces farfalle (bow-tie) pasta
- 1 tablespoon extra-virgin olive oil
- About 1 cup diced ham
- 1 cup (about 4 ounces) shredded sharp Cheddar or Swiss cheese
- 1 large tomato, diced
- ¼ cup chopped fresh flat-leaf parsley
- 6 ounces salad greens
- 2 hard-cooked eggs, finely chopped
- Salt and freshly ground black pepper

VINAIGRETTE

- 2 tablespoons Dijon mustard
- 2 tablespoons cider vinegar
- 1 tablespoon light or dark brown sugar
- ½ teaspoon salt
- ½ cup extra-virgin olive oil

BOIL THE PASTA. Bring a large pot of salted water to a boil. Add the pasta and cook according to the package instructions or until it is al dente. Drain, transfer to a large bowl, and toss with 1 tablespoon of olive oil.

PREPARE THE VINAIGRETTE. While the pasta cooks, make the vinaigrette. Whisk the mustard, vinegar, sugar, and salt together in a large bowl. While whisking, slowly drizzle in the olive oil and set aside.

TOSS THE SALAD. Add the vinaigrette to the pasta and toss to coat. Add the ham, cheese, tomato, parsley, and greens and toss to incorporate. Transfer the pasta salad to a serving bowl, sprinkle the egg on top, season with salt and pepper, and serve.

D2D

Sometimes I wonder what people did before the Internet! The Web can be a great source for deals, especially when you're buying in bulk. If you're partial to a certain brand, whether it's tea, good-quality baking chocolate, or dried pasta, try finding it in bulk online. Even when you factor in shipping, the savings can be immense.

**$6.20/
$1.55**

Ham & Provolone Melts with Cranberry Relish

Between you and me, my ham leftovers rarely make it into soup or a salad because my family just gobbles them up in sandwiches. I slice leftover ham and freeze it in individual portions, so anyone can defrost some for a sandwich anytime. When you consider that sliced deli ham costs upwards of $7 per pound, and your whole ham cost $2.40 per pound, you'll feel really good about stacking a few slices on bread. This sandwich is a bit more work than your basic ham and Swiss, but it's so much tastier.

CRANBERRY RELISH

1 tablespoon olive oil

1 yellow onion, finely chopped

1 garlic clove, finely minced or pressed through a garlic press

½ teaspoon finely chopped fresh rosemary

½ teaspoon salt

¼ teaspoon freshly ground black pepper

¾ cup orange juice

1 cup dried cranberries

SANDWICHES

8 bread slices

¾ pound (about 12 slices) sliced deli ham or homemade baked ham (page 13)

4 slices provolone (or Swiss)

2 tablespoons unsalted butter

MAKE THE RELISH. Heat the olive oil in a small saucepan over medium-high heat. Add the onion, garlic, rosemary, salt, and pepper and cook, stirring often, until the onion is golden brown, 8 to 10 minutes. Pour in the orange juice and add the cranberries, bring to a simmer, cover, and lower the heat to medium-low. Simmer gently until the cranberries are plump and most of the juice has been absorbed, 10 to 12 minutes. Use an immersion blender or small food processor to pulse the cranberry mixture until it resembles jam, about 10 seconds.

 MAKE IT A MEAL
+ Simple Salad with Honey-Mustard Dressing (page 180)

ASSEMBLE THE SANDWICHES. Heat the oven to 250°F. Spread each slice of bread with 1 heaping tablespoon of the cranberry relish. Stack the ham on 4 slices, cover each with a piece of cheese, and top with another slice of bread.

COOK THE SANDWICHES. Melt 1 tablespoon of butter in a large, nonstick skillet over medium heat. Add 2 sandwiches to the pan and cook, covered, until the bread is golden brown and the cheese has melted, about 3 to 4 minutes per side. Place the sandwiches on a baking sheet and keep warm in the oven while you cook the remaining sandwiches. Slice in half and serve immediately.

 D2D
Store meat, poultry, and fish on the lowest shelf in your refrigerator toward the back of the cabinet to keep it at its freshest. That's where it's the coolest and where the temperature fluctuates the least.

Play It Again, Panini

What did we ever do before the panini? Well, for one thing, we called it a "melt"! I have a soft spot for these warm griddled sandwiches. You can easily make one if you have a nonstick skillet, a metal bowl, and something heavy (such as a 28-ounce can of tomatoes) to weigh the bowl down. Voila, a jury-rigged panini press!

Pretty much any leftover meat, from sliced chicken to crumbled meatballs, can be turned into a panini. Just add a melting component (you know, cheese), plus 1 or 2 additions for flavor and texture. Here are some of my favorite combos:

Ham + Cheddar + Red Onions + Apple Butter
Roast Chicken + Swiss + Tomatoes + Bacon
Meatloaf + Mozzarella + Pickles + Ketchup
Meatballs + Taleggio + Roasted Peppers
Roast Turkey + Stuffing + Jalapeño Jack + Cranberry Sauce
Roast Turkey + Havarti + Apples + Honey-Mustard
Roast Pork + Provolone + Pepperoncini
Roast Pork + Queso Oaxaca + Pickled Jalapeños + Chipotle Mayo + Cilantro

Ham & Black Bean Soup

If you have time, consider making this hearty soup with 1 pound of dried black beans instead of canned beans. Using the quick-boil method instead of soaking overnight (see page 158) will save a ton of time as well as the $2.50 you would have spent on 4 cans of beans. The soup amply feeds 4 for dinner, but if you're serving it as a first course, you can easily stretch it to 6 servings.

2   tablespoons olive oil

1   medium yellow onion, finely chopped

1   medium carrot, trimmed, peeled, and finely chopped

    About 2 cups diced ham

6   cups chicken broth, homemade (page 36) or store-bought

4   cans (15 ounces each) black beans, drained and rinsed

    Ham bone from the baked honey ham (page 13, optional)

1   teaspoon dried thyme

¾   teaspoon salt

¾   teaspoon freshly ground black pepper

MAKE THE SOUP BASE. Heat a large soup pot or Dutch oven over medium-high heat. Add the olive oil, onion, carrot, and ham and cook, stirring often, until the onion is soft and just starting to brown, 5 to 7 minutes.

SIMMER. Pour in the chicken broth and then add the beans, ham bone (if using), thyme, salt, and pepper and bring to a boil. Reduce the heat to low and gently simmer until the onion and carrot are soft and tender, about 20 minutes.

D2D
Stretch the last little bit of leftover soup by adding steamed white rice or boiled orzo to it for a nice, complete meal, perfect for 1 serving. Or add another can of rinsed black beans and spoon it over nachos or a hot dog as you would chili.

D2D
Once a month, try making a recipe you've never cooked before, preferably using a few ingredients you might not regularly use. Before you know it, you have a pantry stocked with interesting ingredients and a new repertoire of recipes to call on.

Roast Pork Shoulder with Salsa Verde

THE
BIG
BANG

SERVES 8

$13.20/
$1.65

At 99 cents a pound, pork shoulder is an absolute steal! It is so tender, juicy, and satisfying that I often get more pleasure out of eating slow-cooked pork than I do from a fancy, expensive steak. The 6 pounds you roast here can be turned into a ton of different recipes. One of my favorites it to just wrap some meat in a fresh-steamed tortilla with some sliced onions and salsa. Now that's a fabulous leftover. I used to smoke pork shoulders at the restaurant, but it took too long and the meat shrunk a lot in the process. Now I leave smoking to the barbecue joints and slow-roast the pork instead. It has since become one of my family's favorite meals.

MARINATE THE PORK. Use a paring knife to make ½"-deep slits all over the pork and insert a garlic sliver into each one. Place the onion, lime juice, orange juice, oregano, cumin, paprika, salt, and pepper in a large plastic bag (even a small garbage bag will work) and shake to combine. Add the pork, turn it over a few times in the marinade, knot the bag shut, and refrigerate for at least 24 hours or up to 2 days.

SLOW-ROAST THE PORK. Heat the oven to 400°F. Strain the pork, save the onion and seasonings, and discard the liquid. Place the pork, onion, and spices in a 13" x 9" baking dish. Cover with foil and bake for 1 hour. Reduce the oven temperature to 275°F and cook until the pork is tender and pulls apart effortlessly, an additional 2 to 2½ hours.

MAKE THE SALSA VERDE. Place the parsley, olive oil, lime juice, anchovies, garlic, sugar, red-pepper flakes, and ¼ teaspoon salt in a food processor and blend until smooth. Taste and add additional salt if necessary (the salsa verde can be made up to 5 days in advance; it can also be frozen to use at a later time).

PORK

- 1 pork shoulder (5–6 pounds)
- 3 garlic cloves, halved lengthwise and thinly sliced crosswise into slivers
- 1 large yellow onion, halved and thinly sliced
- 1 cup fresh lime juice (from 12–16 limes)
- 1 cup orange juice (preferably fresh, from 3–4 oranges)
- ¼ cup finely chopped fresh oregano
- 2 teaspoons ground cumin
- 2 teaspoons sweet paprika
- 1 tablespoon salt
- 1 teaspoon freshly ground black pepper

MAKE IT A MEAL
+ Straight-Up Cornbread (page 167)
+ Ranch-Style Beans (page 159)

(continues...)

SALSA VERDE

2 cups packed fresh flat-leaf parsley leaves

½ cup extra-virgin olive oil

Juice of 1 lime

4 anchovy fillets

2 garlic cloves, finely minced or pressed through a garlic press

1 tablespoon sugar

¼ teaspoon red-pepper flakes

¼–½ teaspoon salt

SHRED THE PORK. Heat the broiler to high. Transfer the pork to a rimmed baking sheet and use 2 forks to shred and pull the pork into long strands. (Save the pan juices for another use; I like to use them to make rice for a side dish.) Spread the shredded pork on the baking sheet, sprinkle with a little of the reserved cooking liquid, and broil until it gets a little crispy on top, about 10 minutes. Remove from the oven and serve with the salsa verde.

 SHOP SMART
A pork shoulder (from the front leg of a pig) is divided into 2 sections: the upper butt roast and the lower picnic roast. Both are great and inexpensive, though the butt roast (sometimes called a Boston butt) is often favored as the more tender and flavorful of the two.

Love Your Slow Cooker

If you've got a slow cooker collecting dust in a closet, now's the time to pull that baby out! Start it up in the morning with a big hunk of meat, and by suppertime you have a tender and delicious meal. The best slow-cooker cuts are the ones that need a long time in the oven to become tender. Usually, they're the same ones that cost just a few dollars a pound like beef brisket.

Shredded brisket makes excellent sandwiches and tacos, or it can be used in any of the pork shoulder spin-offs on pages 21 through 23. To make barbecued brisket, rub the meaty side of a 5-pound brisket with 1 tablespoon of Tex-Mex Rub (page 118) and ½ teaspoon of salt. Wrap in plastic wrap and refrigerate overnight. Place the brisket meat-side down in the slow cooker, pour 2 cups of homemade (page 21) or store-bought barbecue sauce over the top, and cook on low until it pulls apart easily, 9 to 10 hours. Shred the brisket or let it cool and slice it. Freeze what you don't serve in quart-size resealable freezer bags.

Pulled Pork Sandwiches with Homemade Barbecue Sauce

This sandwich is one of the Rock's most popular dishes. I used to order barbecue sauce from my food purveyor, but one day I ran out and just mixed up my own. It was so simple, and costs $1 to $2 less (depending on the brand) than buying a bottle at the store. The twinge of acid from soda pop or orange juice gives it just the right kick. Make a big batch and store it in 2-cup portions in the freezer.

MAKE THE BARBECUE SAUCE. Whisk together the ketchup, soda or orange juice, honey, liquid smoke or adobo sauce (if using), Worcestershire, and the Tex-Mex Rub in a medium saucepan over medium heat. Bring the mixture slowly to a boil, then reduce the heat to medium-low and simmer until slightly thickened, about 5 minutes, stirring occasionally. Stir in the pulled pork and cook until heated through, 3 to 5 minutes, stirring often.

FRY THE ONION AND TOAST THE BREAD. Heat the oil in a medium skillet over medium-high heat. Add the onion, salt, and pepper and cook, stirring often, until the onion is browned and soft, 5 to 7 minutes. Transfer the onion to a small bowl. Brush the cut sides of each roll with ½ tablespoon of butter and place them, split-side down, in the pan. Reduce the heat to medium and cook until toasted, 1 to 2 minutes. Repeat with the remaining rolls. Place each roll on a plate and top the bottom half with some meat. Cover with onion, cheese, and the top half of the roll, and serve.

BARBECUE SAUCE

- 2 cups ketchup
- ¼ cup cola or orange juice
- ¼ cup honey
- 2 teaspoons liquid smoke or adobo sauce from 1 can chipotle chiles (optional)
- 2 teaspoons Worcestershire
- ¼ cup Tex-Mex Rub (page 118)

PORK

- 5¼ cups shredded roast pork (page 19)
- 1 tablespoon canola oil
- 1 small yellow onion, chopped
- ⅓ teaspoon salt
- ¼ teaspoon freshly ground black pepper
- 4 kaiser rolls
- 2 tablespoons unsalted butter at room temperature
- ½ cup shredded Monterey Jack cheese

D2D
When you take your next road trip, be sure to stop at a country store, where you'll often find local honey at bargain prices. Buy the monster-big jar—honey lasts forever, and if it crystallizes, just place it in a bowl of hot water until the solid mass becomes pourable again.

MAKE IT A MEAL:
+ Cucumber Refrigerator Pickles (page 194)

Pork, Currant & Pine Nut Ragout over Fettuccine

This pasta dish is a great way to stretch less than 1 pound of meat into 4 servings, and is delicious with just about any kind of roast meat from lamb to turkey, chicken, and even brisket. Before draining the pasta, reserve ½ cup of the cooking water and set it aside. If the finished dish seems dry after tossing the ragout with the fettuccine, stir in some of the pasta water, taste, and add a little salt if needed.

1 tablespoon + ½ teaspoon salt

8 ounces fettuccine

2 tablespoons olive oil

1 yellow onion, finely chopped

1 garlic clove, finely minced or pressed through a garlic press

2 cups shredded roast pork (page 19)

1 cup canned diced tomatoes, with juice

¼ cup dry red wine

½ cup dried currants

½ cup toasted pine nuts

½ teaspoon dried thyme

½ teaspoon freshly ground black pepper

BOIL THE PASTA. Bring a large pot of water and 1 tablespoon of salt to a boil over high heat. Add the fettuccine and cook according to the package instructions until it is al dente. Drain, set aside, and place the pot back on the stovetop.

MAKE THE RAGOUT. Heat the oil in the pot over medium-high heat. Add the onion and cook until soft, stirring occasionally, about 5 minutes. Stir in the garlic and cook until fragrant, about 30 seconds. Add the pork, tomatoes, wine, currants, pine nuts, thyme, pepper, and ½ teaspoon salt. Bring to a simmer and cook until the currants are plump, about 10 minutes. Add the fettuccine, toss together, and serve.

 D2D

Nuts stay freshest when you keep them in the freezer. They keep well for up to 1 year if you wrap them well (sometimes you can get away with longer—just taste one before using them to make sure they haven't absorbed freezer flavors).

 COOK SMART

The ragout can be made several days ahead of time and even frozen in resealable quart-size freezer bags. Defrost, heat through, and add cooked fettuccine.

Roast Pork, Beans & Bangers

Franks and beans can evoke memories of the school cafeteria, which is a shame, because stripped down to its humble beginnings, it's a great, economical dish that feeds a crowd easily. This version is a little more upscale than the campfire classic, but like gussied-up meatloaf, it is reminiscent enough of the original for my kids to gobble it up like there's no tomorrow. It's great with crusty bread on the side.

HEAT THE OIL in a Dutch oven or large pot over medium-high heat. Add the onion and cook until it's soft, stirring often, about 5 minutes. Add the garlic and cook until fragrant, about 30 seconds. Add the sausage and pork and cook until slightly browned, about 5 minutes. Add the beans, orange juice, ketchup, mustard, cumin, sugar, and salt, and bring to a boil. Reduce the heat to medium-low and simmer until slightly thickened, about 15 minutes. Stir in the orange segments and serve.

 D2D
Buy canned beans in the ethnic food aisle of your grocery store, where they're often much less expensive.

- 1 tablespoon canola oil
- 1 yellow onion, diced
- 2 garlic cloves, finely minced or pressed through a garlic press
- ¾ pound "sear and serve" sausage, such as chicken sausage, andouille, or kielbasa, sliced ½" thick
- 2 cups shredded roast pork (page 19)
- 3 cans (15 ounces each) kidney, pinto, or cannellini beans, drained and rinsed (or 4½ cups cooked dried beans, see page 158)
- ½ cup orange juice
- ½ cup ketchup
- 2 teaspoons dry mustard
- 1 teaspoon ground cumin
- 1 tablespoon dark brown sugar
- ½ teaspoon salt
- 1 orange, peeled, segmented, and coarsely chopped

THE
BIG
BANG

SERVES 12

$16.25/
$1.35

Meatball Evolution

One day, as I was mixing up a batch of meatballs, I realized I basically had the makings of a meatloaf or kebabs right in front of me. Why not double (or even triple) the batch and have a head start on a couple more meals at the ready? I did just that, and have been using this shortcut ever since. You can use the entire recipe for meatballs and freeze half for another meal down the line. Also, if you prefer not to fry the meatballs, bake them at 400°F for 20 to 25 minutes. Half of this recipe will make 24 meatballs, serving 6; save the rest for one of the relay recipes.

1   cup dried bread crumbs

1   cup whole or low-fat milk

2   large eggs

1½ cups (about 6 ounces) finely grated Parmesan cheese

1   large yellow onion, finely chopped

¼   cup finely chopped flat-leaf parsley

4   garlic cloves, finely minced or pressed through a garlic press

2   teaspoons salt

1   teaspoon finely ground black pepper

3½ pounds ground beef (preferably 90% lean)

1   tablespoon olive oil

MAKE THE MEAT MIXTURE. Place the bread crumbs and milk in a small bowl, stir together, and set aside. Whisk the eggs and 1 cup of the Parmesan together in a large bowl. Stir in the onion, parsley, garlic, salt, and pepper and then add the beef and the breadcrumb mixture. Stir with a wooden spoon or your hands until the mixture is well combined. Use your hands to roll golf ball–size pieces into smooth balls.

COOK THE MEATBALLS. Heat the oil in a large, nonstick skillet over medium-high heat. Add enough meatballs to fill the pan without overcrowding and cook, covered, until browned on all sides, 10 to 12 minutes total. Transfer the meatballs to a paper towel–lined plate, sprinkle with some of the remaining Parmesan, and set aside. Repeat with the remaining meatballs. Stir the meatballs into sauce or serve as is, sprinkled with the remaining Parmesan.

MAKE IT A MEAL
+ Pasta with Spicy Arrabbiata-Basil Sauce (page 44)

D2D
Ground beef has a lot of flavor and stays nice and moist once cooked. To save a few cents per pound, grind your own the next time chuck roast is on sale. Leave most of the fat on, and either ask the butcher to grind it or grind it yourself if you have a meat grinder or an attachment for your stand mixer.

Spicy Glazed Meatloaf

I take pride in my meatloaf and serve it for family dinners and to dinner guests. Shaping a meatloaf free-form on a broiler pan allows it to get browned and crusty on the outside, a nice contrast to the tender, moist interior. To get my meatloaf to cook more quickly, I use a skewer or a long toothpick to poke holes through the loaf from top to bottom. This also helps the spicy honey glaze to seep into the interior.

GLAZE

- ½ cup ketchup
- 1 tablespoon honey
- 1 teaspoon–1 tablespoon hot sauce, to taste
- 1 teaspoon ground cumin
- ¼ teaspoon salt
- ¼ teaspoon finely ground black pepper

MEATLOAF

- ½ recipe meatball mixture (about 2½ pounds, page 24)
- 6 fresh sage leaves, chopped
- 3 bacon slices

MAKE IT A MEAL
+ Homestyle Smashed Potatoes with Dill (page 182)

D2D
Crumble leftover meatloaf and freeze it. Use later in lasagna, for tacos, a quick sloppy Joe, or in your favorite marinara sauce.

MAKE THE GLAZE. Whisk the ketchup, honey, hot sauce, Worcestershire, cumin, salt, and pepper together in a small bowl and set aside.

PREPARE THE BROILER PAN. Heat the oven to 350°F. Line a broiler pan top (the part with the open slits in it) with foil, using a paring knife to cut through the foil so the slits in the broiler top are visible (this allows the fat to drain off while the meatloaf cooks). Line the broiler pan bottom with foil and fit the top part onto the bottom.

MAKE THE MEATLOAF. Mix the meatball mixture and sage together until it's well combined (a stand mixer fitted with a paddle makes this a clean, quick, and easy job). Place the mixture onto the broiler pan top and form into a 9" x 5" loaf. Use the handle of a wooden spoon to poke a few holes into the meatloaf, going all the way through (this is so the fat can drain off and so the meatloaf cooks more quickly). Lay the bacon strips over the loaf lengthwise, tucking the ends under the loaf. Bake until the internal temperature of the loaf reads 155°F on an instant-read thermometer, about 1¼ hours.

GLAZE THE MEATLOAF. Remove the loaf from the oven and slather it with the glaze. Return the meatloaf to the oven and bake until the meatloaf is 165°F, about 10 more minutes. Remove from the oven and cool for a few minutes before slicing and serving.

Split a Steer

If you eat a lot of meat, have the freezer space, and want to save money and time shopping for beef, consider buying a steer. You can buy a whole steer, half of a steer, or a quarter of a steer—or cowpool with a group of friends, buy a cow, and then split it up (no fighting over the T-bones!). The savings can be significant, since the price per pound for all of the meat, from brisket to tenderloin, averages somewhere between $3 and $3.50.

This is an especially good option if you prefer your beef grass-fed. While most steers are raised on grain and corn, grass-fed cattle graze on grass—it's better for the cow and for the environment. Whether it tastes better is a matter of personal preference. Some say grass-fed beef has a stronger flavor and tougher texture. A way around this is to find a rancher who raises his cattle on grass, then finishes them on grain before slaughtering so you get the best of both worlds.

If you don't know where to go to buy a cow, your farmers' market is a great place to start—just ask around and see if anyone knows anyone. Another option is to call up the agriculture teachers at local schools and universities, or get in touch with 4-H clubs.

How much are you going to get? Well, the average steer provides around 500 to 600 pounds of meat. Split it between 4 friends and you're looking at a little more than 100 pounds of all kinds of cuts, such as shanks, flanks, rib eyes, ground beef, and yes, even offal (it would be a good idea to include friends who are not just fans of filet!). Oftentimes the rancher you buy it from either has a processing facility on-site or can refer you to a licensed one (my supermarket processes and wraps cuts for folks). Many ranchers will freeze, vacuum-seal, and label your meat, too. Do keep in mind that frozen beef should be consumed within 1 year.

Mozzarella-Stuffed Burgers with Arugula Pesto

Bite into this mild-mannered-looking burger and you'll get a cheesy surprise and the big flavors of garlicky arugula pesto. My burgers come off the same grill that has been at the Rock since it first opened 70 years ago (it was the only piece of the kitchen that was unharmed from the fire), and it has probably grilled about 2½ million burgers since then. I mean, off of that grill came burgers to feed our boys going off to World War II and coming home from 'Nam. It served the hungry during the Depression. When I think of all the people who have been comforted by the food coming off of that grill, it gives me perspective and makes me happy that I can keep the Rock and its amazing history alive.

MAKE THE PESTO. Place the Parmesan, arugula, pine nuts, olive oil, garlic, and pepper in a food processor and blend for 15 seconds. Stop and scrape the sides of the bowl, and process until the pesto is smooth, about 10 seconds more. Taste and add the salt if necessary.

STUFF THE BURGERS. Take ⅓ cup meat mixture and form it into a flat circle, about 4" in diameter. (Make the patty slightly larger or smaller depending on the width of your mozzarella cheese slice—the patty should be just slightly wider than the cheese slice.) Place a piece of cheese in the center and top with another ⅓ cup meat mixture, also flattened into a circle. Seal the edges shut and repeat with the remaining meat and cheese, until you have 6 filled hamburger patties.

COOK THE BURGERS. Heat the canola oil in a large, nonstick skillet over medium-high heat. Place the burgers in the pan (as many as will fit), cover, and cook until browned, about 3 to 6 minutes per side. Place each burger on the bottom half of a bun, top the burger with about 2 tablespoons pesto, cover with the bun top, and serve.

PESTO

- 1 cup (about 4 ounces) finely grated Parmesan cheese
- About 2 cups arugula
- ½ cup toasted pine nuts
- ¼ cup extra-virgin olive oil
- 4 garlic cloves, roughly chopped
- ½ teaspoon freshly ground black pepper
- ¼–½ teaspoon salt

BURGERS

- ½ recipe meatball mixture (about 2½ pounds, page 24)
- 6 slices fresh mozzarella cheese
- 2 teaspoons canola oil
- 6 hamburger buns, toasted

MAKE IT A MEAL
+ Spiced Sweet Potato Fries with Dijon Dip (page 184)

Middle Eastern Kebabs & Cucumber-Radish Salad

$13.60/ $1.70

Burgers go from ho-hum to fancy when you form the mixture around a skewer. This recipe is a great one for parties and entertaining—it offers that wow factor without you having to shell out big bucks on shrimp or filet. The kebabs are fantastic cooked on the grill, too.

SALAD

- 10 radishes, trimmed, washed, and thinly sliced
- 2 large cucumbers, washed and thinly sliced
- Juice of 1 lemon
- 3 tablespoons extra-virgin olive oil
- ¼ cup finely chopped fresh flat-leaf parsley
- 1 tablespoon chopped fresh mint (optional)
- ¼ teaspoon salt

KEBABS

- ½ recipe meatball mixture (about 2½ pounds, page 24)
- ¼ cup toasted pine nuts
- 1 tablespoon sugar
- 1 teaspoon ground cumin
- 1 teaspoon dried oregano
- ½ teaspoon ground allspice
- ¼ teaspoon ground cinnamon

MAKE IT A MEAL
Pilaf with Almonds and Golden Raisins (page 153)

MAKE THE SALAD. Place the radishes, cucumbers, lemon juice, olive oil, parsley, mint (if using), and salt in a large bowl and toss together. Cover with plastic wrap and refrigerate up to 4 hours.

MIX THE MEAT. Adjust an oven rack to the top position and heat the broiler to high. Line a baking sheet with foil and set aside. Place the meatball mixture, nuts, sugar, cumin, oregano, allspice, and cinnamon in a large bowl and mix to combine.

SHAPE AND BROIL THE KEBABS. Divide the meat into 24 pieces and shape into oblong torpedoes. Thread 3 lengthwise onto each of 8 wooden or metal skewers and place the skewers on the baking sheet. Fold a sheet of foil in half lengthwise and place over the skewer bottoms to keep them from burning if using wooden skewers. Broil the kebabs until browned, 5 to 6 minutes, turn the skewers over, and broil the other side until browned, another 4 to 5 minutes. Serve hot or at room temperature with the salad on the side.

SHOP SMART
When I see a sale on ground turkey (preferably dark meat), ground pork, ground veal, or even ground bison, I'll buy a few pounds and freeze it for a rainy-day meatball marathon. Cutting other types of ground meat into the beef keeps the mixture flavorful, tender, and moist.

THE
BIG
BANG

SERVES 8

😊

$20.40/
$2.55

Not-Just-for-Thanksgiving Turkey with Simplest Pan Gravy

In December 2007, Central Oklahoma got hit with a devastating ice storm that left hundreds of thousands of people from Tulsa to Oklahoma City without power for days upon days. Fred had to take a chain saw to a tree that fell across our entryway during the storm so that my daughter, Alexis, and I could head to the Rock and cook up breakfast (fortunately, our grill, oven, and fryer were all gas-fueled). I offered to make coffee and breakfast for the Red Cross team that had taken over a senior center near the cafe, and somehow, and I'm not quite sure how, that turned into breakfast, lunch, and dinner for 5 days running. Folks came from as far as Oklahoma City once they heard on the radio I was cooking up food. The local McDonald's, Sonic, and our grocery store all brought cases and cases of food that would have spoiled, what with no refrigeration and such, and even the locals started leaving food from their own freezers and refrigerators at the Rock's back door. You wouldn't believe how many frozen turkeys we wound up with! We ended up feeding more people than even the Red Cross in Oklahoma City. Now, whenever I go to roast a turkey, I can't help but think of the ice storm of '07 and the generosity and good intentions that came together at the Rock during that time. I didn't have time to brine the turkeys then, but under saner circumstances, I always try to make time. Though it's not essential, I think it makes a big difference.

1 cup + 1 tablespoon salt

1 turkey (10–12 pounds), tail, neck, and giblets removed

¼ cup fresh lemon juice (from 2 lemons)

1 small yellow onion, quartered

2 carrots, trimmed, peeled, and roughly chopped

Leafy tops of 1 bunch celery (save the stalks for another use, such as stuffing)

BRINE AND AIR-DRY THE TURKEY (OPTIONAL). Bring 8 cups of water and 1 cup of salt to a boil in a tall, 20-quart stockpot (if you don't have a stockpot, bring the water to a boil in a large pot), turn off the heat, and set aside to cool. Add the turkey and enough cold water to cover it to within 1" from the top of the pot. (If you're not using a stockpot, transfer the salt water to a large cooler and add the turkey and enough water to cover it. Note that if you have to add more than 2 gallons of water to cover the turkey, you need to dissolve extra salt in some warm water: ¼ cup for each extra quart.) Cover the pot and refrigerate the turkey for 12 hours or overnight. Remove the turkey (discard the water), pat dry with paper towels, and place breast-up on a roasting rack set over a rimmed baking sheet or roasting pan. Refrigerate overnight.

PREP THE TURKEY. Take the turkey out of the refrigerator 30 minutes before heating the oven to 325°F. Pour the lemon juice into the cavity of the turkey, and then rub the remaining 1 tablespoon salt into the cavity. Stuff the turkey with the onion, carrots, celery leaves, parsley, rosemary, and thyme, and then plug the cavity with a bunched-up piece of foil. Cross the legs one over the other and use butcher's twine to tie them together at their base. Tuck the wings underneath the breast and, if you have a trussing needle, stitch the neck opening closed; if you don't, use wooden toothpicks or small wood skewers to bring the skin together as much as possible. Brush the turkey with the melted butter (sprinkle with an additional 2 teaspoons of salt if you didn't brine it).

ROAST THE TURKEY. Roast the turkey until the thickest part of the thigh reads 165°F on an instant-read thermometer, about 3½ hours. Transfer the turkey to a cutting board (or serving platter if you're carving it at the table) and let it rest for at least 10 minutes before carving. Serve with the gravy.

D2D
Turkey wings are a great value, often up to $1.50 cheaper than chicken wings. They're fun to make buffalo-style (see the recipe on page 76) and serve as the main event! They're also great for quick turkey stock.

1 bunch flat-leaf parsley

6 sprigs fresh rosemary

6 sprigs fresh thyme

4 tablespoons unsalted butter, melted

   Homemade gravy (page 34)

MAKE IT A MEAL
+ Creamy Broccoli Gratin (page 55)

COOK SMART
Buy a turkey and split it in half using poultry shears or a sharp chef's knife to slice right through the breastbone. Roast half for dinner tonight and cut the other half into parts to freeze. Slice the breast off the bone, then remove the drumstick, thigh, and wing. Wrap well and freeze for another meal, another time. FYI: A skinless, boneless turkey breast half often weighs around 3 pounds, and can easily feed up to 8 people!

Gravy 101

Homemade gravy is so delicious, silky, and rich that I love it on just about anything from ham to roast chicken, fluffy biscuits, and of course turkey. Gravy is an easy, low-cost accompaniment that takes just minutes to make but really ups the ante on the plate.

MEASURE OUT THE JUICES AND DRIPPINGS. Tilt the turkey cavity-side down over the roasting pan to drain out the accumulated juices. Place the turkey on your cutting board, tent with foil, and set aside. Pour the drippings and juices from the roasting pan into a large measuring cup. Skim off the fat and add enough chicken broth to equal 2 cups of liquid.

MAKE A ROUX. Melt 4 tablespoons of butter in a medium saucepan over medium heat. Reduce the heat to medium-low and stir in ¼ cup of flour a little at a time, working out any lumps before adding the next addition. Cook the roux for at least 3 minutes, stirring constantly. If you like a darker, nutty-tasting gravy, continue to cook the roux for up to 10 more minutes, stirring often and keeping the heat at a very gentle bare simmer.

ADD THE LIQUID. Slowly whisk in the liquid, salt, and pepper, stirring thoroughly between additions to work out any lumps. Cook until silky and thick, about 5 minutes. Salt to taste.

Confident Carving

To carve a turkey, begin by separating the drumstick where it meets the bottom of the breast. Slice down and into the thigh so the leg and thigh lie at a 90-degree angle to the breast. Pop out the leg joint and carve through the thigh to detach it from the breast. Separate the drumstick from the thigh. Remove the skin from the thigh and carve the meat from the thigh parallel to the bone. Slice the skin into thin strips. Repeat with the other leg and thigh. To carve the breast, slice straight down along the breast bone. Starting at the top and outer edge of the breast, cut across the breast to create nice slices. Repeat with the other breast. Cut through the wing joints where they connect to the breast and pull the wings off. Cut off the wing tips, and separate the wings through the drummette joints. (Make sure you save the carcass to make turkey broth.)

Turkey & Sausage Strata

We used to go to Fred's mom's in Oklahoma City for Christmas, and on Christmas Eve, we'd make this breakfast dish together as a family. It's perfect because you leave it in the fridge overnight and the next day just pop it in the oven. In the morning, while the kids zip down to the tree to stare at their gifts, Fred zips to the kitchen, where he does his happy dance for this casserole!

COOK THE VEGETABLES AND SAUSAGE. Heat the oven to 350°F. Melt 2 tablespoons of butter in a large skillet over medium-high heat. Add the onion, bell pepper, jalapeño (if using), scallions, salt, and pepper, cooking just until the vegetables are soft, 3 to 4 minutes. Add the sausage and paprika and cook until browned, stirring often, about 5 minutes. Drain off any excess fat from the skillet, stir in the turkey, and set aside.

ASSEMBLE AND BAKE THE CASSEROLE. Grease a 13" x 9" baking dish with the remaining butter. Line the bottom of the baking dish with the bread (you may need to squish the slices together to make them fit) and sprinkle the sausage-turkey mixture evenly across the top. Whisk the eggs and milk together and pour over the sausage layer. Evenly sprinkle the cheese over the top, cover with plastic wrap, and refrigerate overnight. Cover the baking dish with foil and bake until the edges are puffed and crisp and the center is cooked, 1 hour to 1 hour and 10 minutes. Cool slightly before slicing into squares and serving with hot sauce or salsa.

> **$ D2D**
>
> A pound of whole-bean coffee is usually cheaper than ground coffee. What I do is just open up the bag and use the grinder that's right there in the store. So I still get the convenience of ground along with the savings of whole-bean.

3 tablespoons unsalted butter

1 yellow onion, finely chopped

1 green, orange, red, or yellow bell pepper, seeded, ribbed, and finely chopped

1 jalapeño, seeded, ribbed, and finely chopped (optional)

3 scallions, white and light green parts only, thinly sliced

$\frac{1}{2}$ teaspoon salt

$\frac{1}{4}$ teaspoon freshly ground black pepper

1 pound bulk mild Italian or breakfast sausage, crumbled

1 teaspoon sweet paprika

About 1½ cups roughly chopped home-cooked (page 32) or store-bought cooked turkey

5 slices (½" thick) sandwich bread (if you have different types, mix them)

6 large eggs

1½ cups whole or low-fat milk

1 cup (about 8 ounces) shredded Monterey Jack or Cheddar cheese

Hot sauce or salsa, for serving

Making Broth from a Carcass

MAKES 3½ QUARTS

Try this once—I know it sounds like a little bit of extra effort, but I guarantee that you'll be hooked at the something-from-nothing fringe benefits! After carving away all the meat from a chicken's or turkey's frame, save those bones for soup. Sure, the soup stock won't be quite as rich and deep as it would be if you made it from necks and backbones, but it's still delicious and much better than store-bought. For extra flavor, I brown my veggies before adding the bones and water. I use dried herbs here, but if you have fresh on hand, by all means double the quantity and toss them in. This broth can also be made with chicken carcasses, but you'll need 2 to make a good broth.

- 1 tablespoon canola oil
- 1 yellow onion, roughly chopped
- 2 carrots, roughly chopped
- 2 celery stalks, roughly chopped
- 1 teaspoon dried basil or thyme
- 1 teaspoon dried parsley
- 1 teaspoon salt
- 6 whole black peppercorns or ¼ teaspoon freshly ground black pepper
- 1 turkey carcass from a 10- to 12-pound turkey, split in half with poultry shears or a chef's knife, or 2 to 3 split chicken carcasses

HEAT THE OIL IN A LARGE DUTCH OVEN OR SOUP POT OVER MEDIUM-HIGH HEAT. Add the onion, carrots, and celery and cook, stirring often, until soft and browned, 5 to 8 minutes. Stir in the basil or thyme, parsley, salt, and pepper, add the turkey or chicken bones, and cover with 2 quarts of water. Bring to a boil, reduce the heat to medium-low, partially cover the pot, and gently simmer until the broth is rich and flavorful, about 2 hours. Strain through a fine-mesh sieve and cool before refrigerating (it will keep for 5 days) or freezing in quart-size resealable freezer bags, plastic containers, or ice cube trays (transfer the frozen cubes to plastic bags once they're frozen solid).

Turkey Tortilla Soup

What would Thanksgiving weekend be if you didn't cap it off with a steaming bowl of turkey soup on Sunday? This soup transforms a bare minimum of leftover turkey into a big pot. If you have leftover gravy, dilute it with chicken broth or even water and add it to the pot. Roasted chicken works, too!

MAKE THE SOUP. Heat 1 tablespoon of the oil in a Dutch oven or soup pot over medium-high heat. Add the onion and garlic and cook, stirring often, until soft, about 3 minutes. Pour in the broth and tomatoes (with liquid), and add the chile pepper, chili powder, cumin, salt, and black pepper. Bring to a boil, stir in the turkey, reduce the heat to medium-low, and simmer for 10 minutes. Add the corn and continue to simmer until the turkey is heated through, 8 to 10 minutes longer.

MAKE THE GARNISH AND SERVE. Meanwhile, heat the remaining ¼ cup of oil in a large skillet over medium-high heat. Add the tortilla strips to the oil one by one (you will have to do this in batches so the pan doesn't get overcrowded) and fry until both sides are golden and crisp, about 2 minutes total. Transfer to paper towels to drain and fry the remaining strips. Serve the soup with a handful of tortilla strips, some avocado slices (if using), cheese, and cilantro on top, and a lime wedge on the side.

- 1 tablespoon + ¼ cup canola oil
- 1 yellow onion, finely chopped
- 2 garlic cloves, minced
- 4 cups chicken or turkey broth, homemade (page 36) or store-bought
- 1 can (14.5 ounces) diced tomatoes with liquid
- 1 jalapeño or small poblano chile pepper, seeded, ribbed, and finely chopped
- 2 teaspoons chili powder
- ½ teaspoon ground cumin
- ½ teaspoon salt
- ¼ teaspoon freshly ground black pepper
  About 3 cups cooked and shredded turkey (page 32)
- 1 cup frozen corn
- 6 corn tortillas, sliced into ½"-wide strips
- 1 ripe avocado (optional), halved, pitted, and sliced
- ½ cup (about 2 ounces) shredded Monterey Jack or Cheddar cheese
- ¼ cup finely chopped fresh cilantro leaves
- 4 lime wedges

> **$ D2D**
>
> Chips made from fresh tortillas are much cheaper than tortilla chips by the bag, and they taste a whole lot better, too. Just cut them into wedges and fry the wedges in hot vegetable oil until crisp and brown; drain, and sprinkle them lightly with salt. To oven-bake them instead of frying, just brush each tortilla with a little oil before toasting in a 400°F oven until golden-brown and crisp.

Turkey Pot Pie with Cheddar Streusel

Frozen pot pies are cheap because they are made with cheap ingredients—not much meat, tired veggies, and lots of floury gravy—not to mention the thick, soggy crust. Fortunately, making them at home is even cheaper—especially if you are using up leftover dibs and dabs that might otherwise get tossed! And since no one relishes the idea of whipping up a pie crust on a weeknight, I top mine with a cheesy cobbler mixture that requires no rolling. Lots of times I'll make a double batch of filling and freeze half in a gallon-size resealable freezer bag. If I don't feel like making the streusel, I whip up biscuits (page 222) for the topping, or just cover it with a few butter-brushed sheets of thawed phyllo dough.

COBBLER TOPPING

- 2 cups all-purpose flour
- 2 tablespoons sugar
- 2 teaspoons finely chopped fresh thyme or 1 teaspoon dried thyme
- ½ teaspoon salt
- ½ teaspoon freshly ground black pepper
- 1 cup (about 4 ounces) finely grated Cheddar cheese
- 8 tablespoons unsalted butter, melted

TURKEY

- 2 tablespoons unsalted butter
- 1 white onion, very finely chopped
- 1 celery stalk, trimmed and thinly sliced on a diagonal
- 10 ounces button mushrooms, stemmed and thinly sliced

MAKE THE COBBLER TOPPING. Whisk the flour, sugar, thyme, salt, and pepper together in a large bowl and then stir in the Cheddar. Drizzle in the melted butter. Using your hands (or a fork), work the butter into the dry ingredients until just a few dry patches remain and the mixture resembles wet sand.

MAKE THE TURKEY FILLING. Melt the butter in a large saucepan or Dutch oven over medium-high heat. Add the onion and celery and cook until the vegetables are soft, stirring often, about 5 minutes. Add the mushrooms, thyme, salt, and pepper, cooking until the mushrooms are cooked through, stirring often, about 5 minutes. Stir in the garlic and cook until fragrant, 30 seconds to 1 minute. Stir in the flour and cook for 30 seconds, stirring often, then begin adding the broth, ¼ cup at a time, working out lumps as you see them. Once all of the broth is added, stir in the turkey or chicken and the peas.

BAKE THE COBBLER. Heat the oven to 350°F. Pour the turkey filling into a 2-quart baking dish and sprinkle with the topping. Bake until the filling is bubbly and the topping is golden brown, 30 to 40 minutes (if the topping becomes too brown too quickly, cover it with a piece of foil). Cool slightly before serving.

D2D

Here's a fun way to stock your freezer with new ideas—host a food swap. Invite some friends over, the catch being that each person needs to bring 2 frozen dishes to swap. Let your guests know that each dish should feed at least 6 to 8 people, and make sure that not everyone brings beef chili!

2 teaspoons finely chopped fresh thyme or 1 teaspoon dried thyme

1 teaspoon salt

½ teaspoon freshly ground black pepper

2 garlic cloves, finely minced

¼ cup all-purpose flour

2 cups chicken broth, homemade (page 36) or store-bought

About 2 cups shredded cooked turkey (page 32)

1 cup frozen peas

covering your bases

When it comes to weeknight dinners at home, I have a rotating collection of sauces that helps me get dinner on the table. Even if I'm serving something simple, such as broccoli, a quick and creamy cheese sauce can make it taste really special and get everyone at the table jazzed to eat it. I like to think of this as on-the-fly cooking with a safety net. Once you have your sauce made and tucked away in the freezer or fridge, adding a protein, veggie, or starch is a snap. With very little effort, you have a dish that tastes like you spent hours slaving over it.

It all started with leftover marinara sauce. Now let the record show, given their druthers, my kids would take their pasta straight with nothing but a little butter and a bit of Parmesan. So trying to sell spaghetti with red sauce twice in 1 week was going to be a long shot. Instead, I used that marinara sauce to make chicken Parmesan, which my kids gobbled up without even realizing that what they turned their noses up to the night before was making a reappearance on the dinner table. Hey, was I on to something here?

I started thinking about what else I could use marinara sauce for, and for that matter, a few other easy-to-make, inexpensive sauces that are tried-and-true favorites at the Rock. I began making double and triple batches of creamy Parmesan sauce and chunky, fresh vegetable sauce, keeping some in the fridge and some in the freezer. I came up with a ton of meals, from a cheesy white lasagna to a speedy summer gazpacho and even red snapper oven-steamed in fresh vegetables and herbs.

Now, I *always* have a few sauces stashed in the freezer, and perhaps one in the fridge, too. Having these last-minute dinnertime go-tos at the ready means that no matter what kind of day I've had, I know I've got half the work of dinner done already.

Classic Basil Marinara

THE SAUCE

3 ½ QUARTS

$9.24/ $.22

This basic marinara recipe yields 3 sauce variations and lots of meal ideas, from family-friendly pizza to a veggie-packed summer ragout. I started making my own marinara when I evaluated the savings of doing so—ounce per ounce, making your own marinara saves $1 per cup compared to the jarred stuff, and it is *so* much healthier. Look at the nutrition label on the back of your favorite brand next time you're at the supermarket, check the sodium and sugar content, and prepare to be shocked! It's easy to dress up a batch of straight-up marinara with other ingredients, such as black olives, red-pepper flakes, and capers, to turn it into arrabbiata, puttanesca, or a vodka sauce. This makes seven 2-cup portions, each of which serves 6.

MAKE THE SAUCE. Heat the oil over medium-low heat in a large pot and add the garlic, basil, and oregano. Cook until the herbs are simmering and the oil is infused with their flavor, 10 to 12 minutes. Add the onions and increase the heat to medium, cooking until they are soft and translucent, about 5 minutes, stirring often. Add the tomatoes and the remaining ingredients to the pot and bring to a boil over medium-high heat. Reduce the heat to medium-low and simmer, covered, stirring occasionally, until the tomatoes have completely broken down and the sauce is thick, about 1 hour.

DIVIDE AND STORE. Cool the sauce to room temperature, remove and discard the oregano sprigs, and then divide into 4 quart-size resealable zip-top bags (you'll get 3 bags with 4 cups in each, and 1 bag with 2 cups). Refrigerate for up to 1 week or freeze for up to 3 months (if freezing, place freezer bags on their side on a baking sheet so they freeze flat for easy stacking and storage).

- ¼ cup olive oil
- 5 garlic cloves, finely minced or pressed through a garlic press
- 10 fresh basil leaves, finely chopped
- 2 large sprigs fresh oregano
- 2 large yellow onions, finely diced
- 3 quarts (a #10 can) crushed or diced tomatoes (or eight 14-ounce cans) (see "Shop Smart" on page 44)
- 1 tablespoon light brown sugar
- ½ cup (2 ounces) finely grated Parmesan cheese
- 1½ teaspoons salt
- 1 teaspoon freshly ground black pepper

 D2D

In the summertime, my garden overflows with tomatoes and herbs, so instead of buying canned tomatoes to make marinara, I use about 10 large and juicy sun-ripened ones instead. You can peel and seed the tomatoes if you like (I don't bother), and you may have to cook the sauce just a bit longer to compensate for all the juiciness you're adding to the pot. Add whatever fresh herbs you have or need pruning.

Spicy Arrabbiata-Basil Sauce

Heat 1 tablespoon of olive oil in a large pot over medium-high heat. Add 1 teaspoon of crushed red-pepper flakes (or less, depending on how hot you like it) and ¼ teaspoon of freshly ground black pepper. Cook for 30 seconds, then add 2 cups of marinara sauce. Once warmed, stir in 2 tablespoons of finely chopped fresh basil. **Serves 6.**

Black Olive and Caper Puttanesca

Heat 1 tablespoon of olive oil in a large pot over medium-high heat. Add 1 tablespoon of rinsed capers, ⅓ cup of pitted and chopped black olives (preferably an oil-cured variety), and 1 thinly sliced garlic clove. Cook, stirring often, until the garlic is fragrant, 1 to 1½ minutes. Add 2 cups of marinara sauce and cook until warmed through. **Serves 6.**

Vodka Sauce

Heat 1 tablespoon of olive oil in a large pot over medium-high heat. Add 1 finely minced garlic clove (or press through a garlic press) and ¼ teaspoon of crushed red-pepper flakes, and cook until the garlic is fragrant, about 1 minute. Pour in ¼ cup of vodka and let it come to a simmer, then add 2 cups of marinara sauce. Reduce heat to medium and simmer for 10 minutes. Stir in 1 tablespoon of finely chopped fresh basil and 2 tablespoons of heavy cream. Cook for 1 minute (don't let the sauce bubble) and serve. **Serves 6.**

SOS: Save (Y)Our Sauce!

Half the reason to make a big batch of sauce, whether it's marinara or the peanut sauce on page 62, is to store some away for later. When it cools, divide the big batch into 2 or 3 quart-size resealable plastic bags. They don't take up as much room in the freezer as plastic containers, and they're easier to defrost in the microwave (place the bag in a bowl first, and be sure to open the bag a little so the sauce can breathe while it thaws). Plus, if you don't need the whole bag of sauce, you can just place the bag in a bowl and run cold water over it for 10 minutes or so until it just begins to thaw. Then break off as much as you need and transfer it to a pot to warm up, while rezipping the bag and returning the rest to the freezer.

THE
SPIN-
OFF

SERVES 4

$8.40/
$2.10

Oven-Baked Crispy Chicken Parmesan

I am a crispy girl all the way, meaning the crumb coating on chicken Parmesan better be crisp and crunchy, not soggy. Over the years of making chicken Parm, my absolute favorite dish ever, I've come up with a few tricks for getting the chicken super-crispy—without frying. Yes, without frying. Not only does oven-baking save you from an oily cooktop, but it really shows off the flavors in the bread crumbs and marinara sauce while staying on the (somewhat) lighter side.

The trick is to bake the chicken in a single layer on a baking sheet instead of layered in a baking dish. The heat circulates around the chicken more thoroughly, ensuring the most surface area comes into contact with that hot air. I also bake the chicken part way without sauce, which really helps that crumb coating to crisp up.

1   cup bread crumbs

½   teaspoon each dried basil and dried oregano or 1 teaspoon Italian Rub (page 118)

½   teaspoon salt

4   boneless, skinless chicken breasts (6 to 8 ounces each)

1   large egg

1½ cups homemade (page 43) or store-bought marinara, warmed

1   cup grated whole-milk or part-skim mozzarella cheese

    Parmesan cheese, for serving (optional)

    Pasta, for serving

 MAKE IT A MEAL
+ Garlic Toasts (page 103)

SEASON THE BREAD CRUMBS. Place the bread crumbs in a medium bowl and toss with the herbs and salt.

POUND THE CHICKEN BREASTS. Preheat the oven to 400°F. Line a cutting board with a large sheet of plastic wrap. Place 1 chicken breast on top and cover with another sheet of plastic. Pound the breast until it's super-thin, about ¼" thick. Remove the plastic and set the cutlet aside; repeat with the remaining breasts.

BREAD THE CUTLETS. Set a rimmed baking sheet at one end of your work surface. Place the bread crumbs next to the baking dish. Beat an egg in a shallow pie plate or bowl and place next to the bread crumbs. Set the chicken next to the egg. Using 1 hand (this will be your "breading" hand—try to keep the other hand clean), dip a cutlet into the egg, making sure the egg coats both sides, and then place it in the bread crumbs. Sprinkle crumbs over the cutlet, making sure both sides are evenly coated, and then place the breaded cutlet on the baking sheet. Repeat with the remaining chicken and place in the baking sheet (try to fit all of the chicken on the baking sheet in 1 layer).

BAKE, SAUCE, AND BAKE SOME MORE. Bake the cutlets until lightly browned, about 20 minutes. Remove the baking sheet from the oven and pour the sauce over the top. Sprinkle evenly with the mozzarella and bake until the cheese is bubbly and golden brown, about 20 minutes longer. Serve immediately, sprinkled with Parmesan, if using, and with some pasta on the side.

D2D

Save money by purchasing regular boneless chicken breasts and pounding them into thin cutlets yourself. Sure, you can buy already pounded chicken cutlets or scaloppine (the name changes from market to market), but they'll cost you a pretty penny. Doing it yourself is kind of fun, anyway. Just think of it as therapy with benefits—dinner!

D2D

One of the best things you can do for your cooking and your bank account is to grow your own herbs. They're easy to maintain— just keep watering and pruning them. Plus, they'll grow just about anywhere, from in the ground to hanging planters and window boxes. When you compare the price of $2 to $3 for a little bundle of herbs from the store to $3 for a pint-size cluster from a nursery that keeps on growing for months and months, it just makes plain sense.

Caramelized Onion & Sausage Pizza with No-Knead Dough

I got my first taste of the restaurant business at 14, when I worked in a pizzeria in my hometown of Yukon, Oklahoma. I was the waitress and shift supervisor, and believe it or not, none other than Garth Brooks was the assistant manager! To this day, I still love pizza (Garth's music is pretty good, too). Making your own is really fun, especially with this pizza dough that gets buzzed together in a food processor—no kneading required. If I'm going to the trouble of making my own pizza, I like to top it with something kind of special. Sweet, tender, caramelized onions alongside sweet or spicy Italian sausage is just the ticket to ride.

DOUGH

- 1 teaspoon olive oil
- 1 teaspoon active dry or instant yeast
- 1 tablespoon sugar
- 1 teaspoon salt
- 3 cups all-purpose flour + extra for dusting

COOK SMART

You can make the dough up to 2 days ahead of time. Just refrigerate the dough in an oiled, resealable gallon-size plastic bag after the dough comes out of the food processor. On the day you plan to make pizza (or calzones or a pizza roll), transfer the dough to an oiled bowl and let it sit out at room temperature for 1½ to 2 hours until it has doubled in size. Then proceed with the pizza recipe.

MAKE THE DOUGH. Use the oil to grease a large bowl and set aside. Place the yeast, sugar, salt, flour and 1 cup of just-warm-to-the-touch water in the bowl of a food processor fitted with the steel blade. Pulse to combine, scraping down the sides as necessary. Turn the processor on and work the dough until a ball forms, about 1 minute, stopping the processor halfway through to scrape down the sides of the bowl. Lightly flour your work surface and turn the dough out onto it. Give it a few kneads until the dough ball is smooth, and then place it into the oiled bowl, turning it over a couple of times to oil the surface. Cover with plastic wrap and set aside in a warm, draft-free spot until doubled in size, about 1½ hours.

CARAMELIZE THE ONIONS AND BROWN THE SAUSAGE. Heat the olive oil in a large skillet over medium heat. Add the onions, salt, and sugar and cook, stirring occasionally, until the onions start to turn brown, about 10 minutes. Add the sausage and cook, stirring often, until the sausage is lightly browned, about 7 minutes. Turn off the heat and set aside to cool slightly.

BAKE THE PIZZA. Adjust the oven rack to the lower-middle position and heat the oven to 400°F. Grease an 18" x 13" baking sheet with some olive oil. Pick up the dough and start stretching it into a rectangular shape, and then place it onto the greased baking sheet and stretch the dough to cover the entire pan. Spread the sauce over the dough and sprinkle evenly with the cheeses and onion/sausage mixture. Bake until the cheese is browned and bubbly, about 30 minutes. Remove from the oven and add basil, if using. Slice into squares and serve hot.

PIZZA

- 2 tablespoons olive oil + more for greasing the pan
- 2 yellow onions, halved and thinly sliced
- ½ teaspoon salt
- 1 teaspoon sugar
- 8 ounces bulk Italian sausage, crumbled, or sausage links with the meat squeezed from the casings
- 1½ cups marinara, homemade (page 43) or store-bought
- 1½ cups (6 ounces) shredded mozzarella or provolone cheese
- ½ cup (2 ounces) shredded Parmesan cheese

  Roughly chopped fresh basil leaves, for serving (optional)

 D2D
Many pizzerias are happy to sell you balls of raw pizza dough for as little as $1. It's also available in some Italian bakeries. All you have to do is ask!

Artichoke, Black Olive & Ricotta Calzone

This is super fun to make with the kiddos—it's also a great way to use up a fridge full of random odds and ends. Give each child a dough ball to stretch out (or do it for them if they're too young). Then, arrange a table full of filling options with different kinds of sautéed or roasted veggies and meats (sausage, pepperoni, ham, meatballs). If your kids aren't into ricotta, you can substitute a couple of handfuls of shredded cheese instead, or the shredded Cheddar-Jack mixture from the white lasagna on page 57.

FILLING

- 1 pound whole-milk or part-skim ricotta cheese
- 4 cups (about 16 ounces) grated mozzarella cheese
- 2 large eggs, lightly beaten
- ½ cup finely chopped basil leaves
- 1 tablespoon finely chopped fresh oregano
- 1½ teaspoons salt
- 1 cup frozen artichoke heart halves, thawed and cut into thirds
- ½ cup sliced black olives

CALZONE

- 2 teaspoons canola oil
- 1 recipe pizza dough (page 48), divided into 4 equal pieces

  All-purpose flour for stretching the dough
- 1 large egg, beaten with 1 tablespoon water
- 2 cups marinara, homemade (page 43) or store-bought, heated

MAKE THE FILLING. Adjust an oven rack to the lower-middle position and heat the oven to 400°F. Mix together the ricotta, mozzarella, eggs, basil, oregano, and salt in a large bowl. Stir in the artichokes and olives and set aside.

FILL AND BAKE THE CALZONES. Grease a baking sheet with the oil. Lightly dust the 4 pieces of dough with flour and then hand-stretch them each into a 6" circle. Brush the edges with the egg wash. Place 1 cup of the ricotta filling in the center of each piece and fold the dough over, pinching the edges together with your fingers. Place the calzones on the pan and brush the tops with the remaining egg wash (you will not use all of the egg wash). Using the point of a paring knife or kitchen shears, make three 1" vents in the top of each calzone. Bake until golden brown, 20 to 30 minutes. Serve with the marinara sauce on the side.

 D2D

I'm more than happy to give my biceps a workout and grate bulk blocks of cheese rather than buy it already grated at the store. Not only is the cheese fresher, it costs about 50 cents less per pound than pregrated, and I only have to grate as much as I need, so the rest of the block keeps better.

Salami & Provolone Pizza Rolls

Known in some parts of the country as stromboli, pizza rolls are great for parties or as a twist on a pizza dinner. Save a few slices, wrap, and freeze them, then defrost overnight and pack them into your kid's lunchbox for a fun treat.

STRETCH AND FILL THE DOUGH. Grease an 18" x 13" baking sheet with a little oil. Adjust an oven rack to the lower-middle position and heat the oven to 400°F. Sprinkle your work surface with some flour. Stretch the dough into a rough 16" x 12" rectangle. Brush the edges lightly with the egg wash. Spread the marinara onto the center dough, leaving a 2" border. Cover the marinara with a layer of provolone and top the provolone with the salami.

ROLL AND BAKE. Starting at one long edge, carefully roll the dough into a long tube, gently picking the dough up and folding it over so the filling doesn't slide or seep out. Pinch the edges together with your fingers. Place the roll, seam-side down, on the greased baking sheet. Brush some of the egg wash onto the dough (you will not use all of the egg wash), and, using the tip of a knife or kitchen shears, cut five 1" vents in the top of the dough. Bake until the roll is golden brown, 20 to 30 minutes. Remove from the oven, and cool 5 minutes before using a bread knife to slice diagonally into twelve 1"-thick pieces.

Canola oil for greasing the pan

All-purpose flour

1 recipe pizza dough (page 48)

1 large egg, lightly beaten with 1 tablespoon water

½ cup marinara, homemade (page 43) or store-bought

8 slices provolone cheese

5 ounces sliced salami

D2D

If your family drinks a lot of sparkling water or soda, consider investing in a countertop seltzer machine. The cost per liter is about half the price of a liter of seltzer, plus you're not creating as much waste, since you reuse the bottles included with the seltzer maker. You can create natural flavored "sodas" by mixing your seltzer with juice, too.

Summer Vegetable Ragout

I came up with this chunky ragout as a way to use up vegetables from my summer garden. More substantial than a sauce, it's awesome with pasta or ravioli, rice, or a few wedges of crusty country bread. Depending on the weather and my whim, I'll either broil the vegetables, like I do here, or grill them. Grilling adds an extra-special layer of smoke and char to the ragout.

1 pound eggplant (globe, Italian, or Japanese), trimmed and sliced lengthwise into ½"-thick planks

1¼ teaspoons salt + extra for pasta

1 pound zucchini or summer squash, trimmed and sliced lengthwise into ½"-thick planks

2 tablespoons olive oil

4 cups marinara, homemade (page 43) or store-bought

1 pound green beans, trimmed and sliced into 1" pieces

2 fresh tomatoes, cored, seeded, and cut into 1" pieces

1 pound farfalle or rotini pasta or cheese ravioli

2 tablespoons finely chopped fresh basil

Parmesan cheese, for serving

SALT THE EGGPLANT. If using a globe eggplant, place the slices in a colander and toss with ½ teaspoon of the salt. Set aside for 30 minutes (skip this step if using Italian or Japanese eggplant). Rinse and pat dry.

BROIL THE EGGPLANT AND ZUCCHINI. Adjust an oven rack to the top position and heat the broiler to high. Toss the eggplant and zucchini with the olive oil and the remaining ¾ teaspoon of salt in a large bowl. Arrange cut-side down on a baking sheet in a single layer and broil until browned but still firm, about 4 minutes on each side. Set aside until cool, then roughly chop into 1" pieces.

MAKE THE RAGOUT. Place the marinara in a large saucepan and bring to a simmer over medium-high heat. Stir in the eggplant and zucchini along with the green beans and tomatoes. Bring the sauce back to a simmer, reduce the heat to medium-low, cover, and cook until the green beans are just tender, 7 to 10 minutes.

BOIL THE PASTA. Bring a large pot of salted water to a boil. Add the pasta and cook until al dente. Drain and set aside. Taste the ragout and adjust the seasonings if needed; stir in the basil. Serve the ragout over the pasta with some grated Parmesan.

Creamy Parmesan Sauce

After tasting one too many underwhelming and pricey Alfredo dishes in restaurants, I decided to create my own recipe for a perfectly creamy Parmesan sauce, one bursting with garlic and cheese. Of course, it's yummiest made with heavy cream or half-and-half, but most of the time I'll go for what's in the fridge, whole or 2% milk, for a lighter sauce that's just as tasty. It's fantastic simply tossed with pasta and some pan-seared shrimp and steamed broccoli, or made into delicious Spinach and Portobello Stuffed Shells (page 54). This yields three 2-cup portions, each serving 6.

MAKE THE SAUCE. Melt the butter in a large saucepan over medium-low heat. Add the garlic, pepper, and cream or milk, increase the heat to medium-high, and bring it to a simmer (watch the pot—it can boil over in a split second) while stirring often. Stir in the Parmesan-Romano mixture, reduce the heat to medium-low, and let the sauce simmer, stirring often, until the garlic has mellowed, about 12 minutes. Stir in the mozzarella and continue to cook until the cheese is melted. Turn off the heat and whisk the sauce until it is smooth (a blender or immersion blender works great). Stir in the salt.

DIVIDE AND STORE. Cool the sauce to room temperature and then divide it between 2 quart-size resealable freezer bags. Refrigerate it for up to 3 days or freeze it for up to 3 months. (After defrosting it overnight in the refrigerator, rewarm the sauce gently over medium-low heat, being careful not to let the sauce boil—boiling it will cause it to separate. If it separates, use a whisk, blender, or immersion blender to smooth it out.)

1 ½   sticks (¾ cup) unsalted butter

6   garlic cloves, finely minced or pressed through a garlic press

½   teaspoon white pepper

1   quart (4 cups) cream, half-and-half, whole milk, or low-fat milk

1   cup (4 ounces) grated Parmesan-Romano cheese blend or ½ cup each of Parmesan and Romano

2   cups (8 ounces) grated whole-milk or part-skim mozzarella cheese

1   teaspoon salt

MAKE IT A MEAL

+ Fettuccine
+ Seared shrimp and/or steamed broccoli

D2D

Save money by mixing your own half-and-half from equal parts of light cream and whole milk. You'll save an average of 20 percent per quart, believe it or not!

THE
SPIN-
OFF

SERVES 8

$16.00/
$2.00

Spinach & Portobello Stuffed Shells

Covered with the creamy Parm sauce, these shells are a great way to get your kids (and green-averse adults) to eat their vegetables. The sky is the limit when it comes to filling the shells. If you're craving meat, add some shredded chicken or even lump crabmeat. Broccoli, Swiss chard, and asparagus can all stand in for spinach, and if you're not big on mushrooms, lose them.

12	ounces jumbo shells
2	tablespoons olive oil
3	ounces (about 1 cup) finely chopped cremini mushrooms
2	garlic cloves, finely minced or pressed through a garlic press
6	ounces frozen or fresh spinach, thawed
1	pound whole-milk or part-skim ricotta cheese
4	cups (16 ounces) grated whole-milk or part-skim mozzarella cheese
2	large eggs, lightly beaten
½	cup finely chopped fresh basil leaves
1	tablespoon finely chopped fresh oregano (from about 1 large sprig)
1½	teaspoons salt
3	cups homemade Parmesan sauce (page 53) or store-bought Alfredo sauce
⅓	cup grated Parmesan cheese

BOIL THE PASTA. Preheat the oven to 350°F. Bring a large pot of salty water to a boil over high heat. Add the shells and boil them until just shy of al dente, about 10 minutes. Drain and rinse under cool water and then set aside.

MAKE THE FILLING. Heat the oil in a large skillet over medium-high heat. Add the mushrooms and garlic and cook, stirring often, until the mushrooms get juicy, about 5 minutes. Add the spinach and cook, stirring often, until wilted and most of the liquid is gone, about 5 minutes longer. Transfer the mixture in an even layer to a baking sheet to cool. Meanwhile, stir together the ricotta, 3 cups of the mozzarella, the eggs, basil, oregano, and salt in a large bowl. Stir in the cooled vegetables and set aside.

STUFF THE SHELLS. Pour a third of the sauce into the bottom of a 13" x 9" baking dish. Use a small spoon to fill each shell with 1 heaping tablespoon of the cheese/spinach mixture, and then place it in the baking dish. Once all of the shells are filled, cover them with the remaining sauce, the remaining 1 cup of mozzarella, and the Parmesan. (At this point, the dish can be frozen for up to 3 months; defrost it overnight in the fridge before baking.)

BAKE THE SHELLS. Cover the baking dish with foil and bake until bubbly, about 40 minutes. Uncover the dish and bake until the cheese is bubbling and golden brown, another 10 to 15 minutes. Remove it from the oven and let the stuffed shells rest for 5 minutes before serving.

Creamy Broccoli Gratin

THE
SPIN-
OFF

SERVES 6

$8.10/
$1.35

I never have to urge my kids to eat their vegetables when they are baked together with this sumptuous sauce—one of the best reasons I know to keep a batch of sauce in the freezer. Frozen vegetables are a great bargain, especially when time is of the essence and you need to throw something together quickly. You'll save 30 cents a pound when you choose already-cut frozen broccoli instead of precut fresh broccoli crowns at the market. Frozen cauliflower, frozen corn, and frozen green beans would all be delicious in this recipe, too.

HEAT THE OVEN TO 375°F. Mix the cheeses together in a small bowl. Mix together the broccoli, Parmesan sauce, scallions, and salt in a large bowl. Transfer the broccoli mixture to a 13" x 9" baking dish and top with an even layer of the cheese, followed by the bread crumbs. Bake until the center of the casserole is bubbling and the top is golden brown, 30 to 40 minutes. Cool 5 minutes before serving.

- ½ cup (2 ounces) grated Cheddar cheese
- ½ cup (2 ounces) grated Parmesan cheese
- 2 pounds frozen broccoli (or fresh broccoli cut into bite-size pieces)
- 3 cups homemade Parmesan sauce (page 53) or store-bought Alfredo sauce
- 2 scallions, thinly sliced
- ⅓ teaspoon salt
- ½ cup seasoned bread crumbs (or ½ cup panko or fresh bread crumbs seasoned with ¼ teaspoon of salt and ½ teaspoon of Italian Rub, page 118)

D2D

Buying fresh vegetables trimmed and prepped saves you time, but always costs you money (and cuts down significantly on their shelf life as well). To save both time *and* money, trim and cut up a whole head of broccoli or cauliflower, or a pound of mushrooms, beans, etc. Use half right away, and the rest later in the week.

MAKE IT A MEAL
+ Rosemary and Thyme Roasted Chicken (page 3)

Three-Cheese White Lasagna

THE SPIN-OFF

SERVES 6

$12.60/
$2.10

Extra creamy and decadent, this casserole is like macaroni and cheese dressed up for company. Many kids and even adults aren't fans of ricotta cheese, which is how I came up with this Cheddar and Monterey Jack–loaded alternative to the traditional lasagna. Sautéed onions and a mix of beef and pork give the dish some backbone, while a little Parmesan sprinkled over the top offers up an irresistible golden-brown crust. You could make this even more like macaroni and cheese if you wanted by using elbow macaroni or even ziti in place of the lasagna noodles.

MAKE THE SAUCE. Heat the oven to 375°F. Heat the olive oil in a large skillet over medium-high heat. Add the onion and cook until soft and translucent, 3 to 4 minutes. Stir in the garlic, salt, and pepper and cook until the garlic is fragrant, about 1 minute longer. Add the beef and pork and cook 2 to 4 minutes until the meat is browned. Pour off the extra fat from the pan.

ASSEMBLE AND BAKE THE LASAGNA. Stir together the milk and Parmesan sauce and evenly spread ½ cup over the bottom of a 13" x 9" pan. Lay 3 lasagna noodles in the pan lengthwise. Stir together the Cheddar and Monterey Jack cheeses in a medium bowl with the egg. Pour ¾ cup of the sauce over the noodles and top with 2 cups of the cheese-and-egg mixture. Pour ¾ cup of the sauce evenly over the cheese, and follow with 3 more noodles, the meat mixture, ¾ cup of the sauce, 3 more noodles, the remaining 1 cup of the cheese mixture, and the remaining ¾ cup of sauce. Sprinkle evenly with the Parmesan.

BAKE AND SERVE THE LASAGNA. Cover the pan with foil and bake until the cheese is bubbly and brown, about 30 minutes. Cool 5 to 10 minutes before slicing.

2 tablespoons olive oil

1 large yellow onion, finely chopped

2 garlic cloves, finely minced or pressed through a garlic press

½ pound lean ground beef

½ pound ground pork

¾ teaspoon salt

½ teaspoon freshly ground black pepper

½ cup low-fat or whole milk

3 cups homemade Parmesan sauce (page 53) or store-bought Alfredo sauce

9 no-boil egg lasagna noodles

1½ cups (6 ounces) grated Cheddar cheese

1½ cups (6 ounces) grated Monterey Jack cheese

1 large egg, lightly beaten

½ cup (2 ounces) grated Parmesan cheese

No-Cook Garden Vegetable Sauce

If you like salsa, you'll find a million ways to use this sauce aside from the obvious taco topping or dip for chips. I turn it into a gazpacho base (opposite page) or use it as a light, fresh dressing for pasta (page 61). Make this sauce in the summertime when inexpensive and bursting-ripe tomatoes are available, and don't be afraid to let your garden (or neighbor's garden!) inspire you to make your own additions and variations based on whatever is growing gangbusters. I like this a little on the spicy side, but you can certainly eliminate the jalapeños if you prefer. This will make seven 2-cup portions, each serving 6.

5 pounds ripe tomatoes, cored and chopped into ½" cubes

2 large, sweet onions (such as Vidalia), finely chopped

1 orange, red, or yellow bell pepper, seeded and ribbed and finely chopped

2 garlic cloves, finely chopped

1–2 jalapeño peppers to taste, seeded and ribbed

½ cup finely chopped basil, cilantro, and/or oregano

1 cup white wine vinegar or fresh lime juice

2 teaspoons salt

1 teaspoon freshly ground black pepper

⅓ cup tomato paste (optional)

STIR TOGETHER AND STORE. Combine the tomatoes, onions, bell pepper, garlic, jalapeño peppers, herbs, vinegar or lime juice, salt, and pepper in a large bowl. If you want your sauce to have a smoother texture, add the optional tomato paste. Refrigerate the mixture overnight to blend the flavors before using. Divide it among quart-size resealable freezer bags and refrigerate it for up to 5 days or freeze for up to 3 months.

 D2D

When fruits and vegetables are individually priced, always choose the largest, heaviest ones for the best value. When priced by weight, though, choose based on how you will use them. In many cases, it's more convenient to have small or medium tomatoes, onions, etc.

Gazpacho with Avocados

Garden Vegetable Sauce becomes a cool, refreshing soup with just the press of a button. If you like thin gazpacho, use 2 ounces of bread; if you prefer thicker gazpacho, use 3 ounces. To fancy this up, you could add some poached shrimp or lump crabmeat. A drizzle of good, extra-virgin olive oil added before serving is nice, too.

PIT AND DICE THE AVOCADO. Place it in a small bowl and gently toss with a teaspoon of lime juice to prevent browning. Puree the remaining ingredients in a blender or food processor (or in a large bowl if using an immersion blender), blending until smooth. Divide among 4 bowls and top with the avocado. Serve with the bottle of hot sauce on the side.

1 avocado

Juice of 1 lime

2–3 ounces stale bread torn into small pieces (about 1½ cups of 1" pieces)

5 cups No-Cook Garden Vegetable Sauce (opposite page)

Your favorite hot sauce, to taste

MAKE IT A MEAL
+ Singed Steak, Herb, and Lettuce Wraps (page 116)

D2D
If you buy an underripe avocado (meaning it doesn't yield to slight pressure), place it in a paper bag at room temperature for a few days. If you need that avocado ripened pronto, then place an apple or banana in the bag alongside it—the ethylene gas the fruit gives off helps speed the avocado along.

Mozzarella & Orecchiette Toss

If your kids are like mine, they would eat pasta every night of the week—and for lunch, too! That's why I know this meal will be a hit with your whole family. My kids go bananas because they're getting pasta, and I'm happy because they're getting some veggies and protein from the olives. (Fred, well, he's just a happy guy in general.) Because it's as delicious warm as it is at room temperature, the dish is a real winner for picnics and barbecues.

BOIL THE PASTA. Bring a large pot of water to a boil with 1 tablespoon of salt. Add the pasta and the olive oil and cook until the pasta is al dente. Drain, reserving ¼ cup of the pasta cooking water.

TOSS IT ALL TOGETHER. Place the orecchiette in a large serving bowl and add the warmed sauce. Toss to combine, then add the mozzarella, olives, and herbs (if using), and the remaining ¼ teaspoon salt. Toss a couple of times so that the mozzarella gets a little melty (you can add a few tablespoons of the reserved pasta cooking water to make the pasta saucier or get the cheese to melt a little more). Serve right away or at room temperature.

- 1 tablespoon + ¼ teaspoon salt
- 1 pound orecchiette pasta
- 2 tablespoons olive oil
- 5 cups No-Cook Garden Vegetable Sauce (page 58), slightly warmed in a microwave
- 8 ounces fresh mozzarella, cut into ½" cubes
- ½ cup sliced black olives (preferably the oil-cured kind)

  Finely chopped fresh basil or oregano (optional)

 MAKE IT A MEAL
+ Lemon-Rosemary Roasted Salmon (page 96)

 D2D
Pasta is amazing for breakfast! Microwave leftover cooked pasta from the night before with some butter and a touch of olive oil. Top with a fried or poached egg, and if you're really feeling decadent, some crumbled bacon.

Easy Basic Peanut Sauce

This sauce is actually a base—a thick, rich, peanutty base to which you can add coconut milk for a dip, soy sauce and chicken broth for a noodle sauce, or curry powder and chicken broth for an African-style soup. It's packed with protein, so even a spoonful thinned with water would be delicious over steamed white rice as an after-school snack.

Since it's made from wallet-friendly peanut butter, you can stir this base together for less than $1.50 per cup. One batch will make at least 2, if not 3, of the recipes on pages 63 through 66.

1   cup creamy peanut butter

¼   cup light brown sugar (see Note)

2   garlic cloves, finely minced or pressed through a garlic press

2   tablespoons soy sauce

2   tablespoons fresh lime juice (from 1 to 2 limes)

1   tablespoon grated fresh ginger

1½ teaspoons Asian chile paste, such as Sriracha, or hot sauce

PLACE THE peanut butter, brown sugar, garlic, soy sauce, lime juice, ginger, and chile paste or hot sauce in a food processor and process until well blended, 15 to 20 seconds, scraping down the sides once or twice. The peanut sauce can be refrigerated in an airtight container for up to 2 days or frozen for up to 2 months.

Note: If you're using unsweetened peanut butter, add an extra 2 tablespoons of brown sugar.

D2D

At my house, we try to take a few nights off from meat every week. It's not only a healthier way to eat, but eating tofu saves us more than $1 per pound when compared to other proteins.

Peanut Soup with Sweet Potatoes

THE
SPIN-
OFF

SERVES 4

$5.05/
$1.25

If you're searching for a hearty, inexpensive, meat-free option for dinner, look no further. This simple soup is loaded with protein, vitamins, and minerals from the peanut–sweet potato combo. It's comforting and rich, just the ticket on a crisp fall night. I cut the sweet potatoes into bite-size pieces so they cook quickly, providing a quick meal you can make in under 30 minutes. Besides sweet potatoes, this soup takes well to any hard winter squash (though you might need to cook it a tad longer). Make a big batch and freeze it in smaller portions for lunches or quick weekday meals. For a vegetarian version, use vegetable broth or even water. This soup is so big on flavor that I like to keep the side dish basic with plain white or brown rice.

SIMMER THE VEGETABLES. Heat the oil in a Dutch oven over medium-high heat. Add the onion and celery and cook, stirring occasionally, until softened, about 7 minutes. Add the curry powder and cook until fragrant, about 30 seconds. Add the chicken broth and sweet potato, bring to a simmer, then reduce the heat to medium, cover, and cook until the sweet potato is just tender, about 5 minutes.

FINISH THE SOUP. Place the peanut base in a medium heatproof bowl. Pour in ½ cup of the hot broth and whisk until smooth, then scrape this mixture back into the pot and stir to combine. Cover partially, and continue to simmer to blend the flavors, about 3 minutes. Season the soup to taste with salt and pepper and serve sprinkled with cilantro.

1 tablespoon vegetable oil

1 large onion, finely chopped

1 celery stalk, finely chopped

1 teaspoon curry powder

4 cups chicken broth, homemade (page 36) or store-bought

1 medium sweet potato (about 12 ounces), peeled and cut into ¾" pieces

½ cup Easy Basic Peanut Sauce (opposite page)

Salt

Freshly ground black pepper

3 tablespoons finely chopped fresh cilantro

D2D

Farmers' markets are a great source for seasonal produce. For the best value, go about 30 minutes before closing, when most growers would rather sell their items at a discounted price than load them back on the truck.

Peanut Noodles with Tofu & Scallions

It's easy to get stuck in a pasta rut when you're trying to eat on the cheap, but think beyond red sauce and it won't feel like you're being frugal. This Asian noodle dish is a refreshing alternative, packed with protein, and good for vegetarian friends, too. Served at room temperature or even a little chilled, it's great for lunch boxes, picnics, and summer dinners.

MARINATE THE TOFU. Gently toss the tofu with 1 tablespoon of soy sauce and ½ tablespoon of sesame oil in a small bowl and set aside.

BOIL THE NOODLES. Bring a large pot of water to a boil. Add the noodles and cook until tender (check the package directions for the cooking time). Drain and rinse under cold running water until the noodles are cooled. Drain well, shaking the colander several times, and transfer to a large bowl. Toss the noodles with the remaining 2 tablespoons of sesame oil.

COMBINE NOODLES, SAUCE, AND VEGETABLES. Whisk the peanut sauce base, the remaining 2 tablespoons of the soy sauce, and the chicken broth together in a small bowl until combined. Add to the noodles and toss to coat. Add all but 2 tablespoons of the scallions, the carrot, bell pepper, and sesame seeds and toss well. Drain the tofu, add to the noodles, and toss gently. Divide the noodles among 4 bowls, sprinkle each with the reserved scallions, and serve.

8 ounces extra-firm tofu, cut into ½" cubes

3 tablespoons soy sauce

2½ tablespoons toasted sesame oil

1 pound fresh, Asian-style noodles or 12 ounces dried chow mein noodles or spaghetti (preferably thin noodles such as spaghettini)

⅔ cup Easy Basic Peanut Sauce (page 62)

3 tablespoons chicken broth, vegetable broth, or water

4 scallions, sliced thin on the diagonal

1 carrot, peeled and grated

1 small red bell pepper, cut into matchsticks

2 tablespoons sesame seeds lightly toasted in a skillet

> **Ⓢ COOK SMART**
>
> Whether you're using homemade or store-bought chicken broth (or beef or vegetable broth), get into the habit of pouring leftover broth into an ice cube tray to freeze it. Once frozen, place the cubes in a gallon-size resealable zipper bag. Each cube is equal to 2 tablespoons (1 ounce), great for recipes that call for ½ cup (4 cubes) of broth or less.

Thai-Style Chicken Satay
with Quick Cucumber Pickles

Corn dogs, kebabs, chocolate-covered bananas—food on a stick is just fun to eat, and that goes double for these sophisticated chicken skewers. By cutting the chicken into strips on the bias, I get about 18 pieces from 1½ pounds of chicken—that's 6 servings for about $6. Served with steamed rice and a pickled cucumber salad, that's enough for a nice meal, a fun snack for company, or even for party eats on a buffet table. To cut some time from the recipe, marinate the chicken ahead of time and freeze it in freezer bags for up to 1 month, or vacuum-seal it for up to 3 months. Save any leftover cucumber salad to top sandwiches or serve with the Salmon Teriyaki on page 97.

CHICKEN

- 1½ pounds boneless, skinless chicken breasts or thighs (freeze on a baking sheet or plate for 15 minutes for the easiest slicing)
- ½ cup coconut milk
- 2 tablespoons fish sauce (optional)
- 1 tablespoon lime juice
- 1½ tablespoons light brown sugar
- 2 medium garlic cloves, minced
- 1 teaspoon ground turmeric
- ½ teaspoon ground cumin

PEANUT SAUCE

- ½ cup Easy Basic Peanut Sauce (page 62)
- ⅓ cup coconut milk
- 1 tablespoon fish sauce

MARINATE THE CHICKEN. Holding a sharp chef's knife at about a 45-degree angle to the cutting board, cut each piece of chicken into strips about ¼" thick. Combine the coconut milk, fish sauce (if using), lime juice, brown sugar, garlic, turmeric, and cumin in a bowl and stir until the sugar dissolves. Add the chicken and stir well to coat. Cover and refrigerate for at least 30 minutes or up to 2 hours. Soak eighteen 10" bamboo skewers (you can use metal skewers too, but the chicken will cover only half of the skewer) in water to cover for at least 30 minutes.

MAKE THE PEANUT SAUCE AND PICKLES. Whisk the peanut sauce base, coconut milk, and fish sauce in a small bowl until combined. Transfer the peanut sauce to a serving bowl. Combine the vinegar, 2 tablespoons of water, the sugar, fish sauce (if using), and pepper flakes in another small bowl, stirring until the sugar dissolves. Toss with the cucumber and red onion and transfer to a serving bowl.

GRILL THE CHICKEN. Heat a gas or charcoal grill to high heat. Thread the chicken strips onto the skewers, leaving room at the bottom of each skewer to hold it. Grill the skewers over high heat until nicely grill-marked on both sides, about 5 minutes. Serve right away with the peanut sauce and cucumber pickles.

TAKE IT INDOORS: Instead of grilling the satay, you can broil the skewers or cook them in a grill pan on your stove top. If broiling, adjust the oven rack to the upper-middle position and heat the broiler. Place the skewers on a rimmed baking sheet, lay a doubled sheet of foil over the exposed portion of the skewers, and broil until the chicken is cooked through, about 10 minutes, turning the skewers over midway through. If using a grill pan, heat the pan over medium-high heat. Brush the ridges with some oil and cook the chicken on both sides until cooked through, 6 to 8 minutes total, turning the skewers midway through cooking.

D2D

Boneless, skinless chicken thighs are becoming easier to find in supermarkets as well as warehouse clubs, where they come individually packaged. Not only do they offer more flavor and juiciness than breast fillets, but they'll save you $1.20 per pound. If you can't find them at your store, buy thighs and bone them yourself—just remember to save the bones and skin in a resealable bag in the freezer for chicken stock!

PICKLES

¼ cup rice vinegar

2 tablespoons sugar

½ teaspoon fish sauce (optional)

¼ teaspoon red-pepper flakes

½ large cucumber, peeled, seeded, and cut into ¼" slices

¼ small red onion, thinly sliced

MAKE IT A MEAL
+ Steamed white rice

say good-bye to the same old

Chicken, pork chops, salmon fillets—where would weeknight meals be without these tried-and-true staples? They turn up on our menu—at home and at the Cafe—week in and week out because they are quick to cook, reasonably priced, and just about everyone likes them. At home we usually have beef once a week and at least one meatless night, but the other nights are most often devoted to one of these 3 center-plate items, and no one ever seems to get tired of them.

This doesn't mean I serve them up the same old way each time. While my family definitely has favorites, I'm always trying out new ways to shake up the standards.

Fortunately, running the Rock puts me in a unique position to chat up visitors from all corners of the world who cruise Route 66. I love asking them about their country and traditions (even if they're just up from Texas!). We trade recipes and before you know it, I've got a great new take on chicken paprikash up my sleeve. The 15 chicken, pork, and fish recipes in this chapter are anything *but* "the same old."

5 Ways with Baked Chicken

So many people tell me they've gotten stuck in a chicken rut, falling back on one or two old reliables time after time. Well, I'm here to tell you that by cooking your potatoes differently, or adding some paprika, hot sauce, or a can of crushed pineapple, you can revitalize that chicken recipe and proudly present a whole new low-cost take on chicken 5 nights a week.

Barbecued Pineapple Chicken

When I was a purser on a cruise line, we'd revisit the same Caribbean islands (with a boatload of new visitors) several times in a month. My shipmates and I got into the habit of showing up weekly at the same joints for our favorite meals. Sweetened with canned pineapple, this barbecued chicken became my all-time favorite.

SERVES 4

$5.00/
$1.25

BROWN THE CHICKEN. Heat the oven to 325°F. Heat the oil in a large skillet (preferably cast iron) over medium-high heat. Pat the chicken dry, season with the salt and pepper, and place in the pan, skin-side down. Cook without moving until the chicken skin is browned, 4 to 5 minutes. Turn the chicken over and cook the other side until browned, about 3 minutes longer.

MAKE THE SAUCE. Meanwhile, whisk the flour and barbecue sauce together in a small bowl until smooth. Stir in the pineapple and ginger and set aside.

CHICKEN

- 2 tablespoons canola oil
- 4 chicken leg quarters or 8 chicken legs and/or thighs
- 1 teaspoon salt
- ½ teaspoon freshly ground black pepper

(continues...)

SAUCE

- 1½ tablespoons all-purpose flour
- 1 cup barbecue sauce, home-made (page 21) or store-bought
- 1 can (20 ounces) crushed pineapple in natural juice
- 2 teaspoons ground ginger

MAKE IT A MEAL
+ Straight-Up Cornbread
(page 167)

BAKE THE CHICKEN. Transfer the chicken to a 13" x 9" baking dish. Pour the sauce over the chicken, making sure all the pieces are nicely coated. Bake for 1 hour to 1 hour and 15 minutes, basting every 20 minutes, or until the juices at the leg/thigh joint run clear and an instant-read thermometer inserted into the thickest part of the thigh reads 175°F. Serve immediately.

D2D

Learning to break down a whole chicken into serving pieces is a great investment. Not only are whole chickens less per pound than parts, you can save the backs, necks, wing tips, and breast bones (if you bone out your own chicken breasts) for stock. I love getting something for nothing, and making chicken stock from scratch is the best example of that I can think of. I always keep a stock bag in my freezer. To it I'll add veggie trimmings as well as trimmings from raw chickens (wing tips, backbones, necks, trimmed fat). After a month or so, I usually have enough chicken trimmings (3 to 4 pounds) and veggies to make a great homemade chicken stock, no extra expenditure required! Then I'll strain the homemade broth and freeze it in resealable quart-size freezer bags and in ice cube trays for smaller, 2-tablespoon cubes.

Caribbean Salsa

This salsa is really nice with barbecued chicken, fish, and even grilled pork chops. Place 2 cups of bite-size tropical fruit (mangoes and papayas, or a combination of the two, are really good) in a bowl. Stir in ¼ cup finely chopped red onion (about half of a small onion), ¼ cup finely chopped fresh cilantro or mint (or a combination of the two), the juice of 1 lime, 2 teaspoons sugar, and ¼ teaspoon salt. Serve within 6 hours.

One-Pot Chicken Paprikash & Noodles

This baked chicken dish gives you everything you need in one pot: succulent and tender chicken, mushrooms and onions, and rustic sheets of pasta. I don't always have white wine on hand—when I don't, I just substitute an extra cup of chicken broth with an extra squeeze of lemon.

SERVES 4

$12.80/ $3.20

BROWN THE CHICKEN. Heat the oven to 350°F. Season the chicken with ¼ teaspoon of salt and ¼ teaspoon of pepper. Toss with 2 tablespoons of flour. Melt the butter in a large ovenproof Dutch oven over medium-high heat. Add the chicken, skin-side down, and cook until browned on all sides, 5 to 7 minutes. Remove from the pot and set aside.

MAKE THE PAPRIKA SAUCE. Add the onion and garlic to the pot, reduce the heat to medium, and cook until soft and just starting to brown, 3 to 5 minutes. Stir in the mushrooms, and once they get juicy, add all but 1 tablespoon parsley, the paprika, cayenne, and remaining 1 teaspoon of salt and ¼ teaspoon of pepper. Cook for 1 minute (if the pan looks dry, add 1 table-spoon water) and then stir in the remaining 1½ table-spoons of flour, cooking while stirring constantly for 2 minutes. Stir in the white wine, making sure to work out any lumps, before adding the broth and cream.

BAKE. Stir the broken sheets of pasta into the pot. Return the chicken to the pot and turn the pieces over a few times to coat with sauce. Cover the pot and bake until the chicken and noodles are cooked through, about 1 hour, basting the chicken with sauce about halfway through. Squeeze some lemon juice into the pot and serve sprinkled with the remaining parsley.

1¾ pounds bone-in, skin-on chicken breasts or thighs

1¼ teaspoons salt

½ teaspoon freshly ground black pepper

3½ tablespoons all-purpose flour

2 tablespoons unsalted butter

1 white or yellow onion, finely chopped

2 garlic cloves, finely minced or pressed through a garlic press

8 ounces button mushrooms, stemmed and thinly sliced

¼ cup finely chopped fresh parsley

2 teaspoons sweet paprika

Pinch of cayenne

1 cup dry white wine (such as a Sauvignon Blanc or Pinot Grigio)

2 cups chicken broth, homemade (page 36) or store-bought

¼ cup heavy cream or half-and-half

8 ounces no-boil egg lasagna noodles (about 12 sheets), each sheet broken into 1"–2" pieces

1 lemon, halved

Chicken with Mushroom-Wine Sauce & Roesti Potato Cakes

SERVES 4

I'm always looking for new spins on potato recipes. In this version, shredded potatoes become a giant hash-brown cake, super crispy on the outside and deliciously snowy-soft on the inside.

$13.80/ $3.45

ROESTI

- 5 Yukon gold potatoes (1¾ pounds), peeled
- 2 tablespoons + 1 teaspoon salt
- ½ teaspoon freshly ground black pepper
- 3 tablespoons unsalted butter

CHICKEN

- 1½ pounds bone-in, skin-on chicken breasts or thighs (if using breasts, split them in half crosswise)
- ¼ teaspoon salt
- ¼ teaspoon finely ground black pepper
- 2 tablespoons unsalted butter, quartered

SAUCE

- 1 yellow onion, halved and finely chopped
- 2 garlic cloves, finely minced or pressed through a garlic press
- 8 ounces button mushrooms, sliced

BOIL THE POTATOES. Place the potatoes in a large pot and cover with 2" of cold water. Add 2 tablespoons of salt, bring to a boil, and cook until the potatoes are just tender and a paring knife easily slips into the center, 22 to 26 minutes. Drain and transfer the potatoes to a bowl of ice water for 10 minutes to cool.

BROWN THE CHICKEN. Heat the oven to 400°F. Season the chicken with ¼ teaspoon of salt and ¼ teaspoon of pepper and set it aside. Heat a large ovenproof skillet (preferably cast iron) over medium-high heat for 2 minutes. Add the butter and once melted, add the chicken, skin-side down. Cook until the skin is brown and crisp, 4 to 5 minutes. Turn the chicken over and brown the other side, about 3 minutes longer. Use tongs to transfer the chicken to a large plate (the chicken will still be raw on the inside).

MAKE THE MUSHROOM-WINE SAUCE. Add the onion to the pan and cook until soft and just starting to brown, about 4 minutes, stirring often. Stir in the garlic and cook until fragrant, about 30 seconds, then add the mushrooms and cook, stirring often, until they release their juices, about 5 minutes. Reduce the heat to medium-low and mix in the paprika, cayenne, ½ teaspoon of salt, and ¼ teaspoon of pepper and then stir in the flour (if the pan looks dry, add 2 tablespoons of water). Stir constantly for 2 minutes and then slowly begin adding the wine or beer a little at a time, working out any lumps before adding more. Once all of the wine or beer is added, pour in the broth and cream.

BAKE THE CHICKEN. Bring the sauce to a simmer and return the chicken to the pan skin-side up. Bake until the chicken is cooked through, about 1 hour. Sprinkle with parsley and lemon juice (if using). Cover the pan and set it aside until the roësti are finished.

MAKE THE ROESTI. While the chicken bakes, heat a large, nonstick skillet over medium-high heat. While the pan is heating, shred the cooled potatoes on the large-hole side of a box grater and into a large bowl. Gently mix 1 teaspoon of salt and the black pepper with the shredded potatoes.

PLACE 2 TABLESPOONS of butter in the pan, and once melted, sprinkle in the potatoes, trying to make an even layer no thicker than ½". (Divide the butter and potatoes into 2 batches if you're using a smaller skillet.) Reduce the heat to medium and cook the potatoes until golden brown and crisp on the bottom, about 8 minutes. Slide the potato pancake onto a rimless plate (an upturned pot lid works great and even has a handle!) and invert it onto another rimless plate (the underside of a sheet pan works fine). Add the remaining 1 tablespoon of butter to the pan, and slide the potato pancake, uncooked-side down, back into the pan. Brown for 8 minutes longer, then slide the potato cake onto a cutting board and slice it into 4 wedges. Serve each wedge with some chicken and sauce.

2	teaspoons sweet paprika
	Pinch of cayenne
½	teaspoon kosher salt
¼	teaspoon freshly ground black pepper
1½	tablespoons all-purpose flour
1	cup dry white wine or beer
1	cup chicken broth, homemade (page 36) or store-bought
¼	cup heavy cream
¼	cup finely chopped fresh flat-leaf parsley (optional)
	Juice of ½ lemon (optional)

COOK SMART

I like to boil 4 to 6 potatoes in the beginning of the week and keep them in the fridge for making roesti, hash browns, or mashed potatoes.

COOK SMART

If you have herbs in the fridge, don't let them go to waste. Add a teaspoon or two (finely chopped) to these roesti. You can also add a few sprigs to a stock bag.

Buffalo Chicken Salad

SERVES 4

$8.20/
$2.05

My family is big into salad dinners, especially in the summertime. Buying veggies in their whole form is definitely less expensive than paying a premium for someone else to shred, slice, and dice. I get the whole family into the kitchen and everyone participates, from peeling and cutting carrots to washing greens and spinning them dry (a great task for kids).

2   pounds chicken wings (drummettes and wing sections separated), legs, or thighs

¼   cup hot sauce

1   teaspoon canola oil

2   tablespoons Tex-Mex Rub (page 118)

⅛   teaspoon salt

8   cups roughly torn iceberg or romaine lettuce

2   carrots, trimmed, peeled, and shaved into ribbons with a vegetable peeler

2   celery stalks, trimmed and finely chopped

½   cup blue cheese dressing, homemade (page 180) or store-bought

 COOK SMART
Marinate a double batch of wings and freeze half for game day or movie night.

MARINATE THE CHICKEN. If using chicken legs or thighs, remove the skin before placing them into a gallon-size resealable plastic bag or airtight container with the hot sauce. Wings can go in as is. Turn the chicken a few times in the sauce to coat, and marinate them for at least 4 to 24 hours. (The longer you marinate them, the more flavor they'll have. You can also freeze them in the marinade for up to 3 months.)

BAKE THE CHICKEN. Heat the oven to 375°F. Line a rimmed sheet pan with foil and lightly grease the foil with the oil. Arrange the chicken on the pan. Mix the spice rub with the salt and sprinkle some over each piece, rolling them around a little to try to get some spices onto every side of the chicken. Bake the chicken until the skin gets crisp and the chicken juices run clear (if cooking thighs or legs, an instant-read thermometer inserted into the thickest part should read 175°F), 22 to 25 minutes for wings and 35 to 40 minutes for legs or thighs. Remove from the oven and set aside.

MAKE THE SALAD. Toss the lettuce, carrots, celery, and blue cheese dressing together in a large bowl. Divide the salad and chicken among 4 plates and serve.

Here Chicken, Chicken

I may know that I'm going to make chicken twice during the week, but I never decide which type of chicken until I check out the supermarket's sales flyer. If breasts are on sale, I'll make them, or if there's a great deal on chicken quarters, I'll buy those and split them up when I get home. Whole chickens are almost always cheaper than cut-up chickens or parts, so if I have the time, I'll buy the whole bird and chop it up at home (and of course save the backbones and necks for soup!). Staying flexible keeps my options for saving a buck or two open.

Brown Sugar Rock Chicken

$11.60/
$2.90

This brown sugar–brined chicken has been in the Rock's menu for 15 years. The brine uses pantry ingredients such as brown sugar, salt, and dried herbs, so it's easy to throw together in the morning or even the night before you plan to serve it. That way, all you need to do before dinner is bake it.

1 cup (or ½ cup table salt) +
1 teaspoon kosher salt

1½ cups dark brown sugar

1 yellow onion, quartered

4 garlic cloves, smashed

6 bay leaves

6 whole black peppercorns

2 pounds bone-in, skin-on chicken breasts, legs, or thighs

2 fennel bulbs, fronds and stalks removed, cored, and sliced into ½"-thick wedges

1 red onion, halved and sliced into ½"-thick wedges

3 tablespoons olive oil

½ teaspoon freshly ground black pepper

 MAKE IT A MEAL
+ Pilaf with Almonds and Golden Raisins (page 153)

BRINE THE CHICKEN. Bring 2 cups of water to a boil in a large pot. Stir in 1 cup of salt and the brown sugar until dissolved, and turn off the heat. Let the mixture cool for 15 minutes before adding 12 cups of cold water, the yellow onion, garlic, and spices. Divide the mixture and chicken between 2 gallon-size resealable plastic bags and refrigerate for at least 8 hours or up to 24 hours.

BAKE THE CHICKEN. Heat the oven to 350°F. Toss the fennel and red onion with 2 tablespoons of olive oil, ½ teaspoon of salt, and ¼ teaspoon of pepper in a 3-quart baking dish. Drain the chicken and pat dry with paper towels. Place the chicken pieces skin-side up on top of the vegetables, brush with the remaining oil, and sprinkle with the remaining salt and pepper. Roast until the chicken skin is crisp and golden, and the chicken is completely cooked through, stirring the vegetables halfway through cooking, 50 minutes to 1 hour. Remove the chicken from the oven and adjust the oven rack to the upper-middle position. Transfer the vegetables to a bowl and set aside. Heat the broiler to high and broil the chicken until the skin is crisp, 1 to 2 minutes (watch the chicken carefully, as broiler intensity varies). Divide the chicken among plates and serve the vegetables on the side.

 SHOP SMART
If you're not into fennel, then substitute any other sliced vegetable, such as potatoes, carrots, rutabagas, parsnips, or even Brussels sprouts.

5 Ways with Pan-Seared Pork Chops

I don't know anyone who can resist a pan-seared pork chop, all browned and succulent, served up with a delicious sauce. Pork chops are wonderful not just because they taste amazing—they're also easy on the wallet, especially if you buy them in value packs (freeze what you won't use within a few days). These recipes are based on thin-cut pork chops. You can substitute thick chops if you like; after browning both sides, transfer the chops to a rimmed sheet pan and finish them off in a hot oven.

Apple Chops in Whiskey Sauce

SERVES 4

This nice Southern take on chops uses apple juice and whiskey to create a sauce for browned pork chops, apples, and onions. If you don't have whiskey in the house, you can use chicken broth or even water with a few shakes of Worcestershire sauce instead.

$6.00/ $1.50

- 4 bone-in pork chops (6 ounces each, ½" thick)
- 1 cup apple juice or cider
- ½ cup whiskey
- ¼ cup cider vinegar
- 4 teaspoons Dijon mustard
- 2 teaspoons fresh lemon juice
- 1 teaspoon dried sage
- ¼ teaspoon cayenne

PREP THE CHOPS. To prevent the pork chops from curling as they cook, make 2 or 3 small, vertical cuts into the fat and silver skin surrounding the meat on each chop.

MARINATE THE CHOPS. Whisk the apple juice, ¼ cup of the whiskey, the vinegar, mustard, lemon juice, sage, cayenne, salt, and pepper together in a bowl. Pour the mixture into a measuring cup and transfer half to a gallon-size resealable plastic bag. Add the pork chops to the plastic bag and turn to coat, then refrigerate for at least 30 minutes or up to 24 hours (the chops can also be frozen in the marinade for up to 3 months). Use plastic wrap to cover the remaining brine (which becomes the sauce for the chops) and refrigerate it until you're ready to cook the chops. (You can also pour the remaining brine into a quart-size resealable plastic bag and freeze until you're ready to use it.)

BROWN THE CHOPS. Heat the oven to 250°F. Heat the oil in a large skillet over medium-high heat. Remove the pork chops from the brine and pat them dry (discard any remaining brine). Cover and cook the pork chops until nicely browned, 3 to 4 minutes. Turn over and brown the other side, cooking the chops until they're no longer pink in the middle, an additional 3 to 4 minutes. Place the chops on an oven-safe platter, cover with foil, and place in the oven to keep warm.

FINISH THE CHOPS. Add the apple and onion to the pan (if the pan is dry, add a little oil), cover, and cook until they both begin to brown, stirring often, about 8 minutes. Pour in the reserved liquid for the sauce and the remaining ¼ cup of whiskey. Bring to a simmer, reduce the heat to medium, and cook, uncovered, until the sauce has reduced slightly, about 3 to 4 minutes. Remove the chops from the oven and pour the whiskey sauce over the top. Serve immediately.

1 teaspoon salt

½ teaspoon freshly ground black pepper

1 tablespoon canola oil

1 Granny Smith apple, cored, halved, and thinly sliced

1 red onion, thinly sliced

MAKE IT A MEAL
+ Spoon-Tender Green Beans with Bacon (page 196)

D2D
Mini-bar-size bottles of liquor and wine are great to have on hand to use in cooking. While ounce per ounce they are more expensive than buying a large bottle, it works out cheaper than leaving the unused bottle of whiskey on a shelf for years.

Maple-Balsamic Chops with Glazed Carrots

SERVES 4

$5.40/
$1.35

Cast-iron skillets are made to last a lifetime—I'll take one over an expensive stainless steel frying pan any day. I've been using mine for years, and instead of showing its wear and tear, it only gets better with time. Tag sale finds are often already broken-in and seasoned.

3 tablespoons + 2¼ teaspoons table salt

3 tablespoons light brown sugar

3 garlic cloves, crushed

4 bone-in pork chops (6 ounces each, ½" thick)

1 pound carrots, trimmed, peeled, and cut on the diagonal into ¼" slices, or 1 pound baby carrots

½ teaspoon freshly ground black pepper

1 tablespoon canola oil

¼ cup balsamic vinegar

¼ cup maple syrup

1½ tablespoons Dijon mustard

2 pods star anise or 1 cinnamon stick

COOK SMART

Real maple syrup is not cheap, so if you don't have any for the glaze, make a quick brown sugar syrup by bringing 5 tablespoons of dark brown sugar to a boil with ¼ cup of water.

BRINE THE CHOPS. Dissolve 3 tablespoons of salt and the sugar in 2 cups of warm water in a large bowl. Add the garlic, 2 cups cold water, and the pork chops. Refrigerate for 30 minutes or up to 1 hour.

PARBOIL THE CARROTS. Meanwhile, bring 2 quarts of water to a boil in a large saucepan over high heat. Add 2 teaspoons of salt and the carrots and cook until the carrots are barely tender, 3 to 4 minutes. Drain and rinse under cold water to stop the cooking. Drain again.

SEAR THE CHOPS. Remove the chops from the brine (discard the remaining brine), rinse under cold water, and pat dry with paper towels. Season the chops on all sides with the pepper. Heat the oil in a large, nonstick skillet or cast-iron skillet over medium-high heat. Add the pork chops and cook until browned on both sides and cooked through, about 5 minutes total. Transfer to a large plate.

GLAZE THE CHOPS AND CARROTS. Whisk the balsamic vinegar, maple syrup, mustard, and the remaining ¼ teaspoon salt together in a small bowl. Pour the mixture into the skillet, add the star anise or cinnamon, and cook over medium-high heat, scraping the pan bottom with a wooden spoon to loosen the browned bits, until a thick, syrupy glaze forms, about 3 minutes. Return the pork chops and any accumulated juices to the pan and turn each chop to coat with the glaze, then transfer the chops to a clean plate. Add the carrots to the pan and cook, stirring occasionally, just until heated through, 2 to 3 minutes. Serve the chops with carrots spooned alongside.

Chops au Poivre & Herbed Spaetzle

SERVES 4

$4.40/
$1.10

In Germany, spaetzle is as popular as French fries, eaten with just about anything. When I started cooking spaetzle at the Cafe, people went so crazy for it that I had to start making extra batches to freeze because diners were stopping in and buying the uncooked spaetzle right off me so they could cook it up themselves at home for dinner! If only they knew how easy they are to make, based on simple pantry ingredients and some fresh herbs. They really class up a simple dish of pork chops, though!

CHOPS

- 4 bone-in pork chops (6 ounces each, ½" thick)
- ½ teaspoon salt
- ¼ cup coarsely ground black pepper
- 2 teaspoons canola oil

SPAETZLE

- 4 cups all-purpose flour
- 3 large eggs
- 1 cup low-fat or whole milk
- 2 teaspoons lemon juice (optional)
- ¼ teaspoon salt
  All-purpose flour
- 3 tablespoons unsalted butter at room temperature
- 1 tablespoon finely chopped tender herbs (such as basil, chives, or tarragon)

SEASON THE CHOPS. To prevent the pork chops from curling as they cook, make 2 or 3 small, vertical cuts into the fat and silver skin surrounding the meat on each chop. Season the chops with the salt. Place the pepper on a plate and shake the plate a little to evenly disperse it in a single layer. Dip one side of each chop in the pepper, then place the chop on a plate. Cover with plastic wrap and refrigerate.

MAKE THE SPAETZLE. Place the flour in a large bowl and make a well in the center. Whisk the eggs, milk, lemon juice (if using), and salt together in a small bowl and pour into the well. Combine using a wooden spoon to create a dough. Generously flour a sheet pan. Break off pieces of dough (about ⅓-cup knobs), roll into a ¼"-thick rope, flatten slightly, and cut into ¼"-long pieces. Repeat with the remaining dough.

BOIL THE SPAETZLE. Bring a large pot of salted water to a boil. Boil the spaetzle until cooked all the way through, 10 to 15 minutes, and then drain in a colander and rinse under cold water. Line a sheet pan with paper towels and place the spaetzle on it to drain for a few minutes before cooking or freezing (if freezing the spaetzle, leave it on the sheet pan and freeze for 1 hour, then transfer to a few quart-size resealable freezer bags for up to 3 months).

(continues...)

COOK THE PORK CHOPS. While the spaetzle boils, start the chops. Heat a large skillet (preferably cast iron) over medium-high heat for 1 minute. Add the oil and then the pork chops, pepper-side down. Cover and cook the chops until the pepper is browned, 3 to 4 minutes. Reduce the heat to medium, turn the chops over, and continue cooking until the chops are cooked through, an additional 3 to 4 minutes. Transfer to a platter to rest.

BROWN THE SPAETZLE. Melt 1 tablespoon of butter in a large skillet over medium-high heat. Add enough spaetzle to fill the pan in a single layer (you will need to brown them in batches) and cook, stirring occasionally, until browned on all sides, about 4 minutes. Repeat with another tablespoon of butter and the remaining spaetzle. Transfer the spaetzle to a serving bowl and toss with the remaining butter and herbs and add a pinch of salt if needed. Serve with the chops.

Spiced Chops over Braised Red Cabbage

Cabbage is such a great value; red or green, I cook it up all kinds of ways, from coleslaw to corned beef and cabbage, and stuffed cabbage. In this recipe, I pair red cabbage with red wine and red wine vinegar, both of which match up nicely to a warm, allspice-rubbed, and clove-studded chop.

$8.60/
$2.15

BRAISE THE CABBAGE. Heat the oven to 325°F. Place all of the cabbage ingredients in a 13" x 9" baking dish, cover with foil, and cook until the cabbage is very soft, about 1 hour.

SEAR THE PORK. About 10 minutes before the cabbage is done, heat the olive oil in a large skillet (preferably cast iron) over medium-high heat. Sprinkle both sides of the chops with the salt and pepper and brown on both sides, about 5 minutes total.

ROAST THE PORK WITH THE CABBAGE. Remove the cabbage from the oven and arrange the browned chops on top. Sprinkle the allspice and thyme over the chops and stick 1 clove in each. Cover the dish, return it to the oven, and bake until the pork chops are cooked through, about another 20 minutes. Use a slotted spoon to transfer the cabbage to a serving dish. Top with the chops (remove the cloves) and cover to keep warm.

MAKE THE SAUCE. Pour the juices from the baking dish into a small saucepan, add the cream (if using), and bring to a gentle simmer over medium-low heat. Cook until the sauce is slightly thick, 5 to 7 minutes. Pour over the pork and cabbage before serving.

 D2D
Place any leftover cabbage in a saucepan with some chicken broth and a few diced potatoes for quick cabbage soup.

CABBAGE

- 1 head (1½ pounds) red cabbage, cored and thinly sliced
- 2 celery stalks, trimmed and sliced ½" thick
- 1 large white or yellow onion, halved and thinly sliced
- 1 cup dry red wine
- 2 tablespoons red wine vinegar
- 1 tablespoon unsalted butter
- 1 teaspoon salt
- ½ teaspoon freshly ground black pepper

CHOPS

- 4 bone-in pork chops (6 ounces each, ½" thick)
- 2 teaspoons olive oil
- ¾ teaspoon salt
- ¼ teaspoon freshly ground black pepper
- 1 teaspoon ground allspice
- 1 teaspoon dried thyme
- 4 whole cloves

SAUCE

- 1 tablespoon heavy cream (optional)

Mushroom- & Onion-Smothered Chops

SERVES 4

$6.60/
$1.65

Generally, my rule of thumb is that if a vegetable is pre-trimmed, diced, peeled, or shredded, it's going to cost you extra. Sometimes this isn't the case, though. Always compare apples to apples (or mushrooms to mushrooms in this case) to see which is the best value. If your market is overloaded with sliced mushrooms, you may get them for a steal and save money and prep time; just be sure to use them soon after you buy them, as prepped veggies always have a shorter shelf life than whole ones.

4 bone-in pork chops (6 ounces each, ½" thick)

¾ teaspoon salt

½ teaspoon freshly ground black pepper

4 tablespoons canola oil

8 ounces mushrooms, thinly sliced

2 medium yellow onions (or 1 large), thinly sliced

2 garlic cloves, finely minced

2 tablespoons all-purpose flour

2 cups chicken broth, homemade (page 36) or store-bought

1 bay leaf

1 teaspoon finely chopped fresh thyme leaves or ½ teaspoon dried thyme

1 teaspoon Worcestershire

2 tablespoons finely chopped flat-leaf parsley (optional)

MAKE IT A MEAL
+ Homestyle Smashed Potatoes with Dill (page 182)

SEASON AND SEAR THE CHOPS. To prevent the pork chops from curling as they cook, make 2 or 3 small, vertical cuts into the fat and silver skin surrounding the meat on each chop. Season the pork chops with ¼ teaspoon of salt and ¼ teaspoon of pepper. Heat 1 tablespoon of oil in a large skillet over high heat. Add the pork chops and cook until browned on both sides, about 3 minutes total (the chops won't be fully cooked). Transfer the chops to a large plate.

COOK THE MUSHROOMS AND ONIONS. Reduce the heat to medium-high, add 1 tablespoon of oil to the pan, the mushrooms, and ¼ teaspoon of salt and cook, stirring occasionally, until the mushrooms begin to brown, about 5 minutes. Transfer the mushrooms to a bowl. Heat the remaining 2 tablespoons of oil in the pan, add the onions, and stir in the remaining ¼ teaspoon of salt. Cook, stirring occasionally, until the onions are soft and pale golden, 8 to 10 minutes (reduce the heat if they're browning too quickly). Add the garlic and cook until fragrant, about 30 seconds. Sprinkle the flour over the onions and stir to evenly coat the onions. Pour in the chicken broth and stir, scraping the pan bottom with a wooden spoon to loosen any browned bits. Add the bay leaf, thyme, Worcestershire sauce, the remaining ¼ teaspoon of pepper, and the mushrooms, and bring to a simmer.

SMOTHER THE CHOPS. Nestle the pork chops in the onion mixture, overlapping them slightly if necessary and spooning some of the sauce and onion mixture over the chops to cover them. Reduce the heat to medium-low, cover, and simmer gently, occasionally spooning sauce over the chops, until the chops are tender, 25 to 30 minutes. Discard the bay leaf and transfer the chops to a platter or four plates. Sprinkle with the parsley, if using, and serve.

D2D

Save cleaned mushroom stems in a quart-size, resealable freezer bag and use them for making stew or pasta with mushrooms.

Pork Chops 101

Pork chops come in all kinds of shapes and sizes, from super-thin, $\frac{1}{4}$"-thick chops to husky $1\frac{1}{2}$" chops. For an average midweek dinner, I go for $\frac{1}{2}$"-thick chops that can be cooked start-to-finish on the stovetop, since thicker ones need to be finished in the oven, like a thick steak. Also like a steak, chops come in different cuts, all from the pork loin. Here's a look at what's what:

CHOP	COMES FROM	CHARACTERISTICS	USE
Blade chop	Loin end closest to the shoulder	Rich, high bone-to-meat ratio	Braising, stewing
Rib chop	Center of the loin (curved rib bone on one side)	Juicy, meaty, slightly fattier than other chops (less likely to dry out)	Broiling, grilling, searing
Center-cut loin chop	Part loin, part tenderloin (like a porterhouse steak)	Tender, flavorful	Broiling, grilling, searing
Top loin chop	Like a center-cut chop without the tenderloin muscle (like a strip steak)	Flavorful, lean	Broiling, grilling, searing
Sirloin chop	Loin closest to the hip	Rich, high bone-to-meat ratio	Braising, stewing

5 Ways with Roasted Salmon

Some people only see dollar signs when they hear the word *salmon*. Sure, salmon can be pricey—but there are deals to be had, especially if you can find a good source for frozen (and preferably wild) salmon. Salmon is by no means the cheapest protein on the block, but when I factor in all that heart-healthy flavor and those brain-boosting omega-3s, I think it's worth it. To make it affordable for my family, I balance out a salmon night with other, less-expensive meals during the week (see the menu maker on page 264). When you have a calculator always turned on inside your head, you can have your salmon (even wild salmon) and eat it, too. Think about portion size; often 4 ounces per person is plenty if you have substantial sides.

Coriander Sugar-Rubbed Salmon

SERVES 4

$13.80/ $3.45

The way commercial fishermen freeze salmon these days is nothing short of miraculous. If I put 2 cooked fillets in front of you, one that was fresh and one that was frozen, I'd bet you'd have a hard time telling which was which! There is absolutely no crime in buying frozen fish, especially when it's so convenient to have in the freezer (defrost in a bowl of cool water in about 30 minutes; replenish the cool water every 10 minutes). So good for you, and such a great value.

1½ tablespoons coriander seeds

1½ tablespoons cumin seeds

1 teaspoon black peppercorns

1 tablespoon fennel seeds

3 tablespoons dark brown sugar

1 teaspoon salt

4 salmon fillets (6 ounces each, 1"–1½" thick)

1 teaspoon canola oil

MAKE THE CORIANDER RUB. Toast the coriander, cumin, and peppercorns in a skillet over medium-high heat for 2 minutes, stirring often. Add the fennel seeds and continue to toast until fragrant and the cumin seeds brown, an additional 1 to 2 minutes. Transfer the spices to a rimmed sheet pan or plate to cool, and then place in a coffee grinder along with the sugar and salt and pulverize it to a fine powder. Transfer 2 tablespoons to a wide, shallow dish. (The rest can be stored in an airtight container or jar placed in a cool, dark spot for up to 1 month.)

(continues...)

PREP THE SALMON. Place the salmon on your work surface and feel for pinbones, using tweezers to remove any you find. Holding the salmon on the skin side, press the top into the spiced sugar, making sure the top is evenly coated, then set it on a large plate. Repeat with the remaining fillets, and then cover the plate with plastic wrap and refrigerate for at least 1 hour or preferably overnight.

ROAST THE SALMON. Adjust 1 oven rack to the upper position and 1 to the middle position. Heat the oven to 400°F. Line a rimmed baking sheet with foil and lightly grease the foil with the oil. Place the salmon skin-side down on the foil and roast on the middle rack until the fillets are cooked on the outside but still quite pink in the middle, 5 to 7 minutes. Turn the broiler on, move the salmon to the top rack, and broil until the sugar just starts to bubble, 1 to 2 minutes (watch your salmon carefully, as broiler intensity varies and the sugar can quickly burn). Remove from the oven and transfer the salmon (with or without the skin) to individual plates. Serve immediately.

Scallion & Tarragon Salmon Pockets

This recipe is one you can really tailor to suit your own taste or budget. It works beautifully with all kinds of thick-cut fish fillets, such as cod, halibut, snapper, tilapia, and trout. You can substitute any tender herb, such as chives or basil, for the tarragon. And feel free to add whatever you have in the house, such as diced canned tomatoes, black olives, capers, red onions, fennel, bell peppers, and even a splash of vermouth or wine.

SERVES 4

$13.00/
$3.25

PREPARE THE POCKETS. Heat the oven to 375°F. Place four 12"-square pieces of foil on your work surface. Place 4 scallion halves in the center of each square. Top each pile of scallions with ½ teaspoon of tarragon and ¼ teaspoon of salt. Drizzle ¼ teaspoon of vinegar over each mound.

PREP THE SALMON. Set the salmon flat side down on top of the scallions. Squeeze a lemon half over the fillets and then sprinkle each fillet with ⅛ teaspoon of salt and some pepper. Fold the foil over the salmon, crimping the edges to seal, so you have a packet (the foil shouldn't be flush against the salmon; make sure the fish has some "breathing" room).

BAKE THE SALMON. Set the packets on a rimmed sheet pan and bake for 12 minutes for ½"-thick fillets and 14 minutes for ¾"-thick fillets. Remove the pan from the oven and let the fish rest for 5 minutes before slicing a slit in the top of each packet to let the steam out. Carefully tear open each packet and slide the salmon and scallions out and onto plates. Slice the remaining lemon half into 4 wedges and serve with the salmon.

8   scallions, white and light green parts only, halved lengthwise

2   teaspoons finely chopped tarragon

1½ teaspoons salt

1   teaspoon white wine vinegar

4   salmon fillets (6 ounces each, ½"–¾" thick), skin removed

1   lemon, halved

½   teaspoon freshly ground black pepper

MAKE IT A MEAL
+ Summer Tomato Gratin (page 193)

SHOP SMART
If you're shopping for seafood in the summertime, get into the habit of bringing a small portable cooler or insulated bag with you in the car. Place the fish in the cooler along with other frozen or cold items to keep its chill on during the drive home.

Salmon Penne, Charred Cherry Tomatoes & Basil

SERVES 4

$10.60/
$2.65

Oh, the magic of pasta—with just two salmon fillets, you can feed four hungry people! This dish is a thrifty, quick, and delicious way to get your fish once a week. By tossing it with familiar flavors such as fresh basil and tomatoes, it becomes a great way to initiate kids and others who shy away from fish to the deliciousness of salmon.

1   lemon, zested and halved (if you don't have a microplane grater for the lemon, finely chop the zest with a knife)

3¼   teaspoons salt

2   salmon fillets (6 ounces each, 1"–1½" thick)

1   pound penne pasta

1   tablespoon + 2 teaspoons olive oil

1   pound cherry tomatoes, halved

3   scallions, white and light green parts only, finely chopped

¼   cup roughly chopped fresh basil leaves

¼   teaspoon freshly ground black pepper

MAKE IT A MEAL
+ Summer Corn Soup (page 203)

MARINATE THE SALMON. Squeeze the juice from half a lemon into a large bowl. Whisk with ¼ teaspoon of salt, and then add the salmon fillets, turning them to coat with the juice. Refrigerate the salmon for up to 20 minutes.

COOK THE PENNE. While the salmon marinates, bring a large pot of water to a boil with 2 teaspoons of the salt. Add the penne and cook, following the box instructions, until al dente. Drain, reserving ¼ cup of the cooking liquid, and set aside.

BROIL THE SALMON AND TOMATOES. Adjust an oven rack to the upper position and heat the broiler to high. Toss the cherry tomatoes with 1 teaspoon of olive oil and ½ teaspoon of salt in a bowl. Line a rimmed sheet pan with foil and lightly grease with 1 teaspoon of the oil. Place the salmon skin-side down on the foil. Surround the salmon with the cherry tomatoes, cut-side up, and broil until the salmon is nearly cooked all the way through (it should be a little underdone at its thickest part), 5 to 7 minutes.

TOSS AND SERVE. Remove the pan from the oven. Transfer the tomatoes and the penne to a large serving bowl and toss with the scallions, basil, ½ teaspoon of lemon zest, the reserved cooking water, the remaining 1 tablespoon of olive oil, the remaining ½ teaspoon of salt, and the pepper. Use a fork to chunk the salmon away from the skin and arrange it on top of the pasta. Give it a light toss (be careful not to break up the salmon chunks) and taste for seasoning, adding more salt or lemon juice if needed, then serve.

COOK SMART

Canned salmon can easily stand in for fresh salmon in this recipe and will save you lots.

Freezing

Since my garden yields a huge amount of fresh herbs, I've started preserving what I don't use each summer. Drying works well for many herbs (especially lavender and rosemary, which don't freeze well), but for a fresher, "greener" taste, I prefer freezing (freezing is great for chervil, chives, dill, marjoram, oregano, parsley, tarragon, and thyme).

Place 2 tablespoons of chopped herbs in each cup of an ice cube tray (pack the herbs down), and then cover with about 1 tablespoon of water. Once the cubes are frozen, transfer them to a resealable freezer bag (don't forget to label and date it). When you need a hit of fresh herb flavor, add the frozen cube to what you're cooking (you can also let the cube defrost in a strainer to separate the herbs from the liquid). You can freeze herb pesto the same way, by the way—this is what I usually do with extra basil, which doesn't freeze or dry well.

Lemon-Rosemary Roasted Salmon

SERVES 4

$14.80/
$3.70

When summer is at its peak and my garden's herbs are plentiful, this is the dish I make. It just kind of flavors itself in the oven. All I have to do is remember to take it out!

4   salmon fillets (6 ounces each, 1"–1½" thick)

¾   teaspoon salt

½   teaspoon freshly ground black pepper

2   bunches fresh rosemary

1   red onion, halved and thinly sliced

3   lemons (2 thinly sliced crosswise into rounds, 1 sliced into wedges)

3   tablespoons olive oil

MAKE IT A MEAL

+ Thyme-Roasted Plum Tomatoes (page 191)
+ Crusty bread

PREPARE THE SALMON. Heat the oven to 450°F. Place the salmon on your work surface and feel for pinbones, using tweezers to remove any you find. Rub with ½ teaspoon of salt and the pepper and set aside. Arrange half of the rosemary in a 13" x 9" baking dish. Cover with the onion, sprinkle with the remaining ¼ teaspoon of salt, and place the salmon fillets skin-side down on top of the onions. Arrange the remaining rosemary over the salmon, shingle the lemon slices in neat rows over the rosemary, and drizzle with the olive oil.

ROAST THE SALMON. Roast the salmon until it is barely translucent in the thickest part of the fillet, 8 to 12 minutes (use the tip of a paring knife to move the citrus and herbs and peek in the center of the fillet). Remove from the oven. Using tongs or a fork, gently lift away and discard the lemons and rosemary. Serve the salmon with lemon wedges immediately.

D2D

A whole, fresh side of salmon often costs less than fillets, so it makes sense to buy a side of salmon and cut it into fillets yourself (refrigerate what you'll use within 1 or 2 days, and freeze the rest). It's incredibly easy: Just cut across the salmon to divide it into 6-ounce pieces. When slicing from the thick belly, make the fillets narrow, while fillets from the thinner ends can be on the wide side. Be sure the salmon you buy was not previously frozen; when refrozen and thawed, the quality will suffer.

Salmon Teriyaki

Here's another good entry-level dish for the fish-fearful. The sweet-salty flavor of teriyaki makes this extremely approachable and gives it a beautiful burnished glaze. You'll have some teriyaki sauce left over after making this dish, so save it to serve with grilled, pan-seared, or broiled chicken, or stir it into sautéed veggies and rice.

SERVES 4

$13.00/
$3.25

MAKE THE SAUCE. Whisk the soy sauce, brown sugar, garlic, and sesame oil, and red pepper (if using) together in a saucepan. Add the ginger coins and bring to a boil over medium-high heat. Reduce the heat to medium-low, and simmer until slightly thickened, about 15 minutes. Discard the ginger pieces and set aside (the sauce can be made up to 5 days ahead; refrigerate in a sealed jar).

PREP THE SALMON. Meanwhile, place the salmon fillets on a work surface and feel for pinbones, removing any you find with a pair of tweezers.

BROIL THE SALMON. Adjust an oven rack to the top position and heat the broiler to high. Line a rimmed sheet pan with foil and lightly grease with the oil. Place the salmon skin-side down on the foil. Broil until the salmon is nearly cooked all the way through (it should be a little underdone at its thickest part), 5 to 7 minutes, watching carefully to make sure the salmon doesn't burn. Remove from the oven and brush with the teriyaki sauce. Serve immediately.

SAUCE

- 1 cup soy sauce
- 1 cup light brown sugar
- 2 garlic cloves, finely minced or pressed through a garlic press
- 1 teaspoon toasted sesame oil
- ¼ teaspoon red-pepper flakes (optional)
- 1 piece fresh ginger (2"), peeled and sliced into thin coins

SALMON

- 4 salmon fillets (6 ounces each, 1"–1½" thick)
- 1 teaspoon canola oil

MAKE IT A MEAL
+ Quick Cucumber Pickles (pages 66–67)
+ White rice

D2D
If you have light brown sugar and need dark brown sugar, just add 1 tablespoon of molasses per cup of sugar. On the flip side, if you have dark brown sugar and you need light brown, substitute a few tablespoons of white sugar for the equal amount of dark brown sugar.

eating out at home

Most of the food I cook at home isn't very different from the food we serve at the Rock (except instead of paying for dishwashers, I enlist my kids!), and I love it, but sometimes I like to cook a bit outside the box. Like most people in the food business, I get inspired by eating in restaurants. Aside from the obvious convenience of having someone else do the shopping, cooking, and cleanup, it's a great way to discover interesting ingredients and flavorings, and of course there's the indulgence factor. Even a trip to a "continental" restaurant makes a simple steak or chop dinner seem more festive than the everyday. The obvious downside is the expense: Virtually any meal you cook at home is going to cost you less than a meal in a sit-down restaurant, and even ordering takeout can easily run $30 or more. So once a week I try to shake up the routine and get a little of that restaurant flavor on the table. Sometimes it just means cooking up something a tad more exotic, or using an unfamiliar flavor or ingredient that's sure to get everyone's attention and make dinner seem a little more special than the everyday fare. And while many of the ethnic cuisines that I favor aren't necessarily that expensive, when you make them at home, you control what goes into each dish, how much oil is used, and the quality of ingredients that make it onto the table. It's also a fun reminder of some of the far-flung spots I've been lucky enough to visit.

This chapter offers a global take on what's for dinner, from Belgian-style mussels to Jamaican jerk chicken and, of course, a good ol' American steakhouse meal. Eating in never tasted better, and never saved you more.

Rainy-Day Ribs

When I bought the Rock, I inherited the huge smoker the previous owners had used to make their brisket and ribs. I quickly discovered, though, that smoking meat is a tough business that takes a huge investment of time and money. Instead, I started baking them in the oven, then running them under the broiler with an extra mop of barbecue sauce just before serving. The ribs came out juicy and tender—far better than any that came out of that smoker. And oh yeah, you can make them rain or shine, since there is no grill needed!

SERVES 4

$12.40/ $3.10

PREP THE RIBS. Heat the oven to 300°F. Peel or clip off the membrane on the bony side of the ribs.

RUB, WRAP, AND BAKE. Mix the liquid smoke with a tablespoon of water and brush on both sides of the ribs. Rub the spice blend onto both sides of the ribs. Stack two 30" sheets of foil on your work surface and place the ribs on top. Place two more 30"-long sheets of foil on top and fold up the edges to seal. Set the ribs on a rimmed baking sheet and bake until the meat pulls away from the bones, about 2½ hours.

GLAZE AND FINISH THE RIBS. Remove the ribs from the oven, adjust an oven rack to the top position, and heat the broiler to high. Unwrap the rack and transfer to a foil-lined broiler pan, bone-side up. Brush with ½ cup of barbecue sauce and broil until the sauce is bubbling, about 2 minutes. Use tongs to turn the slab over, and brush ½ cup of barbecue sauce on the meaty side and broil until bubbling, about 2 more minutes. Transfer the ribs to a cutting board. Using a very sharp chef's knife, slice the rack into twelve 2-rib portions, slicing the sections as close to the bone as possible. Place the ribs on a platter, and serve with the remaining 1 cup of sauce on the side.

1 slab (2–2½ pounds) pork spare ribs

1 teaspoon liquid smoke

3 tablespoons Tex-Mex Rub (page 118)

2 cups barbecue sauce, homemade (page 21) or store-bought

MAKE IT A MEAL
+ German Potato Salad (page 186)

COOK SMART
When I am slow-roasting meats, I place an ovenproof casserole dish with 1 cup of water alongside the meat in the oven. The steam it gives up keeps the meat nice and moist, preventing it from toughening. Check the water level every so often throughout the cooking time and replenish it as needed.

Shrimp Pad Thai

SERVES 4

$14.40/
$3.60

The first time you make pad thai, you may have to stock up on ingredients you don't have in the house, such as rice stick noodles, fish sauce, and chili sauce. But once you have them around, making pad thai becomes just as easy as having Thai food delivered. If you prefer chicken or tofu to shrimp, use that instead.

8   ounces rice stick noodles

4   tablespoons canola oil

¼   cup lime juice (from 3 limes)

¼   cup dark brown sugar

¼   cup fish sauce

1½ teaspoons Asian chili sauce (such as Sriracha) or hot sauce

12 ounces extra-large shrimp, peeled and deveined

4   garlic cloves, finely minced or pressed through a garlic press

1   large shallot, finely minced

2   large eggs, beaten

5   scallions, dark green parts only (save the white parts for another use), cut into 1" sections

2   cups bean sprouts

3   tablespoons finely chopped, roasted, salted peanuts

D2D

Save your shrimp shells in the freezer. When you have a few cups, cover with water, add onion and carrot, and simmer for 10 minutes. You have a great broth for risottos, soups, or paella.

BOIL THE NOODLES. Bring a large pot of water to a boil over high heat. Turn off the heat, add the noodles, and stir to make sure they don't stick to the bottom of the pot. Let the noodles soak until they are very pliable, but not fully tender, 3 to 5 minutes. Drain well and transfer to a medium bowl. Drizzle with 2 tablespoons of the oil and toss to coat.

SEAR THE SHRIMP. Stir the lime juice, brown sugar, fish sauce, chili sauce, and ⅓ cup of water in a small bowl until the sugar dissolves. Set aside. Heat 1 tablespoon of the oil in a large, nonstick skillet over high heat until it's just beginning to smoke. Add the shrimp and cook, stirring occasionally, just until firm and opaque, about 3 minutes. Transfer to a plate.

ASSEMBLE THE PAD THAI. Add the remaining 1 tablespoon of oil to the skillet, add the garlic and shallot, and cook, stirring often, until the shallot softens, 2 to 3 minutes. Pour in the eggs and cook, stirring quickly and constantly, until they're fully scrambled, about 45 seconds. Add the noodles and stir to combine, scraping the bottom of the pan to release any bits of egg. Pour in the lime juice mixture and cook, tossing frequently, until the noodles are tender and most of the liquid is absorbed, 3 to 5 minutes. Add the shrimp, scallions, and bean sprouts and cook, tossing constantly, until heated through, 1 to 2 minutes. Sprinkle with the peanuts and serve immediately.

Mussels in Broth with Garlic Toasts

Mussels are such a great deal and so full of flavor I can never understand why they aren't more popular. On top of that, most of the mussels we get these days are farm-raised and don't have the tough, hairy "beards" that wild-harvested mussels do. Just rinse and cook. In this recipe, I steam them with beer to make an outrageous broth that's the perfect excuse for buying a nice loaf of bread to sop up the delicious juices!

SERVES 4

$10.20/ $2.55

HEAT THE BROILER. Adjust the oven rack to the top position (about 3" from the heating element) and heat the broiler to high.

STEAM THE MUSSELS. Melt the butter in a Dutch oven or large pot over medium-high heat. Add the shallots and garlic and cook, stirring occasionally, until the shallots are softened, about 2 minutes. Add the lager, parsley, and pepper and bring to a simmer. Add the mussels, cover, and cook, stirring 2 or 3 times, until most if not all of the mussels open, 5 to 10 minutes, depending on their size (a few may pop open once you turn off the heat; do not overcook).

MAKE THE GARLIC TOAST AND SERVE. While the mussels cook, arrange the baguette slices on a baking sheet in a single layer. Combine the butter and garlic in a small bowl and brush the mixture onto the baguette slices. Sprinkle with salt and pepper and broil until browned and crisped, 1 to 2 minutes. Divide the mussels and broth among 4 bowls, discarding any that have not opened, and serve right away with the garlic toasts.

MUSSELS

- 2 tablespoons unsalted butter
- 3 large shallots, finely minced
- 3 medium garlic cloves, minced
- 1 bottle (12 ounces) lager-style beer
- 2 tablespoons chopped fresh flat-leaf parsley
- ¼ teaspoon freshly ground black pepper
- 4 pounds mussels, scrubbed and debearded

GARLIC TOASTS

- 1 baguette, cut into ½" slices
- 2 tablespoons unsalted butter, melted
- 2 medium garlic cloves, minced
- ¼ teaspoon table salt
- ⅛ teaspoon freshly ground black pepper

$ D2D

Save money on beer by buying cans instead of bottles. Aluminum is also much more ecofriendly, as it is more readily recycled than glass, and because it's lighter, you're more likely to haul it back to redeem the deposit if your area imposes one.

MAKE IT A MEAL

+ Pasta with Summer Vegetable Ragout (page 52)

Homemade Wonton Soup

My kids love to order wonton soup at Chinese restaurants, but I hate the broth many of them use. It's too salty and often loaded with MSG. Imagine my surprise when I realized how easy wonton soup is to make at home, and how much better, too. If your kids are like mine, they'll nearly fall over when you make it for them, from scratch, for dinner! To bulk up the soup for a main-course meal, add 12 ounces of cooked, fresh Chinese egg noodles, dividing them among bowls before ladling in the broth and wontons. The wonton recipe can be easily doubled (or tripled) and frozen. Cook them a few different ways (they can be served in broth, steamed, pan-fried, or deep-fried) and serve with a quick dipping sauce made with soy and a squeeze of chili sauce for a home-style dim sum party. You can find wonton wrappers in most any supermarket, in the produce area near the fresh tofu.

BROTH

2½–3 pounds chicken parts for stock, such as necks and backs and/or wings

1 onion, roughly chopped

1 piece (1½") fresh ginger, peeled and thinly sliced

5 garlic cloves

5 sprigs fresh cilantro

1 teaspoon whole black peppercorns

1 teaspoon salt

 D2D

Stretch your grocery dollars by using the same ingredients in several recipes throughout the week (for example, use the cilantro you buy for this recipe to make Barbecued Pineapple Chicken with Caribbean Salsa on pages 71 and 72 and the Tortilla Scramble on page 226).

MAKE THE BROTH. Place the chicken parts, onion, ginger, garlic, cilantro, peppercorns, and salt in a large stockpot and cover with 4 quarts of water. Bring to a boil over high heat, then reduce the heat to medium and simmer gently until flavorful, 2½ to 3 hours, skimming off any foam as necessary.

STRAIN THE BROTH. Pour the broth through a large, fine-mesh sieve or a cheesecloth-lined colander. Press on the solids with the back of a wooden spoon to extract as much liquid as possible. Let the broth settle for 10 minutes, then skim the fat from the surface using a wide, shallow spoon. (Or let the broth cool to room temperature, then refrigerate until cold, at least 2 hours or up to 3 days; scrape the solid fat layer off of the surface with a spoon.) You should have about 3 quarts of broth. (Refrigerate the broth for up to 5 days or freeze in 4 quart-size resealable freezer bags for up to 6 months.)

SHAPE THE WONTONS. Mix the pork, shrimp, scallions, oyster sauce, sesame oil, and cornstarch together in a medium bowl until well combined. Fill a small bowl with water. Place the wonton wrappers on your work surface and cover with a damp kitchen towel to keep them from drying out. Separate 3 wrappers from the stack. Spoon 2 teaspoons of the filling into the center of each wrapper. Work 1 at a time to form the wontons: Lightly moisten 2 adjacent edges of the wrapper with water (use a pastry brush or your finger) and bring two opposite points of the wrapper together to create a triangle. Press out any excess air and press on the edges to seal. Bring the two narrow ends of the triangle together and press to join; the wonton will resemble a tortellini. Place the wontons on a baking sheet and cover with plastic wrap as you continue to fill and form the remaining wontons.

FINISH THE SOUP. Bring 2 quarts of broth to a boil in a Dutch oven or large pot over medium-high heat. Reduce the heat to medium, stir in the soy sauce, add the wontons, and gently simmer until they're cooked through and float to the surface, 2 to 3 minutes. Ladle the soup into individual bowls, dividing the broth and wontons evenly. Sprinkle with the scallions and cilantro, if using, and serve right away.

WONTONS

8	ounces ground pork
4	ounces shrimp (about 6 medium), peeled, deveined, and minced
2	scallions, white and light green parts only, minced
1½	tablespoons oyster sauce
1½	teaspoons toasted sesame oil
¾	teaspoon cornstarch
28–32	square wonton wrappers

SERVING

1	tablespoon soy sauce
2	scallions, thinly sliced
2	tablespoons chopped cilantro (optional)

MAKE IT A MEAL
+ Salmon Teriyaki (page 97)
+ Veggie-Loaded Fried Rice (page 157)

Shortcut Asian Chicken Broth

Though a bit more expensive than homemade soup stock, canned chicken broth can be doctored with aromatics and spices to make a delicious base for wonton soup—and makes this recipe a lot quicker to the table. Bring 8 cups of canned chicken broth to a simmer with the ginger, garlic, cilantro, and peppercorns (as specified in the recipe), reduce to low heat, and gently simmer, partially covered, for 15 minutes. Strain and proceed with the recipe above.

Fried Catfish, Homemade Tartar Sauce & Hush Puppies

SERVES 4

☺

$18.40/
$4.60

Mild, moist, and flaky, fried catfish is one of the most popular dishes at the Rock, and it's a fish that should be on more home menus, too. It's affordable and, unlike many fish these days, it's a sustainable resource that's farmed domestically using environmentally sensitive methods. The homemade tartar sauce that accompanies it is a snap to make, tastes so much better than store-bought, and saves you money, too. Paired with freshly fried hushpuppies, this trio is a meal straight from heaven.

TARTAR SAUCE

- ½ cup mayonnaise
- ¼ small red onion, very finely chopped
- 3 tablespoons roughly chopped pickles (dill, half-sour, or cornichon)
- 2 tablespoons capers, rinsed and roughly chopped
- 2 teaspoons pickle juice
- ¼ teaspoon salt
- ¼ teaspoon freshly ground black pepper

CATFISH

- 1 cup all-purpose flour
- ½ cup cracker crumbs (I use whatever kind of crackers I have in the house)
- ½ teaspoon garlic powder
- 1½ teaspoons salt
- 1 teaspoon freshly ground black pepper
- 1 cup buttermilk

MAKE THE TARTAR SAUCE. Mix the mayonnaise, onion, pickles, capers, pickle juice, salt, and pepper together in a small bowl, cover with plastic wrap, and refrigerate for up to 1 week (the flavor of the onion will become more pronounced over time).

BREAD THE FILLETS. Whisk the flour, cracker crumbs, garlic powder, salt, and pepper together in a wide, shallow dish. Pour the buttermilk into a wide bowl and set aside. Dip each fillet into the buttermilk and then dredge it through the dry ingredients, making sure both sides are evenly coated. Place the breaded fillets on a large plate and refrigerate until you're ready to fry them.

MAKE THE HUSH PUPPIES. Bring 1½ cups of water to a boil in a small saucepan. Stir together the cornmeal, flour, onion, salt, and pepper in a large bowl, then drizzle in enough boiling water to moisten the mixture evenly. Whisk together the milk, egg, and baking powder, and pour into the cornmeal batter, mixing to combine. Heat the oil in a large, deep skillet (preferably a cast-iron one) over medium-high heat until it reads between 350°F and 375°F on an instant-read thermometer. Drop golf ball–size spoonfuls of the batter into the oil, taking care not to overcrowd the pan (you'll probably have to fry the hush puppies in a few batches, depending on the size of your skillet), frying the fritters until they're golden brown on all sides, about 3 minutes. Transfer to a paper towel–lined baking sheet and place in the oven to keep warm while you fry the remaining batter (using more oil if needed) and catfish.

FRY THE FISH. Add more oil to the skillet if necessary (there should be about 1 inch of oil in the skillet) and let the temperature return to between 350°F and 375°F. If you're using a large skillet, you might be able to fry all of the fillets at once. If not, fry them in batches. Add the fillets and fry until crisp and browned on both sides, 8 to 10 minutes total. Transfer to a paper towel–lined plate to drain, and serve with tartar sauce, hush puppies, and lemon wedges.

COOK SMART

If you have leftover tartar sauce, do what I do at the restaurant—stir in some ketchup (I like to add a few tablespoons of simple syrup, too; to make simple syrup, just bring ½ cup of water and ½ cup of sugar to a simmer in a small saucepan, stirring until the sugar is dissolved) and you have homemade Thousand Island dressing.

SHOP SMART

For the cleanest flavor, look for catfish that doesn't have a lot of dark streaks. If you can't find good-quality catfish in your neck of the woods, any moderately thick and flaky white fish will do, such as tilapia or haddock.

4   catfish fillets (6–8 ounces each)

2   cups canola oil, if needed

2   lemons, cut into wedges

HUSH PUPPIES

2   cups cornmeal

2   tablespoons all-purpose flour

½   small yellow onion, finely minced

2   teaspoons salt

    Freshly ground black pepper

¼   cup whole milk

1   large egg, lightly beaten

2   teaspoons baking powder

4   cups canola oil + extra if needed

Bucket-Style Oven "Fried" Chicken

SERVES 4

$10.80/
$2.70

My oven-fried chicken tastes like the real deal, but is a ton healthier for you. And because the cleanup is a snap (no oil to dispose of or splattered stove top to scrub), you'll think twice before pulling into the drive-thru next time your crew is jonesing for a bucket of take-out chicken. Best of all, not only will you save money, you get to serve it up with your own healthy sides.

1⅔ cups plain, full-fat yogurt

2 tablespoons yellow mustard

1 teaspoon hot sauce

2 teaspoons Tex-Mex Rub (page 118)

1 teaspoon celery salt

1½ teaspoons salt

3 pounds bone-in chicken breasts or thighs, skin removed (if the breasts are very large, cut them in half crosswise)

1 teaspoon canola oil

2½ cups dried bread crumbs, cracker crumbs, or panko

2 tablespoons unsalted butter, melted, or canola oil

MAKE IT A MEAL
+ Spoon-Tender Green Beans with Bacon (page 196)

MARINATE THE CHICKEN. Whisk together the yogurt, mustard, hot sauce, 1 teaspoon of the Tex-Mex Rub, the celery salt, and ¾ teaspoon of the salt in a large bowl. Add the chicken and turn to coat with the marinade, then place the chicken in 1 or 2 resealable gallon-size plastic bags and refrigerate for at least 2 hours or overnight.

COAT THE CHICKEN AND BAKE. Heat the oven to 400°F. Line a rimmed baking sheet with foil and grease with 1 teaspoon of oil. Whisk together the bread crumbs, the remaining 1 teaspoon Tex-Mex Rub, and the remaining ¾ teaspoon salt in a medium bowl. Working 1 piece at a time, remove the chicken from the marinade and roll it around in the bread crumbs until evenly coated, and then place it on the baking sheet. Drizzle the melted butter or 2 tablespoons of oil over the chicken and bake until it is lightly browned and its temperature is 170°F, about 40 to 45 minutes (if you want a little extra color, place the chicken under your broiler for a few minutes until it's more deeply browned). Remove from the oven and serve.

D2D
If you're in a breast meat–only household, split those cuts up. Place your bone-in chicken breast on a cutting board, then, with a sharp chef's knife, cut straight down crosswise through the breast, dividing it in 2. You instantly get 4 pieces of white meat for the price of 2.

Jerk-Style Chicken Thighs & Charred Pineapple Salsa

SERVES 4

$11.80/
$2.95

When I was 18, I took my grandma to Jamaica. We snorkeled (she'd take a break in waist-deep water to smoke a cigarette), danced at reggae clubs, and ate jerk chicken. About a decade later, when I was a purser for a cruise line, we were pulling into port in Jamaica when I got a telegram informing me that my grandmother had passed away. Driving to the airport, I passed many of the places we had visited on our trip. It was an amazing way to say good-bye. When I got home, I found out that she left me 25 acres of land—which ended up being the main reason I ultimately returned to Oklahoma, moved to Stroud, and found my calling at the Rock Cafe. Needless to say, spicy jerk chicken has tagged a special place in my heart.

CHICKEN

- 8 bone-in, skin-on chicken thighs, trimmed of extra skin and fat
- ½ teaspoon canola oil

MARINADE

- 3 scallions, coarsely chopped
- ½ small red onion, cut into large chunks (save the other half for the salsa)

  Juice of ½ lime (save the other half for the salsa)
- 2 tablespoons olive oil
- 1½ teaspoons red-pepper flakes
- 1 medium garlic clove, coarsely chopped
- 1 teaspoon grated fresh ginger

MARINATE THE CHICKEN. Cut 3 small slashes through the skin and into the meat of each chicken thigh, using a sharp knife, cutting all the way to the bone. Place the chicken in a large bowl. Combine the scallions, onion, lime juice, olive oil, red-pepper flakes, garlic, ginger, thyme, allspice, sugar, salt, and pepper in a food processor and puree until smooth. Pour the mixture over the chicken thighs and coat them well, rubbing the marinade into the slashes. Set aside while you prepare the salsa (the chicken can be marinated up to 1 day in advance).

MAKE THE SALSA. Adjust an oven rack to the uppermost position (about 3" from the broiler) and heat the broiler to high. Line a rimmed baking sheet with foil and grease lightly with ½ teaspoon of oil. Place the pineapple rings on the baking sheet, pat dry with paper towels, and brush lightly with half of the remaining oil. Broil until lightly charred, about 10 minutes, flip the rings over, brush with the remaining oil, and continue to broil until the second sides are lightly charred, about 5 minutes. Lower the oven rack to the lower-middle position (the rack should

(continues...)

1 teaspoon dried thyme

1 teaspoon ground allspice

1 tablespoon sugar

1 teaspoon salt

1 teaspoon freshly ground black pepper

SALSA

2 teaspoons canola oil

1 can (20 ounces) pineapple rings in juice, drained, juices reserved

½ small red bell pepper, seeded and finely diced

½ small red onion, finely chopped (about 3 tablespoons)

2 scallions, trimmed and thinly sliced

Juice of ½ lime

¼ teaspoon grated fresh ginger

¼ teaspoon sugar

¼ teaspoon red-pepper flakes

¼ teaspoon salt

Freshly ground black pepper

MAKE IT A MEAL
+ White rice

be about 7" from the broiler) and heat the oven to 450°F. Cut the cooled pineapple into ¼" pieces and place in a large bowl. Add the bell pepper, onion, scallions, lime juice, ginger, sugar, red-pepper flakes, 2 tablespoons of the reserved pineapple juice, salt, and pepper, toss to combine, and set aside while you cook the chicken.

BAKE THE CHICKEN. Line the bottom of a broiler pan with foil, set the top in place, and grease with ½ teaspoon of oil. Using a sharp knife, cut 2 or 3 small slashes into each thigh, cutting all the way through to the bone. Remove the chicken from the marinade and place skin side up on the broiler pan. Bake until the surfaces are dry and the edges are beginning to brown, about 20 minutes, rotating the pan halfway through. Turn on the broiler and broil until the skin is crisped and deeply browned, about 5 minutes. Arrange the chicken thighs on a platter and serve with the salsa.

TAKE IT OUTSIDE: The chicken and pineapple can also be cooked on a charcoal or gas grill. Build a 2-level fire with medium-high heat on one side and medium-low on the other, and make sure that the grill grate is well oiled. Sear the chicken over the hotter side until well browned, about 3 minutes on each side, then move the pieces over to the cooler side to finish cooking, 10 to 12 minutes longer. When the hotter side is free, char the pineapple rings (brush each side with oil first) on each side. The chicken is great served hot, but it can also be served warm or at room temperature.

COOK SMART
I'll often marinate the chicken and pop it into a freezer bag and freeze. Defrost it in the microwave and it's ready to cook.

Chicken-Fried Steak & Bacon Gravy

Chicken-fried steak is the official state meal of Oklahoma, and it's the signature dish on the Rock Cafe's menu, with diners traveling hundreds of miles on Route 66 just to get a taste. Like many Oklahomans, I make mine with cube steak (also called a minute steak), an inexpensive and already tenderized cut from the round of the cow. I dip the steaks in buttermilk first, then dredge them through a spiced cracker-crumb mixture that turns beautifully golden and crisp in a cast-iron skillet. Served up with old-fashioned bacon gravy (which is also great with biscuits), it doesn't get much better than this.

SERVES 4

$12.80/
$3.20

BREAD THE STEAKS. Whisk the flour, cracker crumbs, garlic powder, salt, and pepper together in a wide, shallow dish. Pour the buttermilk into a wide bowl. Dip each steak into the buttermilk, then dredge it through the dry ingredients, making sure both sides are evenly coated.

MAKE THE GRAVY. Cook the bacon over medium-high heat in a medium skillet until crispy, stirring often, 4 to 5 minutes. Use a slotted spoon to transfer it to a paper towel–lined plate and set aside. Add the onion to the pan and cook, stirring often, until soft and just starting to brown, about 3 minutes. Stir in the mushrooms and the salt and cook, stirring often, until the mushrooms release their juices, about 5 minutes. Mix in the garlic, paprika, cayenne, and black pepper, and cook until the garlic is fragrant, about 30 seconds. Reduce the heat to medium, add the butter and let it melt, stirring often. Use a wooden spoon to mix in the flour. Cook, stirring constantly, for 2 minutes, then slowly begin to add the milk a little at a time, mixing well between additions to avoid lumps. Cook until slightly thickened, 1 to 2 minutes, then reduce the heat to low and cover, stirring occasionally, to keep the gravy warm. Just before serving, stir in the reserved bacon.

STEAK

- 1 cup all-purpose flour
- ½ cup cracker crumbs (about 30 saltines)
- ½ teaspoon garlic powder
- 1½ teaspoons salt
- 1 teaspoon freshly ground black pepper
- 1 cup buttermilk
- 4 cube steaks (6 ounces each)
- 4 cups canola oil

GRAVY

- 3 slices bacon, sliced crosswise into ½"-wide pieces
- 1 small yellow onion, finely chopped
- 3 ounces button mushrooms (about ⅔ cup), stemmed and thinly sliced

(continues...)

FRY THE STEAKS. Heat the oil in a large, deep skillet (preferably a cast-iron one) over medium-high heat. Once the oil reaches between 350°F and 375°F on an instant-read thermometer, reduce the heat to medium and carefully slide the steaks into the hot oil. Fry on both sides until the coating is golden brown, about 10 minutes. Transfer to a paper towel– or brown bag–lined plate to drain. Serve the steak immediately covered with the bacon gravy.

D2D

When I have just a few strips of bacon left in a package, I like to chop it into narrow strips (what the French call lardons) and stow it away in a quart-size resealable bag in the freezer. It comes in handy when I don't have bacon in the house (a rarity, but it does happen!) and want to make home fries, gravy, or even bacon bits for a salad with blue cheese dressing and juicy garden tomatoes. No need to thaw, just use the bacon pieces straight from the freezer.

¼ teaspoon salt

2 garlic cloves, finely minced or pressed through a garlic press

1 tablespoon sweet paprika

Pinch of cayenne pepper

¼ teaspoon freshly ground black pepper

2 tablespoons (¼ stick) unsalted butter

3 tablespoons all-purpose flour

3 cups whole milk, warmed but not hot

MAKE IT A MEAL
+ Biscuits (page 221)

COOK SMART
To make cracker crumbs, place some crackers in a food processor and pulse until very fine. Or, for a more low-tech approach, place the crackers in a resealable plastic bag and crush them with a meat mallet, rolling pin, or the bottom of a heavy skillet until fine and mealy. A 15-ounce box of saltine crackers makes about 4½ cups of cracker crumbs.

Singed Steak, Herb & Lettuce Wraps

SERVES 4

$17.00/
$4.25

Judging by the popularity of upscale steakhouses from coast to coast, just about everyone likes a good steak now and then. Steakhouse prices, on the other hand, make me lose my appetite. When I'm craving a steak dinner but have a quesadilla budget, these wraps are just the thing. For a heartier dish, do as the men in my house do and opt for a tortilla-style wrap instead.

½ cup soy sauce

5 garlic cloves, finely minced or pressed through a garlic press

6 tablespoons sugar

3 scallions, thinly sliced

1 tablespoon toasted sesame seeds

1 tablespoon toasted sesame oil

½ teaspoon freshly ground black pepper

1½ pounds flank, hanger, or skirt steak

1 head red or green leaf lettuce, separated into leaves

Fresh mint leaves, for serving (optional)

Fresh cilantro leaves, for serving (optional)

MARINATE THE STEAK. Combine the soy sauce, garlic, sugar, scallions, sesame seeds, sesame oil, and pepper in a large baking dish, and stir until the sugar dissolves. Measure out 2 tablespoons of the marinade and set it aside. Place the steak in the baking dish with the marinade (if you're using a skirt steak, slice it in half crosswise and marinate the two pieces side by side). Prick the steak all over with a fork, then flip it and prick the second side. Marinate at room temperature for at least 30 minutes (while the grill heats) or in the fridge for up to 1 hour, turning the steak once or twice.

GRILL THE STEAK. Grill the steak over medium-high heat until deeply browned and cooked to medium-rare, about 4 minutes on each side. Transfer to a cutting board and let rest for 5 minutes. Slice the steak thinly across the grain and arrange on a platter. Drizzle the reserved marinade over the steak. Serve the sliced beef with the lettuce leaves and herbs for wrapping.

 MAKE IT A MEAL
+ Peanut Noodles (without tofu, page 65)

 COOK SMART
Thin, quick-cooking, affordable, and packed with lots of big, beefy flavor, flank steaks, hangers, and skirt steaks are a fantastic alternative to pricier cuts. They aren't the most tender steaks around, though. That's why they're best served thinly sliced against the grain.

Save with Homemade Spice Blends

Premixed spice blends can be a huge rip-off—not only are you paying a ridiculously high price per ounce for spices (compare it to the cost of buying the same spices in bulk and you'll see what I mean), but you have no idea how long those spices have been sitting on the shelf. For cost and flavor, it's much better to mix spices yourself. They keep for up to 4 months if stored in an airtight container or jar in a cool, dark, and dry spot. For blends with whole spices (such as the French and Italian rubs), pulse them in a spice grinder for a finer texture if you like.

FRENCH RUB: 2 tablespoons dried basil, 1 tablespoon dried marjoram, 1 tablespoon dried thyme, 2 teaspoons dried rosemary, 2 teaspoons dried lavender, 2 teaspoons dried fennel seeds
USE to flavor a vinaigrette; as a rub for lamb chops; for the bruschetta on page 128

ITALIAN RUB: 2 tablespoons dried oregano, 1½ tablespoons dried thyme, 1 tablespoon dried rosemary, 2 teaspoons dried sage, 1 teaspoon freshly ground black pepper, 1 teaspoon garlic powder
USE in tabbouleh; in the Chicken Parmesan on page 46; or in meatballs

TEX-MEX RUB: 3 tablespoons chili powder, 1 tablespoon ground cumin, 1 tablespoon dried oregano, 2 teaspoons garlic powder, 2 teaspoons sweet paprika
USE in the buffalo chicken salad on page 76; the ribs on page 101, or to make baked beans

INDIAN RUB: 3 tablespoons ground coriander, 2 tablespoons ground cumin, 1 teaspoon ground cinnamon, 1 teaspoon freshly ground black pepper, 1 teaspoon ground turmeric, ½ teaspoon ground cloves, ½ teaspoon cayenne, and ¼ teaspoon ground nutmeg
USE in lentil soup; to flavor steamed basmati rice; as a rub for chicken breasts

MOROCCAN RUB: 3 tablespoons paprika, 1 tablespoon ground cumin, 1 tablespoon ground coriander, 1 tablespoon ground ginger, 1½ teaspoons cayenne, 1½ teaspoons ground cinnamon, 1½ teaspoons ground turmeric
USE in the Moroccan chicken on page 136; as a rub for pork kebabs; or to flavor broiled fish

My Bistro Steak with Balsamic Pan Sauce

SERVES 4

$16.60/
$4.15

My husband, Fred, believes in grilling over hardwood briquettes, using a chimney starter to ignite them (never lighter fluid), and that the more you stare at that steak—preferably with a beer in one hand and spatula in the other—the better it's going to taste. I like to pan-sear steaks. I have more control over the heat of the pan, and I love building a rich pan sauce from the browned bits left in the pan. Either way, one thing is for sure: Even when you splurge on rib eyes or strips, you're still spending a heck of a lot less than you would in a steakhouse.

STEAKS

- 2 rib eye or strip steaks (12 ounces each)
- ½ teaspoon salt
- ½ teaspoon freshly ground black pepper
- 2 teaspoons canola oil

PAN SAUCE

- 3 tablespoons unsalted butter
- 1 large shallot, finely minced
- ⅓ cup chicken broth or beef broth, homemade (page 36) or store-bought
- ⅓ cup balsamic vinegar
- ½ teaspoon finely chopped fresh thyme leaves
- ¼ teaspoon salt
- ⅛ teaspoon freshly ground black pepper

MAKE IT A MEAL
+ Creamed Spinach (page 187)

SEAR THE STEAKS. Season the steaks on both sides with the salt and pepper. Heat the oil in a large skillet over medium-high heat until just beginning to smoke. Add the steaks and cook until well browned on both sides, about 10 minutes total for medium-rare. Transfer the steaks to a cutting board and let them rest.

MAKE THE PAN SAUCE AND SERVE. In the same pan, melt 1 tablespoon of the butter over medium heat. Add the shallot and cook, stirring occasionally, until softened, about 2 minutes. Add the broth, balsamic vinegar, thyme, salt, and pepper. Increase the heat to medium-high and simmer, stirring occasionally, until the mixture is slightly thickened and reduced to about ⅓ cup, about 4 minutes. Turn off the heat, and whisk in the remaining 2 tablespoons of butter until the sauce is glossy. Spoon some of the sauce over each portion of steak and serve.

D2D

When porterhouse steaks are on sale, buy a couple. At home, cut away the meat from both sides of the T-shaped bone. The long side of meat is what is labeled as a New York or Kansas City strip steak. The smaller, round side is a filet mignon. So for the price of 2 steaks, you just got 4 super-premium steakhouse cuts.

Pozole Rojo Pork Stew

SERVES 6

$11.70/
$1.95

Country-style pork spareribs are meatier than regular spareribs and higher in fat. They come from close to the pork shoulder, and like that big cut, they do very well simmered slowly in liquid for a good, long while. Because they take a little more time to nudge into spoon-tender territory, you can often find them for less than spareribs, too. I like pozole rojo served with warmed corn tortillas, and a combination of whatever of the following I have on hand: diced avocado, Cotija or queso fresco cheese, diced red onions, sliced radishes, and sour cream.

2½   pounds boneless country-style pork spareribs

1   large onion, quartered

12   garlic cloves, unpeeled

¾   teaspoon dried oregano, preferably Mexican oregano

1¼   teaspoons salt

8   medium (about 1¾ ounces) dried New Mexico chiles

3   garlic cloves, chopped

½   teaspoon ground cumin

2   tablespoons canola oil

1   can (29 ounces) hominy, rinsed and drained

¼   cup chopped fresh cilantro

1   lime, cut into 6 wedges

COOK THE PORK. Combine the spareribs, 3 of the onion quarters, 12 garlic cloves, the oregano, and ½ teaspoon of salt in a Dutch oven or large pot. Cover with 8 cups of water and bring to a boil over high heat. Reduce the heat to medium, cover partially, and simmer for 45 minutes. Uncover the pot and continue to simmer until the pork is tender, about 45 minutes longer. Use tongs to transfer the pork to a large plate and let it cool slightly. When it's cool enough to handle, shred the pork and discard any fat. Strain the broth through a fine-mesh sieve and let it stand until the fat rises to the surface. Then, using a wide, shallow spoon, skim off as much fat as possible. Rinse out the pot.

SOFTEN THE CHILES. While the pork is simmering, if the chiles appear dusty or dirty, wipe them with a damp paper towel. Place the chiles in a medium heatproof bowl and cover with 3 cups of boiling water, pushing the chiles down to make sure they are submerged (place a plate on top of the chiles if they keep floating up). Set aside until softened and plump, about 30 minutes.

D2D

Canned hominy (dried and soaked corn) is very economical and quick to use. It's delicious served in stews and braises instead of potatoes or rice.

SHOP SMART

Dried New Mexico chiles are moderately hot; if you can't find them or prefer a milder flavor, you can use ancho chiles (dried poblanos) instead. Store dried chiles in a cool, dark place for up to 6 months. Any longer than that and they'll begin to dull in color and flavor.

PURÉE THE CHILES. Remove the chiles from the water and reserve the soaking water. Remove and discard the stems and seeds from the chiles and place the pods in a blender or food processor. Pour in 1 cup of the soaking water, the remaining onion quarter, the chopped garlic, and the cumin, and purée until smooth.

FINISH THE POZOLE. Add the oil to the empty pot and heat the pot on medium-high. Add the chile paste and cook, stirring frequently, until slightly thickened and darkened in color, about 6 minutes. Add the broth, the remaining ¾ teaspoon of salt, the shredded pork, and the hominy and bring to a boil. Reduce the heat to medium and simmer, stirring occasionally, to blend the flavors and heat through, 5 to 10 minutes. Divide the pozole among 6 bowls, sprinkle with cilantro, and serve with lime wedges.

the door-bell dash

One of the things that makes me the happiest in life is a house full of people, be they friends, family, or teenyboppers who hang out after school and into the evening. I love when my home is the center of the storm, and people in my town know this, so I am always ready to receive drop-in visitors. As we chat and hang out, we get hungry, and offering something to munch on, whether it's a quick snack or a full-blown dinner, is just the natural, hospitable thing to do. I guess that's why I love running the Rock Cafe so much, where it's like one giant, impromptu party from the first cup of coffee served to the last burger and fries.

At home, though, I try to make these spur-of-the-moment meals as effortless as possible, drawing on a few "in case of emergency" items I keep ready to go. If you have a freezer in the basement or garage, use it to stockpile ingredients for these last-minute occasions. If you don't have that much extra freezer space, choose one or two recipes from this chapter and stock up on just those ingredients. Knowing that I have some easy-to-prep proteins tucked away in the freezer guarantees I won't ever be caught off guard when the hungry hordes descend. Freezing meat in single-serving portions helps it to defrost more quickly, so when I buy a bulk or value-size package, I rewrap the chops or chicken pieces separately (first in plastic wrap and then a freezer bag). This also makes it easy to pull out just enough for the number of people I aim to feed.

I like to keep a few kinds of bread in the freezer, too, from small rolls (kids love sliders) to country bread and sliced baguettes. After warming them in the oven, I top the baguette pieces with a smear of pesto or a dollop of tapenade (I always keep both handy in my pantry) or the herb-tossed tomatoes and goat cheese on page 128. Add some seared steak, caramelized onions, and lightly dressed greens, and I have a nice meal.

When it comes to hosting, I'd much rather visit with my guests than slave over a stove, so all of the recipes in this chapter are simple and speedy. They may need 30 or 40 minutes in the oven, but that's all hands-off time. What better opportunity to uncork a bottle of wine and enjoy an impromptu meeting of the minds?

When the doorbell rings, this is what I'm cooking!

Top 2 for Friends

Broiled Shrimp with Feta, Orzo, and Tomatoes (page 132)

Moroccan Chicken, Chickpeas, and Lemon (page 136)

Top 2 for Kids

Turkey BLT Sliders (page 138)

Fajitas on the Fly (page 144)

Top 2 for Company

Garlic-Rosemary Pork Loin and Crisp Salt-Pepper Potatoes (page 146)

Crispy Cod and Caper-Butter Sauce (page 134)

Top 2 for "Just Dropping By" Family Visits

Open-Face Steak Sandwiches with Caramelized Onions and Parmesan (page 141)

Cajun Shrimp Boil with Garlic Dunking Butter (page 130)

Goat Cheese Tomato-Herb Bruschetta

MAKES 24

$12.00/
$.50

All you need to make this quick bruschetta are some baguette slices (which you should always have in your freezer for impromptu snacks) and a few tomatoes. If I have some No-Cook Garden Vegetable Sauce (page 58) in the freezer, I might take a shortcut and use it in place of the herbed tomatoes. Pesto, tapenade, or even a simple drizzle of good olive oil and flaky salt work, too. However you choose to put it together, this little bite is quick and simple. To make a meal, serve it with a tossed salad or before a bowl of soup.

3   ripe tomatoes, cored, seeded, and finely chopped

1   teaspoon balsamic or red wine vinegar or fresh lemon juice

2   teaspoons finely chopped fresh herbs (such as basil or chives) or ½ teaspoon herbes de Provence or French Rub (page 118), pulsed through a spice grinder

    Coarse sea salt

¼   cup extra-virgin olive oil

1   baguette, sliced on the diagonal into ½"-thick pieces

1   garlic clove, halved lengthwise

1   log (8 ounces) soft goat cheese, crumbled

 D2D

Out-of-season tomatoes are expensive and tasteless. In the winter and spring, I'll make this with a can of rinsed white beans or chickpeas (lightly mash after tossing with oil and herbs).

PREPARE THE TOMATO TOPPING. Place an oven rack in the highest position and heat the broiler to high. Toss the tomatoes, vinegar or lemon juice, herbs, and salt together in a medium bowl. Drizzle with 1 tablespoon of the olive oil, stir to combine, and set aside.

TOAST THE BAGUETTE SLICES. Rub one side of each baguette slice with the cut side of the garlic. Brush or drizzle a little olive oil over the bread and then place the slices on a baking sheet. Broil just long enough to get some color around the edges, about 30 seconds. Turn the baguette slices over and toast the other side until they're golden, an additional 30 seconds to 1 minute (depending on your broiler—watch the toasts carefully—this isn't the kind of thing you want to walk away from).

ASSEMBLE THE BRUSCHETTA. Remove the bread from the oven and cover each with about 1½ tablespoons of the tomato mixture. Top with some goat-cheese crumbles and place the bread back under the broiler just long enough to warm the cheese and give it a little color, about 1 minute. Transfer the bruschetta to a platter, drizzle a little oil over each, and finish with a sprinkle of coarse salt.

Roasting Peppers

Roasted peppers are fantastic for sandwiches, to wrap around fresh mozzarella cheese, or to chop and add to a rice dish or salad. Buzz them with a little olive oil, garlic, salt, and pepper for a fantastic bruschetta spread or dip for raw veggies. This is a great way to use up past-their-prime peppers, whether you bought them on sale at the market or they've been sitting in your crisper too long.

Adjust an oven rack to the upper-middle position and heat the broiler to high. Place whole peppers (any color and size) on a sheet pan and roast, using tongs to turn them often, until all the sides are blistered and blackened (check them often). Transfer the peppers to a large bowl and cover with plastic wrap until they're cool enough to handle, about 20 minutes. Peel the charred skin away and remove the stem and seeds. Slice the peppers into strips and place in an airtight container. Submerge in olive oil and add a few garlic cloves, red-pepper flakes, or sprigs of rosemary. Cover and refrigerate for up to 2 weeks.

SHOP SMART

Grocery stores often have two kinds of red-peppers for sale: bell peppers and Holland or hothouse bell peppers. The former are often longer and a deeper red, while the latter are squatter and more perfect looking. The other difference is price—cheaper bell peppers are often $1.50 to $2 less per pound.

Freezer Fresh

I always have bread in the freezer, such as whole-wheat sandwich bread, brioche for French toast, hot dog buns, and sliced country-style bread or baguettes. You can let the bread defrost at room temperature for 10 to 20 minutes or toss it into a warm oven to warm up before using. Whatever you do, make sure to slice your bread before freezing it—freezing a whole loaf is like the kiss of death! It takes longer to defrost and is just less convenient in general. To freeze bread, simply place the whole sliced loaf in a bag in the freezer. Split the loaf into two separate resealable gallon-size freezer bags if the whole loaf doesn't fit into one.

Cajun Shrimp Boil with Garlic Dunking Butter

SERVES 8

$32.00/
$4.00

Louisiana is one of my favorite places in the world. I just love the backcountry, the kindness of the people, and of course the food. This shrimp boil always reminds me of a crab boil free-for-all we were honored to attend in Houma, just southwest of New Orleans. We ended up spending 3 days at a *very* rustic country-side bed-and-breakfast run by a true Cajun lady. When I asked if it would be okay for me to cook up some blue crabs we had purchased, before I knew it, she had phoned what seemed like the whole parish and invited them to come by for a crab boil. Neighbors arrived by foot, car, and boat, each swinging their own bucket of blue crabs. Soon after, we all gathered around a table and cracked, picked, and ate the crabs. Taking what we had and turning it into a party was such spontaneous fun. You can do it, too. All it takes is a little sass—and some Cajun spices, of course.

GARLIC BUTTER

- ½ cup (1 stick) unsalted butter
- 1 garlic clove, finely minced or pressed through a garlic press
- ⅛ teaspoon cayenne
- 1 teaspoon salt

SHRIMP BOIL

- 1 Zatarain's Crawfish, Shrimp & Crab Boil spice pouch or 1 capful Zatarain's Crawfish, Shrimp & Crab Boil liquid concentrate
- 2 garlic cloves, halved
- 2 dried bay leaves
- ½ teaspoon cayenne
- 3 tablespoons salt
- 16 (about 1½ pounds) golf ball–size red creamer potatoes (if using larger red potatoes, halve or quarter them)

MAKE THE GARLIC BUTTER. Melt the butter with the garlic in a microwave-safe dish in 20-second increments. Stir in the cayenne and salt and set aside.

MAKE THE SHRIMP BOIL. Fill a canning pot, lobster pot, or stockpot one-third full of water and bring it to a boil over high heat. Add the spice pouch (or liquid concentrate), the 2 cloves of garlic, bay leaves, cayenne, and salt, followed by the potatoes, lemons, and onions. Boil until the potatoes are just al dente, about 10 minutes (don't stir—you could break the spice pouch). Add the corn and sausage and boil for another 5 minutes (if

D2D

I buy only individually quick frozen (IQF) shrimp packaged in bulk 3- to 5-pound bags. It's a great value, often costing $3 less per pound than fresh shrimp. Buying shell-on shrimp rather than already cleaned shrimp will save you even more and give you shells to make stock with (see opposite page). IQF shrimp aren't frozen in giant ice blocks, either, meaning they're quick to defrost for last-minute meal prep.

you're using frozen corn, it may take a little longer for the liquid to come back to a boil, so adjust the cooking time as necessary). Toss in the frozen shrimp and cook until the shrimp are curled and pink, 3 to 4 minutes. Stir in the ice and let the shrimp boil sit on the stove for 10 minutes to soak up the seasonings.

SERVE THE SHRIMP BOIL. If you have a picnic table outside, spread a whole mess of newspapers or butcher paper across the table (make sure you stack a few layers of paper to soak up the juices). Place a bottle of hot sauce and the garlic butter on the table and carry out the pot with the shrimp boil in it. Using a slotted spoon or long-handled strainer, transfer the shrimp, sausage, and vegetables to the newspaper and let everyone have at it. If you're eating inside, line individual bowls or plates with newspaper and transfer some of the shrimp boil to each. Serve it up while it's hot.

Making Shrimp Broth

Buying shrimp in the shells may add a few minutes to your meal prep, but it is usually cheaper than buying them peeled, and it yields a free bonus of shells for a simple but delicious stock. Just place the shells in a saucepan and bring them to a boil with 2 cups of water. Reduce the heat, cover, and simmer for 20 minutes. Strain out the shells and place the shrimp broth in a large liquid measuring cup. Add enough chicken broth to bring the total amount to 3½ cups and use in the recipe.

2 lemons, halved

2 yellow onions, quartered

4 ears of corn, husked and halved crosswise (or 8 frozen corn cob halves)

1 pound spicy sausage (preferably andouille), sliced 1" thick

3 pounds medium IQF (see D2D tip on opposite page) shell-on shrimp

6 cups ice cubes (about 2 trays)

Hot-pepper sauce, for serving

D2D

For most recipes, it doesn't really make a huge difference what size shrimp you use—if smaller shrimp are a lot cheaper, go for them.

Broiled Shrimp with Feta, Orzo  Tomatoes

SERVES 4

$13.20/
$3.30

I'm a crispy kinda girl, so I always pat my shrimp dry with a paper towel before broiling or pan-searing so they brown better. Buy whatever size shrimp is on sale—if using smaller shrimp, just shave the cooking time by a few minutes so you don't overcook them. And if you don't have feta, don't stress it—you can top the shrimp with grated Parmesan or pecorino, or leave them bare.

1 pound medium IQF shrimp (see D2D tip, page 130), peeled and deveined, thawed

5 tablespoons olive oil

3 garlic cloves, finely minced or pressed through a garlic press

2½ teaspoons salt

¼ teaspoon freshly ground black pepper

8 ounces orzo pasta (about 1¼ cups)

1 can (28 ounces) diced tomatoes, drained

½ teaspoon dried basil or oregano

¼ teaspoon red-pepper flakes

3 ounces feta cheese (about ¾ cup), crumbled

 SHOP SMART
Most warehouse big-box stores offer 5-pound bulk packs of frozen shrimp. These are often a great value when compared to buying frozen 1-pound bags of shrimp.

MARINATE THE SHRIMP. Pat the shrimp dry with paper towels. Stir together 1 tablespoon olive oil, about one-third of the garlic, ¼ teaspoon of the salt, and a pinch of black pepper in a bowl. Mix in the shrimp and marinate for 10 minutes.

BOIL THE ORZO. Stir 2 teaspoons of the salt into a large pot of water and bring to a boil over high heat. Add the orzo and cook until al dente, then drain. Toss with 1 tablespoon olive oil and set aside.

BROIL THE SHRIMP. Adjust an oven rack to the uppper-most position (the rack should be about 3" from the broiler) and heat the broiler to high. Meanwhile, place the tomatoes on a rimmed baking sheet. Drizzle with 1½ tablespoons olive oil and add the remaining garlic, the basil or oregano, the red-pepper flakes, the remaining ¼ teaspoon salt, and black pepper to taste. Stir to combine, and then spread the mixture out in an even layer. Scatter the shrimp over the tomatoes in a single layer. Broil until the edges of the shrimp are beginning to brown and the shrimp are opaque throughout, 5 to 6 minutes, rotating the pan halfway through. Divide the orzo among four bowls. Stir the shrimp into the tomatoes and spoon the mixture over each serving of orzo. Sprinkle with feta, drizzle with the remaining 1½ tablespoons olive oil, and serve.

Crispy Cod & Caper-Butter Sauce

SERVES 4

$14.00/
$3.50

Want to save money and still eat seafood? Get to know your fish. When thinking fish, consider what kind of texture you're looking for, not the "name brand"—here, any thick, flaky, mild fillet will do the job. Haddock, hake, lingcod, and scrod will all work perfectly fine, so buy whatever looks freshest at the best price. Cooking this quickie up in the oven keeps your kitchen smelling fresh, while giving it a blast under the broiler gets the bread-crumb topping nice and crisp. Your friends will be blown away by how quickly you cobbled together such an impressive dish!

FISH

- 2½ tablespoons prepared horseradish
- 1¾ cups panko bread crumbs
- 2 tablespoons unsalted butter, melted
- 2 tablespoons finely chopped flat-leaf parsley
- 1 teaspoon salt
- ¼ teaspoon freshly ground black pepper
- ¼ cup mayonnaise
- 1 teaspoon canola oil
- 6 boneless, skinless cod fillets (6 ounces each and 1" thick), defrosted if frozen (see page 90 for defrosting information)

MAKE IT A MEAL
+ Steamed broccoli with lemon salt

MAKE THE BREAD-CRUMB COATING. Heat the oven to 400°F. Put the horseradish in a fine-mesh sieve and press on it with the back of a spoon to squeeze out the excess liquid. Set aside. Place the panko in a baking dish or shallow pan. Add the melted butter, 1 tablespoon of the drained horseradish, the parsley, ¼ teaspoon of the salt, and a pinch of pepper and toss to combine, breaking up any lumps with your fingers.

COAT THE FISH. Combine the remaining horseradish and the mayonnaise in a small bowl. Line a baking sheet with foil and grease with the oil. Pat the fish dry and season with the remaining salt and pepper. Spread a moderately generous layer of the horseradish-mayonnaise mixture onto one side of each fillet, then lay the fillet mayo-side down in the panko mixture and press so that the crumbs adhere. Turn the fillet panko-side up on the prepared baking sheet. Sprinkle some of the remaining panko over the fillets and press it firmly onto the fish.

BAKE THE FISH. Bake until the fillets flake around the edges but are still undercooked in the center, 10 to 12 minutes. Heat the broiler to high and cook the fish until it is cooked throughout (insert a knife tip into the center of the thickest fillet to check that it's completely opaque) and the panko is browned, another 2 to 4 minutes (watch your broiler closely as broiler intensity varies).

MAKE THE SAUCE. While the fish is cooking, combine the shallot or onion, vinegar, salt, sugar, pepper, and 1 tablespoon water in a small saucepan and bring to a simmer over medium-high heat. Simmer until all but about 2 teaspoons of liquid has evaporated, 2 to 3 minutes. Reduce the heat to low, then whisk in the butter 1 piece at a time, adding another piece only after the last has been fully incorporated. Whisk in the capers, turn off the heat, cover, and set aside. Use a wide metal spatula to transfer the fillets to plates. Spoon some sauce around each fillet and serve right away.

SAUCE

1 small shallot, very finely chopped, or ½ small yellow onion, very finely chopped

2 tablespoons white wine vinegar

¼ teaspoon salt

Pinch of sugar

Pinch of freshly ground black pepper

6 tablespoons unsalted butter, cut into 6 pieces

1½ tablespoons capers, rinsed and drained, coarsely chopped

COOK SMART

Who needs store-bought bread crumbs when it's so easy to make your own? Tear up 3 large slices of sandwich bread and pulse them in a food processor until they form coarse crumbs. If you need dry bread crumbs, toss them with 2 tablespoons of melted butter and bake at 425°F until golden brown, 8 to 10 minutes.

D2D

Frozen fish fillets are often 25 to 50 percent cheaper than fresh ones, and may well be fresher than what you get at the fish counter, since you control how and when they are defrosted. Who knows how long those fillets at the market have been sitting on ice?

Moroccan Chicken, Chickpeas & Lemon

SERVES 6

$11.70/
$1.95

This hearty pot-roasted chicken can be made with whatever chicken parts you have in the freezer. Often times I'll save a few dollars if I buy whole chickens and cut them up myself (save those backbones and necks for chicken broth!), but chicken quarters, legs, and thighs, especially when on sale, are absolutely delicious braised. This dish takes 30 minutes to braise—spend that time hanging out with your guests and enjoying the delicious perfume that fills your home. It's way better than a scented candle!

3	pounds chicken parts
1¾	teaspoons salt
¾	teaspoon freshly ground black pepper
1	tablespoon olive oil
1½	lemons, quartered
1½	onions, thinly sliced
8	garlic cloves (about 1 head), finely minced
1½	tablespoons + 2 teaspoons Moroccan Rub (page 118)
3	cups chicken broth, homemade (page 36) or store-bought
1	can (14.5 ounces) diced tomatoes, drained
1	can (15 ounces) chickpeas, rinsed and drained
3	carrots, peeled and cut into ½" pieces
¾	cup green olives, pitted and halved (optional)
¼	cup chopped fresh cilantro or flat-leaf parsley leaves

BROWN THE CHICKEN. Pat the chicken dry with paper towels and season with 1 teaspoon of the salt and the pepper. If using breasts, cut them in half crosswise. Heat the olive oil in a Dutch oven over medium-high heat. Add the chicken pieces skin-side down and cook until nicely browned, about 5 minutes. Turn the chicken and cook to brown the other side, about 5 minutes. While the chicken browns, thinly slice 2 lemon quarters crosswise into ¼"-thick segments and set aside. Transfer the chicken to a large plate.

MAKE THE SAUCE. Add the lemon slices to the pot and cook, stirring gently, until slightly softened and lightly browned, about 1 minute. Using a slotted spoon, transfer them to the plate with the chicken. Add the onions and ¼ teaspoon of the salt to the pot and cook, stirring occasionally, until softened, about 4 minutes, scraping the bottom of the pot with a wooden spoon to loosen the browned bits. Reduce the heat to medium and add the garlic and Moroccan Rub. Cook, stirring constantly, until fragrant, about 1 minute. Add the chicken broth, tomatoes, chickpeas, and carrots, then squeeze the juice from the remaining lemon quarters into the pot and stir well. Add the lemon slices, then nestle the chicken pieces into the mixture.

BRAISE THE CHICKEN. Increase the heat to medium-high, bring to a simmer, then reduce the heat to medium, cover partially, and simmer until the chicken is cooked through and the carrots are tender, about 30 minutes, turning the chicken pieces over once or twice. Stir in the olives (if using) and cilantro or parsley and serve.

D2D

Don't get price-jacked by those pretty bottles and jars of fancy olives at specialty stores! They're often repackaged versions of econo-sized cans of olives. Ethnic markets or big-box warehouse stores are a great source for olives on the cheap.

Will You Save with a Storage Freezer?

My storage freezer is like my third hand—I depend on it nearly as much as my stove! Keeping an extra freezer in the house really helps me keep my family's food costs down. I can buy meat, seafood, and even cheese in bulk when it's on sale, and I can also freeze in-season fruit such as berries and peaches to use throughout the winter. So much tastier and cheaper (and greener!) than buying out-of-season shipped-in fruit from who knows where. I'll also freeze tomatoes, herbs, and veggies from my garden rather than buying them in the wintertime.

Freezers can run from $150 to more than $800, depending on their size and frills. Remember, though, all you need a freezer to do is keep food cold! Fancy bells and whistles are nice, but by keeping the freezer basic, you're keeping the money in your pocket—or better yet, your stomach. If you save $5 a week on food costs by buying in bulk, even after you factor in the additional energy required to run the freezer, it won't take long to pay for itself. After that, you're looking at pure profit—now that's a return I like!

WHAT YOU NEED	WHAT'S REAL NICE
Ability to keep food frozen if the power fails	An interior light
A light on the outside to let you know the freezer is on	Self defrost
Energy star rating	

Turkey BLT Sliders

SERVES 6

$7.80/
$1.30

Having some ground meat in the freezer definitely comes in handy—especially when I have a kitchen full of hungry kids clamoring for food! Mini burgers are a great solution. They're the perfect handheld size, and grown-ups love them too, so really they're a win-win snack (double the serving for a meal). These turkey burger BLTs are extra-yummy, but you can scratch the BLT part if you don't have the fixings and just top them with ketchup, mustard, pickles, or Swiss. Any kind of ground meat works here, even super-lean and flavorful bison. Oven-cooking the bacon and burgers is a lot less messy than pan-frying, though of course the burgers are great grilled, too.

6   slices bacon, cut in half crosswise

¼   teaspoon salt

⅛   teaspoon freshly ground black pepper

1   pound ground turkey (light or dark meat, or a combo of the two)

6   mini buns or dinner rolls, about 3" in diameter, split

½   cup mayonnaise

½   garlic clove, finely minced

2   teaspoons fresh lemon juice

2   tablespoons (¼ stick) unsalted butter, melted

2–3   lettuce leaves, torn into 3" pieces

2   ripe tomatoes, sliced

MAKE IT A MEAL
+ Spiced Sweet Potato Fries (page 184)

COOK THE BACON. Adjust 1 oven rack to the uppermost position and leave the other in the middle position. Heat the oven to 425°F. Arrange the bacon in a single layer on a rimmed baking sheet and bake until crisped and browned, about 12 minutes. Transfer the bacon to a paper towel–lined plate. Pour the bacon fat from the baking sheet into an airtight container (or top off the bacon fat you already have stored in the fridge) and refrigerate. Wipe off the baking sheet and turn on the broiler.

MAKE THE BURGERS AND THE MAYO. Sprinkle the salt and the pepper over the ground turkey and gently mix to combine (squeezing and compacting meat makes for tough burgers). Divide the turkey into 6 mounds and lightly roll each portion into a ball. Place the balls on the baking sheet and flatten them with your hands into patties slightly larger than the buns (the burgers will shrink a little with cooking). Arrange the buns, cut-side up, on a second baking sheet and place on the middle rack. Broil the burgers on the upper rack until cooked through and lightly browned, 5 to 6 minutes. While the

(continues...)

burgers cook, mix the mayonnaise, garlic, and lemon juice in a small bowl.

TOAST THE BUNS. Take the burgers and buns out; set the burgers aside. Brush the cut side of the buns with some melted butter and broil just until lightly toasted, 30 seconds to 1 minute. Remove from the oven and spread each bun with the garlic mayonnaise. Place a patty on each bun bottom, top with bacon, lettuce, tomato, and the bun top, and serve.

Classic Creamy Slaw

SERVES 10

$2.60/ $.25

In Oklahoma, everyone just kind of learns to make coleslaw by osmosis. When I started making it at the Rock, I just kept adding ingredients and tweaking the recipe until it was perfect—nice and creamy, and so easy to whip up. I bet it's even better than your favorite fried chicken joint's slaw.

1 head (2 pounds) green cabbage, cored, halved, and thinly shredded

2 carrots, trimmed, peeled, and grated on the large-hole side of a box grater

6 tablespoons sugar

1 teaspoon salt

1 cup mayonnaise

⅔ cup white vinegar

PLACE ONE-THIRD OF THE CABBAGE in a large bowl and cover with one-third of the grated carrots. Sprinkle with 2 tablespoons of sugar and ⅓ teaspoon of salt. Repeat with 2 more layers of cabbage, carrots, sugar, and salt. Whisk the mayonnaise and vinegar together and pour over the slaw. Use a wooden spoon to mix it all together and set aside at room temperature for 5 minutes. Cover the bowl with plastic wrap and refrigerate until it's nice and creamy, at least 1 hour, before serving. (The slaw keeps crisp for up to 3 days in the fridge).

Open-Face Steak Sandwiches with Caramelized Onions & Parmesan

SERVES 4

$9.40/
$2.35

I'm always looking for a way to keep all the foods we love on the menu without breaking the bank, and this recipe is a perfect example. By serving the steak as an open-faced knife-and-fork sandwich, I can stretch 1 pound of sirloin to feed 4 people—even 6 if they're not very hearty eaters. Caramelized onions, steak, and Parmesan cheese is a classic combo, making this sandwich hearty, satisfying, and just on the right side of casual. A layer of lightly dressed greens adds crunch and texture. A bitter green like arugula is totally delicious, but spinach or romaine works, too. If you don't have crusty bread or a baguette in the freezer, double up on the greens and you have a nice steak salad.

CARAMELIZE THE ONIONS. Heat 1 tablespoon of the olive oil in a large, nonstick skillet over high heat. Add the onions and ¼ teaspoon salt and cook, stirring occasionally, until the onions soften and the edges brown, about 3 minutes. Reduce the heat to medium-high and continue to cook, stirring frequently, until the onions are deeply browned, about 15 minutes. Add 1 tablespoon of the balsamic vinegar and cook until the liquid evaporates, about 3 minutes. Season with pepper to taste and set aside.

PREPARE THE BREAD AND DRESS THE GREENS. While the onions caramelize, combine 1 tablespoon of the olive oil and the garlic in a small bowl. Place the bread on a baking sheet and brush one side of each slice with the garlic oil. Sprinkle with salt and set aside. In a small bowl, toss the greens with 1 teaspoon of the olive oil, ¼ teaspoon of the balsamic vinegar, and a sprinkle of salt. Adjust the oven rack to the uppermost position and heat the broiler.

SEAR THE STEAK. Season the steak on all sides with salt and pepper. Heat the remaining 2 teaspoons olive

3 tablespoons olive oil

2 medium onions (about 1 pound), thinly sliced

¼ teaspoon salt + extra for seasoning

1 tablespoon + 2¼ teaspoons balsamic vinegar

Freshly ground black pepper

1 garlic clove, finely minced or pressed through a garlic press

4 slices crusty country-style bread (¾" thick), or 8 slices of baguette cut on the bias

2 cups loosely packed salad greens (small leaves work best)

1 top sirloin steak (1 pound, 1" thick)

Parmesan cheese, shaved with a vegetable peeler

MAKE IT A MEAL
+ Summer Corn Soup (page 203)

oil in a nonstick skillet over medium-high heat. Add the steak and cook until well browned on both sides and an instant-read thermometer inserted into the thickest part registers 145°F for medium-rare, 8 to 10 minutes total. Transfer to a cutting board and set aside. While the steak rests, broil the bread until it's toasted, 1 to 2 minutes (keep an eye on the bread as broiler intensity varies).

MAKE THE SANDWICH. Cut the steak into thin slices and sprinkle with salt and pepper. Place 1 bread slice on each of 4 plates. Top each bread slice with about ½ cup of greens, then fan a portion of the steak on the greens. Spoon the onions on top of the steak and top with Parmesan. Drizzle each serving with ½ teaspoon balsamic vinegar and serve.

D2D

When I find a good price on hard cheeses, such as Grana Padano, Parmesan, and pecorino (which are all generally interchangeable in recipes), I stock up. At home, wrap them in a double layer of plastic wrap and store in a freezer bag. They freeze perfectly well for up to 6 months.

Defrosting Meat

For defrosting meat, your microwave is really your best friend. Just don't abuse it by blasting the frozen stuff at 100% power—use the defrost setting! Because microwaves are supposed to be fast, people just want to put their frozen meat in and hit "start." But do it that way and your meat will end up cooked on the outside and frozen in the middle. If you've lost your instruction manual, hop online and go to the manufacturer's Web site, or call the manufacturer and ask them to mail or e-mail you the instructions.

Fajitas on the Fly

SERVES 4

$18.80/
$4.70

Flank and skirt steaks are two of my favorite low-cost, big-flavor meats. Turned into fajitas, one steak easily stretches into four servings (and the recipe can be doubled to serve more), especially when smothered with onions and peppers. Fajitas are super adaptable to nearly any situation, too—if you have tortillas in the fridge (quesadillas are a house favorite so we always do), you're in the clear. If not, serve it as southwestern steak stir-fry alongside some red beans and rice (page 156).

2½   tablespoons olive oil

2   limes, juiced

¼   cup finely chopped cilantro

½   to 2 jalapeño chile peppers, ribbed, seeded, and finely diced (optional)

2   garlic cloves, finely minced or pressed through a garlic press

1   teaspoon ground cumin

1   teaspoon paprika

1   teaspoon dried oregano

½   teaspoon salt

½   teaspoon freshly ground black pepper

1¼   pounds flank or skirt steak, sliced crosswise into ¼"-thick pieces

2   large green or red bell peppers or 1 cup of roasted pepper strips

1   large white onion

8   flour tortillas

     Salsa, for serving

MAKE IT A MEAL
+ Ranch-Style Beans (page 159)

MARINATE THE MEAT. Whisk 1½ tablespoons of the olive oil, the lime juice, cilantro, jalapeños (if using), garlic, cumin, paprika, oregano, salt, and black pepper together in a large bowl. Place the meat in the marinade and toss to coat. Set aside while you slice the peppers and onion into ¼"-thick strips.

SEAR THE STEAK. Heat a heavy-bottomed skillet (cast iron works great) for 3 minutes over medium-high heat. Remove the steak from the marinade. Drizzle ½ tablespoon of the olive oil into the pan and then add half of the steak to the skillet. Cook, stirring occasionally, until the steak is nicely seared on all sides, about 2 minutes. Transfer the steak to a large plate and repeat with the remaining steak slices. Use tongs and a wad of paper towels to wipe out the skillet (be careful—it's hot).

BROWN THE VEGETABLES. Place the skillet back over the heat and drizzle in the remaining ½ tablespoon of olive oil in the pan. Add the onion and bell peppers to the pan and cook until charred and softened, about 5 minutes.

HEAT THE TORTILLAS. While the onion and peppers cook, wrap the stack of tortillas in a kitchen towel or paper towels and place them on a plate. Microwave them until they are soft and supple, 20 to 30 seconds. Transfer the steak and vegetables to a large shallow dish and serve with the warm tortillas and the salsa.

Garlic-Rosemary Pork Loin & Crisp Salt-Pepper Potatoes

This pork roast really pulls through when you need to whip a meal together with just a handful of ingredients. Whole pork loins are often on sale for as little as $1.99 per pound, and when they are, I buy one and then cut it up into smaller roasts when I get home. If I've really got my act together, I'll even season the pork with the garlic-rosemary rub before I freeze it, so all I have to do is pull a roast from the freezer, defrost it in the microwave, and cook. For the juiciest, most flavorful roast, be sure to let it rest for 10 minutes or so before slicing.

6   garlic cloves, finely minced or pressed through a garlic press

1   tablespoon finely chopped fresh rosemary, plus extra sprigs for serving

4½   tablespoons olive oil

1   teaspoon salt + extra for seasoning

½   teaspoon freshly ground black pepper + extra for seasoning

1   boneless center-cut or blade-cut pork loin roast (2 pounds)

    Butchers' twine

6   medium red potatoes (about 2 pounds, halved and cut into 1" cubes)

SEASON THE PORK. Adjust an oven rack to the lowest position, set a rimmed sheet pan on the rack, and heat the oven to 375°F. Combine the garlic, rosemary, 2 tablespoons of the olive oil, ½ teaspoon of the salt, and ¼ teaspoon of the pepper in a small bowl and mix well. Pat the pork dry with paper towels and make a lengthwise cut down the length of the roast, stopping about ½" short of cutting all the way through. Open the roast up like a book, season the inside and outside with some salt and pepper, then spread 1 tablespoon of the garlic-rosemary paste on the inside of the roast. Use twine to tie the roast together at the ends as well as in a few spots in the middle.

SEAR AND ROAST THE PORK. Heat 1½ teaspoons of the oil in a medium or large skillet (whichever fits your roast more snugly) over medium-high heat. Add the roast and brown on all sides, about 8 minutes total. Transfer the roast to a cutting board and spread the remaining garlic-rosemary paste on all sides. Place the roast fat side up on the hot baking sheet in the oven and roast for 15 minutes. While the pork roasts, place the potatoes in a large bowl and toss with the remaining 2 tablespoons olive oil, ½ teaspoon salt, and ¼ teaspoon pepper.

ROAST THE POTATOES AND CARVE. Remove the baking sheet from the oven, scatter the potatoes around the roast in a single layer, and return the baking sheet to the oven. Continue to cook for 10 minutes. Increase the oven temperature to 450°F and cook until the roast is well browned and its center registers about 145°F on an instant-read thermometer, 15 to 20 minutes. Remove the baking sheet from the oven and transfer the pork to a carving board. Scrape up and flip the potatoes, mixing them with the drippings from the roast, then return the baking sheet to the oven and cook until the potatoes are deeply browned, 5 to 10 minutes longer. Carve the roast, removing the strings as you carve, and arrange the slices on a platter. Remove the potatoes from the oven and scatter around the pork. Garnish with rosemary sprigs and serve.

D2D
Center-cut pork roasts are the most expensive. If I see a blade-cut roast, I buy it—it has more fat, and yields a juicier (and less expensive) roast.

SHOP SMART
Buy a 4-pound pork loin and cut it in 2 pieces when you get home. Refrigerate one half to roast within a few days, and freeze the other half for a "free" meal another time.

when the pantry is your BFF

When you need to cook dinner on a shoestring budget, look no further than your pantry. It can be a treasure trove of fast, budget-friendly options if you stock it with the essentials, and even when there's nothing in the fridge, I just know I can count on what's there to pull dinner together in a snap—and for a penny.

Pantry dishes are easy to make because they rely on everyday ingredients as a starting point. Inexpensive building blocks such as flour, rice, beans, and even canned tuna become your kitchen superheroes: Just when you find yourself scratching your head wondering what to make for dinner, they swoop in at the nick of time to help you get food on the table no matter what you have in the fridge.

There are other ways the pantry can save you money, too. When my kids bring friends over after school, the first thing they do is open the cupboards and scrounge around for snacks. Nine times out of ten I'll hear their friends complain "there's nothing to eat in here!" because I don't keep chips, candy, and other "snack" foods in the house. Besides being unhealthy, these foods are extremely expensive. Fortunately, my kids love to prove their friends wrong by showing them there are all *kinds* of things to eat—they just have to add heat.

My Trusty Pantry List

Your everyday pantry is more than just what is in your cupboards. I consider my long-term perishables, such as pickles, eggs, and citrus fruits, to be pantry items too. Just because they need to be refrigerated (or even frozen) doesn't mean they're any less essential. They last a few weeks (or longer), so there's really no point in not keeping them in the house. With these essentials at your fingertips, you can always cook something up. It's a pretty big list, so I'm not suggesting that you go out and buy everything all at once. But if you decide to try some of the recipes in this chapter, you'll build your pantry and before you know it, you'll have everything on the list!

Just a reminder: Don't be afraid to make substitutions. So a recipe calls for currants and all you have are raisins. Sub them in. Same goes for beans, oils, and vinegars—nine times out of ten, compliments will come your way.

Go to myd2d.com to print out Pantry List.

Beans, bread, flours, grains, pastas

All-purpose flour

Bread** (burger buns, sandwich bread, sliced baguette, or country bread)

Bread crumbs (dried, panko, or fresh**)

Brown lentils

Canned and dried beans (pinto, black, cannellini, and/or chickpeas)

Cornmeal

Crackers (graham, saltines, or wheat crackers)

Leaveners and thickeners (baking powder, baking soda, cornstarch)

Noodles and pasta (egg, no-boil lasagna, orzo, rotini, or spaghetti)

Oats (old fashioned and quick)

Rice (basmati, brown, or long-grain white)

Tortillas*

Quick flavor add-ins

Capers*

Chili sauce or hot sauce

Garlic

Ketchup*

Mustard* (Dijon, grainy, or yellow)

Olives*

Pickles* (cornichon, dill, or relish)

Soy sauce

Dried fruits, nuts, and sweeteners

Chocolate chips

Dried fruit (apples, apricots, cranberries, currants, figs, or raisins)

Nuts and seeds (almonds, peanuts, pecans, sesame seeds, or walnuts)

Peanut butter

Sugar (corn syrup, dark or light brown, granulated white, honey, maple syrup)

Dairy and eggs

Butter*

Cheese (Cheddar* or Monterey Jack*, Parmesan*)

Citrus* (lemons or limes)

Dried buttermilk powder*

Dried milk powder

Eggs*

Mayonnaise*

Milk*

Canned goods

Low-sodium chicken broth

Tomatoes (diced, paste)

Tuna

Herbs, oils, spices, vinegars

Dried spices and spice blends (see page 118): basil, bay leaves, black pepper-corns, cayenne, chili powder, ground ginger, herbes de Provence, oregano, red-pepper flakes, sweet paprika, turmeric)

Oil (vegetable oil such as canola or corn, extra-virgin or pure olive)

Salt (kosher and table)

Vinegar (balsamic, cider, red wine vinegar, rice, or white wine)

*REFRIGERATOR ITEM

**FREEZER ITEM

The Price Is Rice

At only 10 cents per serving, rice is an excellent value-staple to have in the pantry at all times. Besides being delicious simply steamed and served plain alongside something stewy or spicy, here are some other ways to take advantage of the low price point of rice.

Use as a mix-in. Stretch out dishes such as meatloaf, meatballs, or even a small amount of leftover stir-fried chicken or pulled pork by mixing in rice.

Use as a foundation. Become a champion of stir-fries. With a small amount of protein and some veggies plus an interesting sauce, such as the peanut sauce on page 62 or the teriyaki sauce on page 97, a few cups of rice with a minimal addition of fresh ingredients becomes a meal.

Use as a stuffing. Moisten cooked rice with canned tomatoes or chicken broth and mix in herbs, spices, dried fruits, nuts, and even bacon or sausage to use as a stuffing. Acorn squash, bell peppers, eggplant (slender Italian or Japanese, not globe), and zucchini are all vegetables particularly suited to stuffing. Grape leaves are wonderful, too. You can also stuff butterflied leg of lamb and pork loins, whole chickens, and Cornish hens with rice.

Pilaf with Almonds Golden Raisins

For a little more than $5, plain white rice gets a makeover and becomes this tasty dish. What really makes it is the toasted angel hair pasta. It cooks with the rice and adds a wonderful texture and appearance to this very simple side dish. You can add nearly any kind of nut or fruit you have in the pantry—some other good combos are pine nuts and currants, pecans and dried cranberries, or pistachios and dried apricots.

SERVES 6

$5.40/ $.90

MAKE THE PILAF BASE. Melt the butter in a large saucepan or Dutch oven over medium-high heat. Add the onion, salt, and pepper and cook until the onion is soft, about 5 minutes. Stir in the pasta and almonds and cook until both are golden-brown, about 3 minutes.

COOK THE PILAF. Mix in the rice, add 3¾ cups of the broth, and the raisins, and bring to a boil. Reduce the heat to low, cover, and cook until the broth is absorbed and the rice is cooked, 20 to 25 minutes (add the remaining ¼ cup of broth if the rice seems undercooked). Turn off the heat and let the rice sit for 5 minutes. Fluff with a fork and sprinkle with parsley before serving.

Oven Pilaf

If you need to free up your stovetop, you can finish the pilaf in the oven (but be sure you start it in an oven-safe saucepan or Dutch oven). Along with the raisins, add the full 4 cups of broth to the recipe above, bring to a boil, and then transfer to a 350°F oven and bake, covered, until the rice has absorbed all of the liquid and is fully cooked, 30 to 35 minutes. Remove from the oven, and let it sit for 5 minutes before serving.

2 tablespoons unsalted butter

1 yellow onion, finely chopped

½ teaspoon salt

¼ teaspoon freshly ground black pepper

2 ounces vermicelli or angel hair pasta, broken into 1" pieces (about ½ cup)

½ cup sliced almonds

1½ cups long-grain white rice

4 cups chicken broth, homemade (page 36) or store-bought

½ cup golden raisins

½ cup finely chopped fresh flat-leaf parsley

 MAKE IT A MEAL
+ Middle Eastern Kebabs (page 30)

Paella with Spicy Sausage  Shrimp

SERVES 8

This is an excellent party dish because it seems fancy, impressive, and expensive. I stretch a pound of shrimp by slicing them in half lengthwise, so it looks as if there is a ton of shrimp in the pan. A nice addition to or substitution for the shrimp is fresh clams and mussels, often priced at between $3 and $6 per pound.

$16.00/ $2.00

2	tablespoons olive oil
1	yellow onion, finely chopped
12	ounces chorizo or other spicy sausage, sliced ½" thick
1	large green bell pepper, finely chopped
4	garlic cloves, finely minced
2	cups long-grain white rice
1	can (14.5 ounces) diced tomatoes, undrained
½	cup dry white wine
3–3½	cups chicken broth, homemade (page 36) or store-bought
¼	teaspoon crushed saffron threads
½	teaspoon salt
1	pound large (26/30) peeled and deveined shrimp
¼	cup chopped fresh flat-leaf parsley
1	lemon, cut into wedges

MAKE THE PAELLA BASE. Heat the oil in a large pot or Dutch oven over medium-high heat. Add the onion and cook until it's soft, about 5 minutes. Add the sausage, bell pepper, and garlic and cook until the sausage is lightly browned, about 5 minutes. Stir in the rice, tomatoes, and wine, scraping any brown bits off the bottom of the pan.

COOK THE RICE AND SEAFOOD. Add 3 cups of the broth, the saffron, and salt, and bring to a boil. Reduce the heat to medium, cover, and simmer until the rice is cooked through but still firm, about 20 minutes, adding the remaining ½ cup broth if the pan seems dry before the rice is done. Add the shrimp, cover, and cook until the shrimp are pink, 2 to 3 minutes longer. Season to taste with salt, sprinkle with parsley, and serve immediately with lemon wedges.

 D2D

Ground turmeric is often used as a stand-in for saffron. The flavor is a little different, but your guests probably won't know the difference.

 COOK SMART

I'm always defrosting seafood on the fly—I just never seem to think far enough ahead to defrost my fish and shrimp in the fridge the night before. To quickly defrost it, I place the bag of shrimp in a large bowl in my sink and cover it with cold water (I weigh the bag down with a plate or a can of beans if it floats to the top) and let it be for 15 to 20 minutes, pouring out the water and recovering it with fresh, cold water 2 or 3 times throughout (for fish, I place the fillet in a resealable bag before setting it under water). Lickety split, it's good to go. While you're defrosting seafood, use your time wisely and prep the other ingredients for the dish.

Cajun-Style Red Beans  Rice

SERVES 4

$3.40/
$.85

This recipe is a great use for leftover rice, and like chili, it's very wallet-friendly. We love it with cornbread on the side. If you don't have any leftover rice, just cook up 1 cup of raw rice to get the 3 cups you need.

1 tablespoon canola oil

1 yellow onion, finely chopped

1 green bell pepper, ribbed, seeded, and finely chopped

½ teaspoon salt

¼ teaspoon freshly ground black pepper

2 garlic cloves, finely minced or pressed through a garlic press

1 tablespoon chili powder

1 tablespoon Tex-Mex Rub (page 118)

1 can (14 ounces) pinto beans, drained and rinsed, or 1½ cups cooked pinto beans (page 158)

3 cups cooked white rice

Hot-pepper sauce, optional

HEAT THE OIL in a large skillet over medium-high heat. Add the onion, bell pepper, salt, and black pepper and cook, stirring often, until the onion is soft, 3 to 4 minutes. Stir in the garlic and cook until fragrant, about 30 seconds, then add the chili powder and Tex-Mex Rub. Cook, stirring often, for 2 minutes, and then mix in the pinto beans and rice. Continue to cook and stir until the beans and rice are heated through, about 5 minutes, adding water if it looks as if the spices or rice are sticking and burning. Serve with hot-pepper sauce on the side if using.

Meaty Red Beans and Rice

This is the version that is on offer at the restaurant, and people go crazy for it. Before sautéing the onion and bell pepper, I brown 1 pound of ground beef and ½ pound of sliced smoked sausage (such as andouille or kielbasa). Once the meat is browned, I add in the onion, bell pepper, salt, and black pepper, and continue with the recipe above.

D2D

Leftover rice loses its tenderness when refrigerated. To replump it, place it in a microwave-safe dish and sprinkle with some water before reheating.

Veggie-Loaded Fried Rice

Frozen vegetables are true assets. Oftentimes, they're less expensive than their fresh veggie twins in the produce department, especially if you're shopping out of season. Since they're usually picked at their peak sweetness and flash-frozen to preserve nutrients and flavor, there's just no reason to turn your nose up at frozen broccoli, carrots, cauliflower, corn, green beans, pearl onions, or peas.

SERVES 4

$3.20/ $.80

HEAT THE CANOLA OIL in a wok or large, heavy-bottomed skillet over high heat for 1½ minutes. Add the onion and cook, stirring constantly, for 1 minute, then stir in the garlic and cook until it's fragrant, about 30 seconds. Stir in the frozen vegetables along with the salt and 3 table-spoons of water and cook, partially covered, until thawed, 3 to 6 minutes (depending on what kinds of frozen vegetables you used). Add the scallions, soy sauce, Asian sauce, and sesame oil, toss with the vegetables to coat, and then stir in the rice and cook until all the grains are coated with sauce. Serve immediately.

- 1 tablespoon canola oil
- 1 yellow onion, finely chopped
- 2 garlic cloves, finely minced or pressed through a garlic press
- 4 cups frozen Asian-blend vegetables (or 4 cups of mixed frozen vegetables such as broccoli florets, carrots, cauliflower, green beans, pearl onions, peas, or snow peas)
- ½ teaspoon salt
- 3 scallions, white and light green parts only, finely chopped
- 2 tablespoons soy sauce
- 2 tablespoons prepared Asian sauce (such as black bean, hoisin, or teriyaki)
- 1 tablespoon toasted sesame oil
- 3 cups cooked brown or white rice

D2D

Boxed pilaf mix is essentially just a few ounces of rice mixed with powdered bouillon and a few dried herbs or spices—dollar for dollar, a huge markup over the cost of the individual ingredients. Why spend the money when it's so easy to make yourself? Add a cup or 2 of raw rice to a skillet of fried onions and then cook in chicken broth (double the amount of the rice), and there you have it, homemade pilaf for a fraction of the price.

MAKE IT A MEAL
+ Thai-Style Chicken Satay (page 66)

A Hill of Beans

Using 1 pound of dried beans that yields about 6 cups of cooked beans can save you up to $3 when compared to the same amount of beans from a can. Once I realized this simple economic reality, I started to cook up a big pot of beans every few weeks. I freeze some to use later and turn the rest into dinners for the week, such as Cajun-Style Red Beans and Rice (page 156) and the Ham and Black Bean Soup on page 18 (though the recipe calls for black beans, any kind of beans are delicious!).

1 pound dried beans

1 smoked ham hock (optional)

Salt

Freshly ground black pepper

COOK SMART

A few cups of beans are all it takes to make a quick bean soup. Sauté some vegetables in oil in a large pot. Add some dried herbs and spices, the beans, and chicken broth or bean broth—or water if you have neither. Bring to a boil and serve, or puree one-third of the soup for a thicker consistency (an immersion blender is useful for this job!).

First boil. Place the beans in a Dutch oven or large pot and cover with ½" of cold water. Bring the beans to a boil over high heat, then drain them and rinse under cool water.
Second boil. Return the beans to the pot and add the ham hock, if using. Cover with 3" of warm water. Cover the pot and bring to a boil.
Simmer until tender. Reduce the heat so the beans are at a gentle simmer and cook for 1 to 1½ hours, checking every 20 minutes to see if you need to add more water to the pot. (Soft beans, such as cannellini, take less time, while hard beans, such

COOK SMART

Instead of thickening soup or stew with cream or cornstarch, add a handful of mashed lentils or beans. They add flavor, heft, and nutrition.

as chickpeas, take longer. Check often toward the end to ensure that the beans don't overcook and split.) When the beans are nearly finished (but are still a little raw in the middle), add a generous pinch of salt and some pepper and continue to cook, checking the pot often, until perfectly tender, another 30 minutes to 1 hour. Remove the ham

hock and set aside (discard the skin and bones and add the shredded meat to the pot of beans or save it for another use). Cool and refrigerate for up to 1 week, or strain (save the cooking liquid to use instead of chicken broth) and refrigerate the beans for up to 1 week.

Ranch-Style Beans

This is a Rock Cafe classic that I usually serve with a big hunk of cornbread. It's wonderful and hearty, and loaded with flavor from garlic and chiles. While you can make this with canned beans, I often have a batch of boiled pintos in the fridge or freezer and will pull them to use here. For my cooking method, see opposite page.

SERVES 6

$4.50/ $.75

HEAT THE OIL in a large skillet over medium-high heat. Add the onion, pepper, and ½ teaspoon of the salt, and cook until they're soft and brown around the edges, about 4 minutes, stirring often. Mix in the garlic and cook until fragrant, about 30 seconds, and then add the beans, Worcestershire, sugar, chili powder, mustard, and the remaining ½ teaspoon of salt (if the beans look dry, add ½ cup of water to the pan). Simmer for 30 minutes and then stir in the diced tomatoes and cook until they begin to break down, another 20 minutes, stirring occasionally. Serve over rice or as a side dish.

COOK SMART

Ranch-Style Beans become bean dip instantly when you transfer the beans and a little liquid to a food processor. Blend until smooth, and serve with home-baked tortilla chips (made from baked tortillas) or raw veggies.

1 tablespoon canola oil

1 yellow onion, finely chopped

1 green bell pepper, ribbed, seeded, and finely chopped

1 teaspoon salt

3 garlic cloves, finely minced or pressed through a garlic press

2 cans (14 ounces each) pinto beans, drained and rinsed, or 3 cups cooked beans

2 tablespoons Worcestershire sauce

3 tablespoons dark brown sugar

1 tablespoon chili powder

½ teaspoon ground mustard

1 can (10 ounces) diced tomatoes with green chiles

Rice, for serving (optional)

MAKE IT A MEAL
+ Tortilla Scramble (page 226)

Pantry Veggie Burgers

These days, I get a lot of requests for veggie burgers at the Rock. I make them Oklahoma-style, with pinto beans and bulgur wheat, and top them off with barbecue sauce. At home, I often make a double or triple batch, shape them, and freeze them for a quick meal or afterschool snack.

1   can (14 ounces) pinto beans, drained and rinsed, or 1½ cups cooked pinto beans (page 158)

½   cup bulgur wheat

1   teaspoon salt

1   tablespoon + 2 teaspoons canola oil

8   ounces cremini mushrooms, stemmed and thinly sliced

½   yellow onion, finely chopped

1   large garlic clove, minced

½   cup walnut pieces

½   teaspoon freshly ground black pepper

⅛   teaspoon smoked paprika (optional)

5   tablespoons mayonnaise

2   teaspoons canola oil

6   hamburger buns, toasted

    Lettuce leaves

1   large or 2 small ripe tomatoes, cored and thinly sliced

6   tablespoons barbecue sauce or ketchup

MAKE IT A MEAL
+ Mozzarella and Orecchiette Toss (page 61)

DRY THE BEANS. Spread the drained pinto beans on a paper towel–lined plate and set aside.

COOK THE BULGUR. Bring 1 cup of water to a boil in a small saucepan over high heat. Stir in the bulgur and ¼ teaspoon of the salt, cover, and turn off the heat. Set aside until the bulgur is tender, about 20 minutes. (If some water remains in the bottom of the saucepan, drain the bulgur in a fine-mesh sieve, then set aside to cool to room temperature.)

COOK THE VEGGIES. Heat 1 tablespoon of the oil in a large skillet over medium-high heat. Add the mushrooms, onion, and ¼ teaspoon of the salt, and cook, stirring often, until the vegetables begin to brown, about 9 minutes. Stir in the garlic and cook until fragrant, about 30 seconds. Transfer the mixture to a plate and let it cool to room temperature.

MAKE THE BURGER MIXTURE. Pulse the walnuts in a food processor until chopped, about five 1-second pulses. Add the beans, bulgur, the mushroom-onion mixture, the remaining ½ teaspoon of salt, the pepper, and the paprika (if using) to the food processor. Pulse about 15 times, or until the mixture holds together when squeezed, but isn't pureed, scraping down the sides of the bowl as necessary. Add 2 tablespoons of the mayonnaise and pulse a couple of times to combine.

SHAPE THE BURGERS. Line a large baking sheet with parchment paper (parchment makes it easier to remove the burgers from the baking sheet). Shape the mixture into 6 equal patties and place them on the prepared baking sheet. Cover with plastic wrap and refrigerate for at least 30 minutes or up to 12 hours (the burgers can also be frozen for up to 6 months).

BROWN THE BURGERS AND SERVE. Heat 1 teaspoon of the oil in a large skillet over medium-high heat. Place 3 burgers in the pan and cook until browned on both sides, 5 to 6 minutes total, using a thin, wide, metal spatula to carefully flip the burgers. Transfer to a large plate and tent with foil. Repeat with the remaining oil to cook the last 3 burgers. Place a burger on each bun bottom and top with lettuce and tomato slices. Spread some mayonnaise and barbecue sauce or ketchup on the bun top, cover the burger, and serve.

D2D
Go grocery shopping with a list of staples that you need, such as milk and eggs, but for produce and meat, keep it broad so that you can take advantage of store specials. For example, instead of writing down "broccoli," note that you need a "Monday night vegetable for pork." This opens you up to a broader range of possibilities, such as cauliflower or cabbage to go with pork rib chops or pork cutlets—whatever is priced most competitively.

D2D
Price groceries by the ounce, not by the unit, to see if the "value" size is really a bargain.

D2D
I'm always searching out the best deal, and one that's often overlooked is buying supermarket private-label brands. More often than not, the brand-name product is just repackaged with the supermarket label. So try it—if you don't like it, you can always switch back. But if you *do* like it, then you're saving some money.

COOK SMART
Turn these burgers into meatballs by making small, golf ball–size rounds and browning them in the skillet. They're great with spaghetti or crumbled and used in place of meat in lasagna or chili.

Route 66 Chili

If there was ever an econo-meal all-star, chili would win that title! Loaded with veggies, meat, and beans, a big pot of this chili serves 4 hungry people for less than $10, making it a real meal deal. Double the batch and freeze the rest for Fry Bread Tostadas (page 164) or chili dogs with grated cheese and relish.

3 tablespoons chili powder

1 tablespoon canola oil

1 yellow onion, finely chopped

2 teaspoons salt

2 garlic cloves, finely minced or pressed through a garlic press

2 pounds ground beef (preferably 85% lean)

1 tablespoon all-purpose flour

¼ teaspoon freshly ground black pepper

1 can (14 ounces) pinto beans, drained and rinsed, or 1½ cups cooked pinto beans (page 158)

1 can (6 ounces) tomato paste

2 tablespoons light brown sugar

Hot-pepper sauce, to taste (optional)

MAKE THE CHILI BROTH. Bring 2½ cups of water to a boil in a large saucepan over high heat. Whisk in the chili powder, cover, turn off the heat, and set aside.

BROWN THE VEGGIES AND MEAT. Heat the oil in a large Dutch oven or pot over medium-high heat. Add the onion and ½ teaspoon of salt and cook until the onion is soft and just starting to brown, about 5 minutes, stirring occasionally. Stir in the garlic and cook until it's fragrant, about 30 seconds, then stir in the ground beef. Cook, stirring often, until browned, 3 to 4 minutes. Mix in the flour, the remaining 1½ teaspoons of salt, and the pepper and cook, stirring constantly, for 1 minute.

COOK THE CHILI. Whisk a little of the chili-water into the meat while stirring to work out any lumps. Add the rest of the chili-water, bring to a boil, reduce the heat to medium-low, and gently simmer for 1 hour. Pour in the beans and add the tomato paste (if the chili doesn't look saucy enough for your taste, add ⅔ cup of water) and the sugar and simmer for another 30 minutes to bring the flavors together. Serve immediately with hot-pepper sauce on the side, if using, or cool and refrigerate for up to 5 days (or freeze in 2 quart-size resealable freezer bags for up to 3 months).

 D2D

When I have just 1 serving of chili left, I'll add a pound of pasta, some extra beans, chopped raw onions, grated cheese, and cilantro, and call it chili mac. Everyone loves it, and it allows me to stretch one $2.20 serving out to feed 4 people.

Bare-Cupboard Lentil Soup

Even though this soup uses only a handful of ingredients, lentils are so rich and flavorful they don't require much fussing with. They're such an incredible source of protein, iron, and fiber, we should all be eating more lentils, whatever our budget. This recipe is definitely slow-cooker friendly—just toss in all of the ingredients and cook on low until the lentils are tender, about 8 hours. Doesn't get any easier than that!

$9.60/ $1.20

MAKE THE SOUP BASE. Heat the olive oil in a large pot or Dutch oven over medium-high heat. Add the onion and cook until soft, about 5 minutes. Stir in the lentils, red-peppers, thyme, salt, and black pepper, cook for 1 minute, and then add the chicken broth and 5 cups of water.

COOK THE SOUP. Bring the soup to a boil, reduce the heat to medium-low, and simmer, covered, until the lentils are soft, about 1 hour. Add the spinach (if using), increase the heat to high, and bring back to a boil until the spinach is warmed through and tender, about 5 minutes. Serve with lemon wedges on the side.

2 tablespoons olive oil

1 yellow onion, finely chopped

1 pound dry brown lentils

1 jar (12 ounces) roasted red-peppers, drained and diced

1 teaspoon dried thyme

1 teaspoon salt

½ teaspoon finely ground black pepper

5 cups chicken broth, homemade (page 36) or store-bought

1 package (1 pound) frozen chopped spinach (optional), thawed, drained, and squeezed dry

Lemon wedges, for serving

D2D

Here's a fun twist on the traditional dinner party: Invite your friends over for a "group soup" night. Have each person bring an ingredient to make soup or stew, such as a vegetable, meat, beans, noodles, chicken broth, herbs, or bread (for eating with the soup or stew), then make soup together.

MAKE IT A MEAL
+ Coriander Sugar-Rubbed Salmon (page 90)
+ Rice

Fry Bread Tostadas

SERVES 6

$7.80/
$1.30

Fry bread is an authentic Native American flatbread similar to Mexican sopapillas. It costs pennies to make and is super-good on its own (my family loves it as a snack or for dessert drizzled with honey) or used as a taco shell—like a base for chili (page 162) or even pulled pork (page 21). I was taught how to make fry bread by an Apache woman who shared her secret: self-rising flour. Even if you don't use it for anything other than this recipe, you'll want to keep a sack in your pantry—fry bread is that good.

2⅓ cups self-rising flour + extra for kneading

⅓ cup sugar

4 cups + 1 teaspoon corn oil

6 cups leftover chili, warmed

Grated Cheddar or Monterey Jack cheese, for serving

Chopped onions or scallions, for serving

Chopped cilantro, for serving

MAKE IT A MEAL
+ Green salad with your choice of dressing (page 180)

D2D
If you don't have self-rising flour but want to make fry bread, you can make your own blend by whisking together 4 cups of all-purpose flour, 2 tablespoons of baking powder, and 2 teaspoons of salt. It won't come out exactly the same, but it's pretty darn close.

MAKE THE DOUGH AND LET IT RISE. Using a wooden spoon, stir the 2⅓ cups of flour and the sugar together in a large bowl. Add 1½ cups of very warm water (between lukewarm and hot) and stir until there are no remaining dry patches. At this point, the bread dough looks more like batter than dough—it's very wet and slack. Set it aside to rise until slightly puffy and evenly moistened, about 30 minutes.

KNEAD THE DOUGH AND RISE AGAIN. Place 1 cup of flour on your work surface in a thick layer. Use a rubber spatula to turn the dough out onto the floured work surface. Flour your hands and slip them under the edges of the dough and fold the edges over onto the dough several times, until a soft, yet cohesive, mass forms (it will be slightly lumpy with some floury streaks). Knead the dough a few times so it looks more like a dough ball. Grease a large bowl with ½ teaspoon of the oil and place the dough in the bowl (leave the flour on your work surface; you'll need it to shape the dough). Grease your fingers with another ½ teaspoon of oil and tap the dough to oil the surface of it, lightly coating it with oil. (At this point, the dough can be refrigerated for up to 3 days.) Set the dough aside and let it rise again until puffy, about 30 minutes.

(continues...)

D2D

For the freshest, crispest greens, never wash them before putting them away in the fridge. If they're especially wet from being spritzed with water at the market, wrap them loosely in a paper towel to absorb extra moisture before putting them away.

SHAPE THE DOUGH, FRY. Heat the remaining 4 cups of oil in a large, deep skillet (preferably cast iron) over medium-high heat until it reaches between 350°F and 375°F. Transfer the dough back to the floured work surface and divide it into 6 equal pieces. Pick each piece up and gently stretch it into a 6" or 7" oval shape (don't worry if it isn't perfect or gets a hole or two). Carefully use your index finger to poke a hole through the center of the dough (this helps it cook evenly—if your dough already has a hole or two in it from stretching, skip that step) and gently slip the dough into the oil.

FRY THE DOUGH AND SERVE. Fry until each side is golden brown, 2½ to 3½ minutes total. Set aside on a paper towel–lined baking sheet to drain and then serve, or keep warm on a baking sheet in a 250°F oven until the rest of the bread is ready. Place about 1 cup of chili in the middle of each, top with cheese, onions, and cilantro, and serve.

Straight-Up Cornbread

Even though you can buy a box of corn muffin mix for less than 75 cents, it's still worth it to make your own. First of all, it tastes so much better. Secondly, it's a lot healthier for you, since you won't be adding shortening or lard. I like my cornbread on the sweet side, but if you prefer it more savory, cut the sugar in half.

PREP THE PAN. Heat the oven to 400°F. Grease a 9" baking pan with 1 tablespoon of oil and set aside.

MAKE THE BATTER. Whisk the flour, cornmeal, sugar, baking powder, and salt together in a large bowl. Whisk the milk and remaining ⅓ cup of oil together in a small bowl, then add to the dry ingredients. Mix together until just combined and no dry patches remain.

BAKE THE CORNBREAD. Use a rubber spatula to scrape the batter from the bowl into the prepared baking pan and give the pan a little shake to even the batter out. Bake the cornbread until it is golden brown, pulls away from the sides of the pan, and resists light pressure, 20 to 25 minutes. Cool for at least 10 minutes before slicing into squares and serving.

⅓ cup + 1 tablespoon canola oil
1 cup all-purpose flour
1 cup yellow cornmeal
⅔ cup sugar
3½ teaspoons baking powder
1 teaspoon salt
1 cup whole milk

MAKE IT A MEAL
+ Cajun-Style Red Beans and Rice (page 156)

D2D

Homemade muffins cost $1.50 less than the average coffee-shop muffin. After baking, cool the muffins completely, then wrap them in plastic wrap. Freeze the muffins in a few gallon-size resealable freezer bags and defrost them at room temperature for about 30 minutes, or defrost in the microwave. Squares of cornbread can be frozen and defrosted in the same manner (or bake the batter in a muffin tin instead of in a baking pan).

Couscous with Dried Fruit, Butternut Squash & Turmeric

SERVES 8

$12.40/
$1.55

Dried fruit and spices turn couscous into an exotic side dish that's delicious with roasted chicken and lamb or even a vegetarian main course. Winter squash is a great keeper; there's often acorn, butternut, or spaghetti squash stashed away in my garage (it lasts for months in a cool, dark, dry spot) ready to be transformed into quick roasted side dishes.

5 tablespoons olive oil

2 leeks, white parts only, cleaned and finely minced

5 garlic cloves, finely minced or pressed through a garlic press

1 teaspoon salt

3 cups chicken or vegetable broth, homemade (page 36) or store-bought

3 cups finely chopped butternut squash

1 cup chopped dried apricots

1 cup chopped dried figs

1 teaspoon turmeric

½ teaspoon ground ginger

¼ teaspoon cayenne

1½ cups couscous

¼ cup finely chopped mint

MAKE THE COUSCOUS BASE. Heat the oil in a Dutch oven or large pot over medium-low heat. Add the leeks, garlic, and ½ teaspoon of the salt, cover, and cook until the leeks are very tender but not brown, about 10 minutes, stirring occasionally. Pour in the broth and then add the squash, apricots, figs, turmeric, ginger, and cayenne. Stir in the remaining salt and bring to a boil. Cover, reduce the heat to medium-low, and simmer until the squash is tender, 10 to 12 minutes.

COOK THE COUSCOUS AND SERVE. Mix in the couscous, cover, turn off the heat, and let it stand for 10 minutes. Add all but 1 tablespoon of the mint and fluff the couscous with a fork to combine. Transfer to a large platter. Serve sprinkled with the remaining mint.

 D2D
If I don't have fresh mint handy, I've been known to steep a bag of herbal mint tea in ¼ cup of water and stir it in.

Crispy Salmon Cakes

I love crab cakes, but canned crabmeat can't hold a candle to the fresh lump crabmeat you get in most restaurant cakes. So unless I'm feeling flush, when the craving for fish cakes hits, I choose a far more economical and tasty alternative, canned salmon. You can often pick up cans of salmon on the cheap, and it is packed with all the same big flavors and nutrients that I turn to fresh salmon for.

MAKE THE SALMON MIXTURE. Mix together the salmon, 1 cup of the panko, the tartar sauce or mayonnaise, scallions or onion powder, the egg, salt, and pepper in a large bowl.

SHAPE THE CAKES. Form the mixture into eight 3" cakes that are about 1" thick. Place the remaining ½ cup of panko in a shallow dish and press the cakes into the bread crumbs until all sides are evenly coated.

FRY THE SALMON CAKES. Heat ½ cup of oil in a large skillet over medium-high heat. Once the oil is shimmering, fry the salmon cakes in 2 batches until golden brown on both sides, 8 to 10 minutes per batch, adding the remaining ¼ cup of oil to fry the second batch if necessary. Place the salmon cakes on a paper towel–lined plate to drain, and serve hot.

- 2 cans (14.75 ounces each) salmon, drained
- 1½ cups panko bread crumbs
- ½ cup tartar sauce (page 106) or mayonnaise
- 2 scallions, white and light green parts only, thinly sliced, or ½ teaspoon onion powder
- 1 large egg
- ½ teaspoon salt
- ¼ teaspoon freshly ground black pepper
- ¾ cup canola oil

MAKE IT A MEAL
+ Summer Corn Soup (page 203)

D2D

When I finish frying neutral-flavored foods, such as French fries, beignets, or rice balls, I'll cool the oil, strain it through cheesecloth or paper towels into a clean container, and reuse it to fry a strong-flavored food, such as these salmon cakes.

Sicilian Pasta with Tuna & Capers

Canned tuna is a great value, so why just use it for tuna salad? Paired with pasta and capers, it makes a great, rustic, and flavorful dinner that seems fancy even though it's pretty bare-bones. When my garden is pushing out tomatoes by the bushel, I chop a few up and use them, often with a handful of fresh basil, instead of canned tomatoes. Oil-cured black olives are a great addition if you have them.

SERVES 4

$8.20/
$2.05

2 tablespoons olive oil

3 garlic cloves, finely minced or pressed through a garlic press

⅓ cup finely chopped flat-leaf parsley

2 tablespoons capers, rinsed and roughly chopped

1 can (28 ounces) chopped tomatoes with juice (about 3 cups)

1 tablespoon + ½ teaspoon salt

1 pound spaghetti

2 cans (6 ounces each) olive oil–packed tuna, drained

Freshly ground black pepper

2 tablespoons unsalted butter

½ lemon

D2D

Buy oil-packed tuna instead of water-packed tuna. It's moister, and you can use the tuna-infused olive oil in place of extra oil called for in recipes.

MAKE THE SAUCE. Pour the oil into a large skillet. Add the garlic and cook gently over medium heat until the garlic is fragrant, about 1 to 1½ minutes. Add the parsley and capers and cook for 30 seconds, then add the tomatoes and their juices. Bring to a simmer and then reduce the heat to medium-low, add ½ teaspoon of the salt, and simmer gently until slightly thickened, about 20 minutes, stirring occasionally.

BOIL THE PASTA. While the sauce simmers, bring a large pot of water to a boil with the remaining 1 tablespoon of salt. Add the pasta and cook according to the package instructions until it is al dente. Reserve ¼ cup of the cooking water, then drain the pasta and return it to the pot.

ADD THE TUNA AND SERVE. Break the tuna into small flakes and add to the sauce along with the pepper. Add the sauce and the butter to the pasta, tossing gently until the butter is completely melted (add a little pasta water if the pasta seems dry). Squeeze the lemon half over the pasta, toss, divide the pasta among 4 bowls, and serve.

5 ways to use up
a handful of pasta

Does your pantry suffer from random pasta syndrome? You know, when 3 or 4 boxes each holding barely 1 serving of pasta begin to clutter the shelves? Don't stress it—there are great ways to use up those odds and ends. Boil it up (cook different shapes separately, as they may have different cooking times) and have fun.

1. Add to a frittata (add the boiled pasta to the egg mixture when it just starts setting up in the pan, top with cheese, and run under the broiler).

2. Mix with canned beans, olive oil, and herbs for a healthy lunch.

3. Toss with a single serving of chili or lentils.

4. Make a kitchen-sink pasta casserole (cook all of your pastas and then layer in a casserole dish with sauce, cheese, and vegetables or chunks of sausage, and top with more cheese before baking until bubbly).

5. Sweeten with cinnamon sugar and butter to satisfy a dessert craving.

love your veggies

I love vegetables and never tire of coming up with new ways to serve them. In the 16 years that I've had the Rock, I've turned them into everything from cheesy gratins to soups, pickles, and simple platters of steamed goodness. I must admit, I'm obsessed with getting kids and grown-ups to eat more veggies, and most of the time I'm pretty successful. The secret is to get them as excited about eating veggies as they are about chocolate cake! It's a challenge that I happily tackle head-on with fierce determination!

At dinnertime I usually set 2 vegetable dishes on the table. That way, if one of the kids doesn't care for the texture of spoon-tender green beans or the heat of spicy roasted cauliflower, I get peace of mind knowing that they'll dig into more familiar offerings, such as a leafy green salad with honey-mustard dressing or quickly steamed broccoli sprinkled with Parmesan and lemon juice. Offering options is a great way to introduce new flavors to your family, and also to guarantee left-overs for future meals. That steamed broccoli is fabulous tossed with pasta, peas, and a creamy Parmesan sauce for lunch, and nothing beats leftover salad (set some aside before you dress it) stuffed into a pita pocket with feta and chopped olives for lunch or a snack.

The price of vegetables varies enormously by season and even week to week, so I pay special attention to prices when I'm in the produce aisle, looking for specials and bargains. When I spot pricey portobello mushrooms or artichokes on sale for 50 to 75 percent less than their regular prices, you better believe I'm doing something with them for dinner in the next few days!

That said, there is nothing wrong with heading to the frozen food aisle for vegetables, especially in winter months when fresh produce is imported, expensive, and often of poor quality. What matters more than frozen or fresh is that my family is eating (and loving) their vegetables every night of the week.

Spicy Roasted Cauliflower

Easy enough for every day and interesting enough to offer to company, cauliflower takes on a different spin when roasted with spicy Indian flavors such as ground turmeric and chile flakes. If your cauliflower is priced by the head rather than by the pound, it pays to search for the biggest head so you get the most mileage from your dollar. Best of all, cauliflower is a keeper in the fridge, so buy a head now to use within the next 10 days.

$6.00/ $1.50

HEAT THE OVEN TO 425°F. Whisk the cumin, coriander, turmeric, cayenne, and salt together in a large bowl. Whisk in the olive oil and then add the cauliflower, tossing it until it is evenly coated with the spiced oil. Transfer the cauliflower to a 2-quart casserole dish and roast until browned and tender, 35 to 40 minutes, stirring twice. Remove the cauliflower from the oven and toss with the scallions, lemon juice, and red-pepper flakes. Serve hot or at room temperature.

2 teaspoons ground cumin

1½ teaspoons ground coriander

½ teaspoon ground turmeric

¼ teaspoon cayenne

1 teaspoon salt

2 tablespoons olive oil

1 head (1½ pounds) cauliflower, cored and separated into florets

4 scallions, white and light green parts only, thinly sliced

Juice of ½ lemon

¼ teaspoon red-pepper flakes

D2D

Leftover roasted vegetables can be turned into quick sauces or soups. Just combine them in a blender with some chicken broth or water (and a little half-and-half or cream for richness) until they're the right consistency (thinner for soup, thicker for a sauce). Pour over enchiladas or quesadillas, pasta, meatloaf, or sautéed chicken. For extra flavor, I'll sometimes add jarred, roasted red-peppers or even jarred salsa.

MAKE IT A MEAL

+ Singed Steak, Herb, and Lettuce Wraps (page 116)

A Simple Salad, Dressed for Dinner

Mixing your own dressings instead of buying them from the grocery store is really easy and saves money big-time compared to bottled dressings. It also has fewer additives than the bottled stuff. Just toss with 6 cups of washed greens. Double or triple these recipes to make enough dressing for a few nights' worth of salads.

Blue Cheese Dressing

Whisk together 1 cup of mayonnaise with 3 tablespoons of whole milk, the juice of half of a lemon, 1 tablespoon of finely chopped onion or shallot, 2 teaspoons of sugar, ¼ teaspoon of Worcestershire sauce, ¼ teaspoon of salt, and ¼ teaspoon of freshly ground black pepper in a large bowl. Stir in 4 ounces of crumbled blue cheese. Cover with plastic wrap and refrigerate for up to 3 days (stir before using). Makes 1½ cups.

Honey-Mustard Dressing

Whisk together ½ cup of mayonnaise with 2 tablespoons of honey, 1 tablespoon of yellow mustard, and ¼ teaspoon of salt in a large bowl. Cover with plastic wrap and refrigerate for up to 1 week (stir before using). Makes 1½ cups.

Greek Vinaigrette

Whisk together ⅓ cup of white wine vinegar, the juice from 1½ lemons, 2 finely minced garlic cloves, 2 teaspoons of dried oregano, ½ teaspoon of salt, and ¼ teaspoon of freshly ground black pepper in a large bowl. Whisk in ¾ cup of extra-virgin olive oil. Cover with plastic wrap and refrigerate for up to 5 days (stir before using). Makes 1½ cups.

Favorite Salad Combos: 6 cups greens (arugula, baby spinach, butter leaf, iceberg, oak leaf, romaine) plus:

1 cup diced ham (baked ham or deli ham) + 1 cup thawed frozen peas + Honey-Mustard Dressing

Crumbled crispy bacon + 2 chopped tomatoes + 1 chopped cucumber + Blue Cheese Dressing

2 grated carrots + ½ cup chopped black olives + 2 sliced scallions + feta cheese + Greek Vinaigrette

Homestyle Smashed Potatoes with Dill

Everyone loves classic smashed potatoes, but I like to shake things up once in a while by adding different flavors. Dill is one of my favorite herbs, and I love it finely chopped and stirred into mashed potatoes. It instantly gives them a fresh, spring-y flavor.

SERVES 4

$2.00/
$.50

5   (about 1½ pounds) Yukon Gold or russet potatoes, peeled and quartered

1   tablespoon + ½ teaspoon salt

¼   cup half-and-half, whole milk, or low-fat milk

2   tablespoons unsalted butter

2   teaspoons finely chopped fresh dill

    Freshly ground black pepper (optional)

BOIL THE POTATOES. Place the potatoes in a large pot with enough water to cover them by 1". Add 1 tablespoon of salt and bring to a boil. Reduce the heat to medium-low and simmer until they're fork-tender and just starting to fall apart, 20 to 25 minutes. Drain in a colander and return to the same pot.

MASH THE POTATOES. While the potatoes boil, combine the half-and-half or milk and the butter in a glass measuring cup. Microwave at 50% power until the butter is melted. Pour over the potatoes, mashing them with a large wooden spoon or potato masher (I like to smash the potatoes against the side of the pot to break them up). Don't mash them any more than necessary; overstirring makes them gluey. Stir in the dill, the remaining ½ teaspoon of salt, and the pepper (if using), and serve hot.

MAKE IT A MEAL
+ Spicy Glazed Meatloaf (page 26)

COOK SMART
Mashed potatoes can be doctored up with all kinds of ingredients: Try basil, buttermilk, Cheddar cheese, chives, crispy fried onions, crumbled bacon, extra-virgin olive oil, jalapeños, fresh chopped rosemary, or smoked Gouda.

D2D
If stored in a cool, dark, and dry place (a cool garage or basement is ideal), potatoes will keep for months. Store them loose in a basket or in a brown paper bag with a few holes punched in it. Don't store them near onions or in plastic or they'll spoil quicker.

Potato Pancakes, Sour Cream & Chives

My strategy is to always have leftover mashed potatoes so they can make their way into these savory, pillowy potato pancakes. They're great with over-easy eggs and mushroom gravy (page 221).

SERVES 4

$4.40/
$1.10

MAKE THE POTATO MIXTURE. Whisk the milk, egg yolks, and salt together in a small bowl. Place the potatoes in a large bowl and stir in the flour and cracker crumbs, and then add the milk mixture, stirring until combined.

WHIP THE EGG WHITES. Using a stand mixer or hand mixer, whip the egg whites on medium speed until foamy, then increase the speed to high and whip until they hold stiff peaks. Whisk one-third of the whites into the potato mixture and then gently fold in the remaining egg whites.

COOK THE PANCAKES. Place a baking sheet in the oven and heat the oven to 250°F. Heat a large nonstick or cast-iron skillet over medium-high heat. Add 1 tablespoon of melted butter and pour ½ cup of the batter per pancake into the pan. Make 1 or 2 pancakes (depending on how large your skillet is), leaving at least enough space between them so they can be easily flipped. Once the edges are golden brown, about 1½ to 2 minutes, use a spatula to flip the pancake over and cook the other side until golden brown, another 1½ to 2 minutes, reducing the heat if necessary. Transfer the pancakes to the baking sheet in the oven to keep warm while you cook the remaining batter, adding more melted butter to the pan as necessary. Serve the pancakes warm with a dollop of sour cream and some chives or dill.

½ cup whole milk

3 large eggs, separated

¼ teaspoon salt

3 cups mashed potatoes (1 batch of Homestyle Smashed Potatoes, made without the dill, opposite page)

½ cup all-purpose flour

¼ cup cracker crumbs

4 tablespoons unsalted butter, melted

Sour cream, for serving

Chopped fresh chives or dill, for serving

MAKE IT A MEAL
+ One-Pot Chicken Paprikash (leave out the noodles, page 73)

D2D
Compare the price of potatoes packed in 5- or 10-pound bags to the price of potatoes by the pound—the bagged potatoes are often a better bargain. But be sure to look closely at the quality in the bag to make sure none of the potatoes are shriveled or sprouting.

Spiced Sweet Potato Fries with Dijon Dip

Once your family tries these fries, restaurant fries won't stand a chance. They're crisp, sweet, and loaded with flavor from a trio of sweet, earthy, and fiery spices. You can definitely use Yukon Gold potatoes in place of the sweet potatoes for a more traditional french fry flavor. If you have a coarse or flaky salt in your cupboard, break it out and use it as the finishing salt instead of table salt.

FRIES

- 1 cup all-purpose flour
- 2 tablespoons ground cumin
- 1 tablespoon ground coriander
- ¼ teaspoon cayenne
- 1 teaspoon salt + extra for finishing
- 4 cups canola oil
- 2 large egg whites
- 3 large (about 3 pounds) sweet potatoes, peeled and sliced into ¼"-thick planks, and then into ¼"-thick fries

DIP

- ½ cup Dijon mustard
- ½ cup packed dark brown sugar
- ¼ cup mayonnaise

MIX THE SPICES AND MAKE THE DIP. Whisk the flour with the cumin, coriander, cayenne, and 1 teaspoon of salt in a large bowl and set aside. Stir together the mustard, sugar, and mayonnaise for the dip and set aside.

FRY THE SWEET POTATOES. Heat the oil in a large pot or Dutch oven until it reaches between 350°F and 375°F. Vigorously beat the egg whites with a pinch of salt in a large bowl until they're foamy. Evenly coat the potatoes in the beaten egg whites and then transfer them to the spiced flour, tossing them with your fingers to make sure the fries are spiced on all sides. Fry the sweet potato fries in batches (taking care not to overcrowd the pot) until golden brown, 5 to 7 minutes, using a slotted spoon or frying spider to turn the fries often so all sides brown. Transfer to a paper towel–lined rimmed baking sheet and sprinkle with more salt. Repeat with the remaining sweet potatoes and serve hot with the dip on the side.

MAKE IT A MEAL
+ Jerk-Style Chicken Thighs (page 110)

D2D
Sweet potatoes provide excellent nutritional value at a very low cost. You can use them in any recipe that calls for white potatoes.

German Potato Salad

Like many families, mine always kept a coffee can full of bacon fat under the sink to be used for frying onions or making popovers. If you don't save your bacon drippings, you will start once you taste this warm potato salad. It is absolutely delicious—savory, meaty, and rich, with just the right balance of tangy cider vinegar. It tastes best served the minute it's ready.

6   thick slices bacon

     Olive oil or additional bacon fat if needed

6   (about 2 pounds) Yukon Gold or red potatoes, peeled and sliced ¼" thick

3   teaspoons salt

¼   cup cider vinegar

1½   teaspoons sweet paprika

¼   teaspoon freshly ground black pepper

1   yellow onion, finely chopped

1   tablespoon finely chopped chives, parsley, or scallions (optional)

MAKE IT A MEAL
+ Rosemary and Thyme Roasted Chickens (page 3)
+ Steamed asparagus

D2D
Set aside $5 a week to buy an interesting ingredient you wanted to try, like jarred artichokes or a special flaky salt. Before you know it, you'll have all kinds of fun extras to play around with.

FRY THE BACON. Heat a large skillet over medium-high heat. Add the bacon strips, reduce the heat to medium, and fry until crisp and browned on both sides, 8 to 10 minutes. Transfer the bacon from the pan to a paper towel–lined plate and set aside; once cooled, crumble into small bits. Pour the bacon grease from the pan into a measuring cup (don't wash the pan, you'll use it to brown the onion). If you don't have ⅓ cup of fat, add enough olive oil or liquefied bacon fat to equal ⅓ cup.

COOK THE POTATOES. Place the potatoes and 2 teaspoons of salt in a large saucepan, add enough water to cover by 1", and bring to a boil over high heat. Reduce the heat to medium and partially cover the pot, allowing a little of the steam to escape. Simmer the potatoes until they are tender but not falling apart, 6 to 8 minutes. Drain the potatoes in a colander and set aside.

FINISH THE SALAD. When the potatoes are nearly finished cooking, return the reserved bacon fat (and oil, if needed) to the skillet you cooked the bacon in. Add the cider vinegar, paprika, pepper, and the remaining 1 teaspoon salt. Add the onion and bring to a simmer over medium-high heat. Add the potatoes and crumbled bacon to the pan and stir carefully, trying not to break up the potatoes. Sprinkle with the chives, parsley, or scallions (if using) and serve immediately.

Creamed Spinach

I could eat creamed spinach every day of the week, maybe because it always reminds me of steakhouse restaurants and big occasions! Even though creamed spinach is easy to make, it really does make a meal feel special.

SERVES 4

$7.60/
$1.90

WILT THE SPINACH. Heat a Dutch oven or large pot over high heat. Add the spinach with the water still clinging to its leaves and cook, turning the spinach with tongs, until fully wilted but still bright green, 2 to 3 minutes. Drain the spinach in a colander (wipe out the pot and set aside), pressing on the spinach with the back of a wooden spoon to extract as much liquid as possible.

CREAM THE SPINACH. Melt the butter in the same pot over medium-high heat. Add the shallot and cook until softened, about 2 minutes. Add the flour and stir well to combine. Whisk in the cream or half-and-half, salt, and pepper and bring to a simmer. Cook, stirring constantly, until very thick, about 2 minutes. Add the spinach and stir well to combine. Serve immediately or cover and reduce the heat to its lowest setting (or turn it off) to keep the creamed spinach warm until serving.

- 2 bags (9 ounces each) fresh or frozen and thawed spinach
- 2 tablespoons unsalted butter
- 1 medium shallot, finely minced
- 2 teaspoons all-purpose flour
- ½ cup heavy cream or half-and-half
- ½ teaspoon salt
- ¼ teaspoon freshly ground black pepper

MAKE IT A MEAL
+ Garlic-Rosemary Pork Loin and Crisp Salt-Pepper Potatoes (page 146)

D2D
Don't throw away dairy products just because their sell-by date has passed. Slightly tangy milk, yogurt, and sour cream are fine to use in baked goods such as cakes, muffins, quick breads, biscuits, and pancakes. If it shows any signs of mold or lumpiness, though, pitch it.

Preserving Now for Later

I am so happy that canning is making a comeback. My grandma taught my mom to can, my mom taught me, and now I'm passing that tradition along to my kids, Alexis and Paul. Preserving doesn't just save you money, it makes you feel smart about being thrifty. I guarantee that when you open up a jar of mixed-berry jam in February, you'll be thinking more about its amazing flavor than about the pocketful of change you saved making it. From salsas to pickles, relishes, jams, chutneys, and fruit butters, canning food is a great way to preserve peak flavor.

Finding a recipe you like and want to stick with is sometimes an edible game of trial and error. Make a small batch of a new recipe at first, open a jar (after the required curing time, as in the case of pickles), and taste it, and then make notes to the recipe to suit your tastes for the next batch. (Note: There are all kinds of products available for making freezer and refrigerator jams, too. These jams don't require processing like traditional "canned" jams do.)

DIY Canned Tomatoes in 6 Simple Steps

Preserve the flavor of your sweet, sun-ripened tomatoes for a jolt of summer during the coldest days of winter.

FOR 1 QUART OF QUARTERED, HALVED, OR WHOLE TOMATOES:

1	2	3	4	5	6
Blanch 3 pounds of tomatoes in boiling water for 30 seconds.	Peel the skin from the tomatoes.	Pack the tomatoes into a sterilized quart-size jar (leave only ½" of headspace at the top).	Add 2 tablespoons of lemon juice (or ½ teaspoon of citric acid) and 1 teaspoon of salt.	Process in a canner according to the manufacturer's instructions (I let mine go for 1½ hours).	Cool jar to room temperature, check to make sure that the lid doesn't flex when pressed, and store in a cool, dark spot.

Canning Basics

While the ingredients change from recipe to recipe, the method for canning—other than the length of time required to process a jar—doesn't. Here are the essentials.

1. **BUY A CANNER.** This is a large, deep pot that can hold many jars—sometimes in two layers—with ample room for water around the jars. Sure, you can use a stock pot or large soup pot, but most hardware stores sell canning sets for $30 or less, and they come with all kinds of handy bonuses, such as magnetic lid lifters (to help pull lids from boiling water), rubber tongs (for pulling jars out of boiling water), a canning rack, a recipe book, and a funnel for getting the jam or salsa into the sterilized jar.

2. **STERILIZE THE JARS AND LIDS.** Boil the jars in a pot of water (keep the water at a bare simmer until you're ready to fill the jars so they don't crack when you fill them with hot fruit or vegetables) and the lids in barely simmering water in a saucepan (boiling lids can cause the seals to fail). Or, you can sterilize both on the top shelf of your dishwasher if yours has a sterilize setting. After washing the bands in hot, soapy water, leave them at room temperature for easy handling. (Note that while you can reuse jars and bands, you should always use new lids to ensure that they seal properly.)

3. **FILL THE JARS** with whatever you're canning, leaving ½" of room (called headspace) at the top. Stir to eliminate any air bubbles, and then wipe the jar rims with a clean cloth. Place the lid on and twist on the band to seal. Don't twist them on too tightly.

4. **PROCESS THE JARS** by setting them in the rack in the canner; they should be entirely submerged in boiling water. Boil them according to your recipe. Once the time is up, turn off the heat and let the jars sit in hot water for 5 minutes before removing them from the canner. Let the jars stand at room temperature for at least 1 day before opening.

For more information about canning, see the Ball Web site at www.freshpreserving.com, or check out *Preserving the Summer's Bounty* by the Staff of the Rodale Food Center (Rodale Press, 1995).

Honey-Roasted Parsnips

Parsnips are often totally overlooked, and they shouldn't be, because when roasted, they're totally amazing. This recipe also works beautifully with carrots or a combo of carrots and parsnips.

HEAT THE OVEN TO 400°F. Place the bacon in a large ovenproof skillet (cast iron works fine) over medium-high heat. Fry the bacon until it is semicrisp, 4 to 6 minutes. Turn off the heat and add the parsnips, honey, salt, and pepper, and toss to coat. Transfer to the oven and roast until the parsnips are tender but still firm, 35 to 40 minutes. Sprinkle with parsley and serve.

3 slices bacon, sliced crosswise ½"-thick pieces

8 medium parsnips (about 2 pounds), peeled and cut diagonally into ½"-thick slices

1 tablespoon honey

¼ teaspoon salt

¼ teaspoon freshly ground black pepper

2 tablespoons chopped, fresh, flat-leaf parsley

Thyme-Roasted Plum Tomatoes

Roasting enhances the flavor of winter tomatoes and brings out their natural sweetness.

HEAT THE OVEN TO 325°F. Place the tomatoes, cut-side up, in a 13" x 9" baking dish. Place the thyme sprigs on top of the tomatoes, drizzle with the olive oil, and sprinkle with the sugar, salt, and pepper. Roast until the tomatoes are soft, 60 to 70 minutes. Cool and serve as a side dish or accompaniment.

10–12 medium (2 pounds) plum tomatoes, cored, halved, and seeded

8 sprigs fresh thyme

2 tablespoons extra-virgin olive oil

1 teaspoon sugar

½ teaspoon salt

¼ teaspoon freshly ground black pepper

Summer Tomato Gratin

$7.20/
$1.20

My garden goes crazy with tomatoes in the summer and fall. Consequently, I've come up with a million ways to use them, this side dish being one of my favorites. You can make it with any kind of tomato you've got, from heirloom Cherokees to beefsteaks or Italian plums. Only one rule applies: The juicier and sweeter your tomatoes, the more delicious the gratin. Extra-virgin olive oil makes this dish really shine.

PREP THE TOMATOES. Heat the oven to 375°F. Slice each tomato in half crosswise along its equator. Using your fingers, scoop the seeds out, then slice the tomatoes into ½"-thick rounds. Place the tomato slices in a large bowl and toss gently with the oil, garlic, sugar, salt, and pepper.

BAKE THE GRATIN. Arrange the tomatoes in a 13" x 9" baking dish in overlapping rows, like shingles on a roof. Sprinkle with the cheese and panko or cracker crumbs, cover with foil, and bake until bubbly, about 30 minutes. Remove the foil and return to the oven to brown the top, another 5 to 10 minutes. Remove from the oven, sprinkle with the basil, and serve hot or at room temperature.

3 large (about 3 pounds) ripe tomatoes, cored

3 tablespoons extra-virgin olive oil

1 garlic clove, finely minced or pressed through a garlic press

1 teaspoon sugar

¼ teaspoon salt

¼ teaspoon freshly ground black pepper

1 cup freshly shredded Parmesan, mozzarella, or provolone (or a blend of all 3)

½ cup panko bread crumbs or cracker crumbs

¼ cup roughly torn fresh basil leaves

D2D

To avoid the super-high cost of tasteless winter tomatoes, can some of your summer bounty to enjoy when your garden is closed for winter (see page 190).

MAKE IT A MEAL

+ Open-Face Steak Sandwiches with Caramelized Onions and Parmesan (page 141)

Cucumber Refrigerator Pickles

MAKES 2 PINTS

$1.70

Back in the day, home cooks always had a jar of pickled something or other in the fridge, be it green tomatoes, zucchini, green beans, or dill pickles. Homemade pickles are so simple to make and so delicious—plus you'll save about 50 percent by making them yourself and avoiding the supermarket big-name varieties. Once you've made this recipe a few times, break out of the recipe box and try adding whatever floats your boat—I've tossed in sliced jalapeños, mint, garlic cloves, and red-pepper flakes. Why not throw a pickle-making party and let all your friends make jars to take home?

2 pint-size canning jars for pickle spears, or 2 pint-size or four ½-pint-size canning jars for pickle rounds, with lids

3 large Kirby cucumbers, sliced into spears or ½" rounds

1 medium yellow onion, finely chopped

1 cup white vinegar

2 cups sugar

2 tablespoons salt

2 teaspoons celery seed

 D2D

There is nothing like the flavor and satisfaction of eating a Kirby you grew yourself. Buy a seed packet, plant, sit back, and watch your garden grow.

PREPARE AND FILL THE JARS. Wash the glass jars and lids in hot, soapy water and let air-dry (or sterilize using the top rack of your dishwasher on the sanitize setting). Divide the cucumbers and onion among the jars and set aside (you want the cucumbers to fit snugly in the jars).

MAKE THE PICKLING LIQUID. Bring the vinegar, sugar, salt, and celery seed to a boil in a medium saucepan over high heat, stirring to dissolve the sugar and salt. Pour the hot liquid over the cucumbers and onion and set the lids in place, twisting the bands tightly to seal. Refrigerate for at least 1 day (I like to wait 2 weeks) before opening and eating. The pickles can be refrigerated for up to 3 months.

Fried Pickles

The Oklahoma state motto should read "fit to be fried," because we fry nearly everything we can get our hands on—from okra to mac and cheese and candy bars. But fried pickles are in a class all their own. Try them with some chipotle mayonnaise—just mix a few tablespoons of mayo with a teaspoon or two of adobo sauce from a can of chipotles in adobo. It has a nice smoky kick that's great on burgers, too.

HEAT THE OIL. Pour the oil into a deep skillet (preferably cast-iron) or medium pot. Heat over medium-high heat until it reaches between 350°F and 375°F on an instant-read thermometer.

BREAD AND FRY THE PICKLES. Whisk the flour, cracker crumbs, dill (if using), garlic powder, salt, and pepper in a large bowl. Whisk the buttermilk, egg, and Worcestershire sauce in a medium bowl. Dunk the pickle spears into the egg mixture and then dredge them through the flour mixture, tapping off any excess. Carefully lower the pickles into the oil and fry until golden brown, 2 to 3 minutes. Transfer to a paper towel–lined plate and eat hot.

4 cups canola oil

1 cup all-purpose flour

½ cup cracker crumbs

1 teaspoon finely chopped fresh dill (optional)

1 teaspoon garlic powder

1 teaspoon salt

1 teaspoon freshly ground black pepper

½ cup buttermilk

1 large egg

1 teaspoon Worcestershire sauce

16 dill pickle spears (or 4 dill pickles quartered lengthwise into spears)

MAKE IT A MEAL
+ Pulled Pork Sandwiches with Homemade Barbecue Sauce (page 21)

Spoon-Tender Green Beans with Bacon

SERVES 4

$2.80/
$.70

I'm not choosy when it comes to green beans—I like them crunchy and raw, semicooked until just tender, or cooked a good, long while until they melt in your mouth. This recipe falls into the latter category (for crisper beans, leave them in long pieces after trimming the ends). Make a triple batch, add the mushroom gravy on page 221, and bake topped with a layer of buttered, fresh bread crumbs for the best green bean casserole ever to hit your table!

BROWN THE BACON AND ONION. Heat a large skillet over medium-high heat. Add the bacon and cook, stirring often, until it's just starting to crisp up, about 8 minutes. Mix in the onion and garlic and cook until the onion is soft, another 4 to 5 minutes, stirring often. If you have more than 1 tablespoon of fat in the pan, carefully pour all but 1 tablespoon out of the skillet (save it for another time).

COOK THE GREEN BEANS. Add the green beans, salt, and pepper to the pan. Add 1 cup of water (the beans should be half submerged—add more or less water if necessary), increase the heat to high, and bring the liquid to a boil. Reduce the heat to medium-low, partially cover the pan, and cook until the green beans are very soft and limp, 20 to 30 minutes (check the water level occasionally, adding more as needed). Serve warm.

4 bacon slices, cut crosswise into ½" pieces

1 small white onion, finely chopped

3 garlic cloves, chopped

1 pound green beans, ends trimmed, cut in 1" pieces

½ teaspoon salt

¼ teaspoon freshly ground black pepper

MAKE IT A MEAL
+ Baked Honey-Glazed Ham (page 13)

COOK SMART
Bacon is a lot easier to cut when it's partially frozen. Before trimming the green beans for this recipe, I'll pop a few bacon slices into the freezer. By the time I'm ready to start cooking, they're semihard and super-easy to snip up using kitchen scissors.

Fruity Stuffed Zucchini with Nuts & Rosemary

I've been known to stuff just about any vegetable—bell peppers, eggplants, acorn squash, potatoes, mushrooms, cabbage leaves—the list is endless. Zucchini is one of my favorites because it retains a nice texture when stuffed and baked—not too soft, not too crunchy. I make this in the summer and fall when zucchinis are a dime a dozen.

SERVES 6

$7.80/
$1.30

MAKE THE STUFFING. Heat the oven to 350°F. Heat the oil in a skillet over medium-high heat. Add the onion and cook, stirring often, until it's soft, about 5 minutes. Stir in the nuts and cook until they're toasted, about 2 minutes more. Add the dried fruit, rosemary, ½ cup of the broth, ½ teaspoon salt, and pepper. Bring the mixture to a boil, reduce the heat to medium, and simmer until the fruit is plump, about 5 minutes. Transfer the onion mixture to a large bowl and stir in the cooked rice. Once the mixture is cool enough to handle, stir in the beaten egg.

STUFF AND BAKE THE ZUCCHINI. Pour the remaining ½ cup of broth into in a 9" x 13" baking pan. Sprinkle the remaining ⅛ teaspoon salt onto the zucchini halves, fill each zucchini half with a generous amount of the rice mixture, and place the stuffed zucchini halves in the pan. Cover the pan with foil and bake until the zucchini is soft, 40 to 45 minutes. Serve hot or at room temperature.

2	tablespoons olive oil
1	small yellow onion, finely chopped
½	cup chopped nuts (almonds, pecans, pine nuts, or walnuts)
½	cup chopped dried fruit (apricots, cherries, cranberries, or raisins)
1	teaspoon chopped fresh rosemary
1	cup chicken or vegetable broth, homemade (page 36) or store-bought
½	teaspoon + ⅛ teaspoon salt
¼	teaspoon freshly ground black pepper
2	cups cooked rice
1	large egg, lightly beaten
6	medium zucchini, ends trimmed, halved lengthwise, and hollowed out with a teaspoon

COOK SMART

If you grow your own zucchini, make use of the zucchini blossoms. Try stuffing them with the cheese mixture from the white lasagna on page 57, dunk in the beignet batter on page 234, and fry in hot oil for a wonderful treat.

 MAKE IT A MEAL
+ Oven-Baked Crispy Chicken Parmesan (page 46)

Everyone's Favorite Potato Soup with Bacon

SERVES 6

$3.30/
$.55

When I first started at the Rock, money was tight, and I had to find ways to make use of absolutely everything in the kitchen. One thing that made me crazy was the sorry sight of a pile of baked potatoes that didn't get sold during dinner service (I'd never sell them the next day; they were too soggy and soft). Then, one day, a lightbulb went off—why not turn them into potato soup? My potato soup became such a hit that I had to start boiling up extra potatoes to augment whatever I had left from the night before. It's still one of the most popular items at the Cafe.

4   thick-cut bacon slices

1   small yellow onion, finely chopped

3   garlic cloves, finely minced or pressed through a garlic press

2   teaspoons salt

9   (about 3 pounds) russet potatoes, peeled and quartered

2   cups whole or low-fat milk

½   teaspoon freshly ground black pepper

    Finely chopped chives, for serving (optional)

FRY THE BACON AND ONION. Heat a large skillet over medium-high heat. Place the bacon in the pan, reduce the heat to medium, and cook until browned and crisp, about 6 minutes. Transfer the bacon to a paper towel–lined plate. Add the onion, garlic, and ¼ teaspoon of salt to the pan and cook until the onion is soft and the garlic is fragrant, about 2 minutes. Crumble the bacon back into the skillet, turn off the heat, and set aside.

BOIL AND SMASH THE POTATOES. Bring the potatoes to a boil in a large pot with 4 cups of water and 1½ teaspoons of salt. Reduce the heat to medium and simmer until they're tender and just starting to break apart, 20 to 25 minutes. Remove from heat. Using a potato masher or wooden spoon, smash the potatoes in the pot with the water until they're mostly broken up (you want to keep some chunky potato bits).

FINISH THE SOUP. Heat the milk in a small saucepan or the microwave until hot, and then add to the potatoes. Stir in the bacon and onion mixture, the remaining ¼ teaspoon of salt, and the pepper. Return to the stove, and continue to simmer until the soup is slightly thickened, about 5 minutes. Sprinkle with chives, if using, and serve hot.

 COOK SMART

Potato soup can be boosted with all kinds of ingredients, such as sautéed carrots, leeks, mushrooms, shredded cheese, cooked pearl barley, or even steamed and shucked fresh or canned clams for a quick clam chowder.

Clean Out the Fridge Soup

Once a week I'm using up my onion halves, bell pepper quarters, and any other veggie odds and ends I have in the fridge, either in the fried rice on page 157 or in this soup. Of course the best part is that the soup is so delicious, no one knows it's really just a delicious form of waste management! I sometimes finish the soup with a cup of croutons; garlic- and oil-rubbed, day-old bread; or shredded Parmesan.

SERVES 6

$11.10/
$1.85

COOK THE HARD VEGETABLES. Heat the olive oil in a large soup pot over medium-high heat. Add the onion and cook, stirring occasionally, until soft, about 5 minutes. Add the hard vegetables and salt, cooking until they start to brown, about 5 minutes, stirring occasionally. Pour in the broth, tomatoes (if using), Parmesan rind (if using), and herb, bring to a boil, and then reduce the heat to low and simmer, covered, until the vegetables begin to soften, 15 to 20 minutes.

COOK THE SOFT VEGETABLES AND LEAFY GREENS. Add the soft vegetables to the pot, bring the soup back to a boil, and simmer until the vegetables are starting to soften, about 10 minutes. Add the leafy vegetables and the beans, grains, or pasta, bring the soup back to a boil, and simmer until the greens are tender, about 15 minutes. Remove the Parmesan rind and discard. Season to taste with black pepper and serve.

D2D

Save your Parmesan cheese heels to add big flavor to soups, stocks, and even marinara sauce. Just add the heel when the liquid is boiling and remove it before serving. Freeze your rinds in a quart-size resealable freezer bag—they keep for ages.

2 tablespoons olive oil

1 red or yellow onion, finely chopped

2 cups hard vegetables (butternut squash, carrot, cauliflower, celery, daikon, parsnip, potato), chopped into bite-size pieces

½ teaspoon salt

6 cups chicken or vegetable broth, homemade (page 36) or store-bought

1 can (14.5 ounces) diced tomatoes (optional)

1 Parmesan rind (optional)

1 teaspoon of your favorite dried herb

2 cups soft vegetables (bell peppers, broccoli, fresh or frozen corn, green beans, fresh or frozen peas, zucchini), chopped into bite-size pieces

2–3 cups leafy vegetables (cabbage, chard, collards, escarole, kale, spinach), roughly chopped

1–2 cups leftover beans, grains, or pasta

Freshly ground black pepper

French Onion Soup with Broiled Swiss Caps

SERVES 6

$10.80/
$1.80

When I was 19 years old, I joined the crew of a cruise line as a purser. Up until that point, the fanciest sit-down meal I had ever experienced was my prom dinner at a banquet hall in Oklahoma. On the cruise ship, I was just like Julia Roberts in *Pretty Woman,* not knowing which fork to use, let alone the proper way to hold it! So, at my first dinner I went for soup, the simplest and most straightforward dish I could think of. Though I'd never had French onion soup before, it was truly love at first bite.

½ cup (8 tablespoons) unsalted butter

4 large (3 pounds) white onions, halved and thinly sliced

1½ teaspoons salt

½ teaspoon freshly ground black pepper

8 cups canned beef broth

3 tablespoons all-purpose flour

CHEESE TOAST

6 slices (1" thick) French bread

2 tablespoons unsalted butter, melted

6 slices Swiss cheese

¼ cup finely grated Parmesan cheese

 COOK SMART

Turn the last bowl of French onion soup into French dip sandwiches. Warm a few slices of roast beef in a saucepan with some soup. Use tongs to place the beef and onions from the soup between a split French roll. Serve with the broth on the side for dunking.

COOK THE ONIONS. Melt the butter in a large, heavy-bottomed pot or Dutch oven over medium-high heat. Add the onions, salt, and pepper and reduce the heat to low. Cook until the onions are soft and golden brown, stirring occasionally, about 20 minutes.

SIMMER THE SOUP. Meanwhile, bring the beef broth to a boil in another pot. Mix the flour into the onions and cook for 1 minute, stirring constantly, then add 1 cup of beef broth, stirring well to work out any lumps. Add the remaining beef broth and bring to a boil. Reduce the heat to a gentle simmer, partially cover the pot, and cook for 40 minutes.

MAKE THE CHEESE TOASTS AND SERVE. Heat the broiler to high. Brush both sides of the bread slices with melted butter and place them on a rimmed baking sheet. Broil until golden on both sides, about 1 minute per side (watch the bread closely, as broiler intensity varies). Top each slice with a piece of Swiss cheese and broil until the cheese is bubbly and browned, about 1½ minutes. Divide the soup among 6 bowls. Add a piece of cheesy bread to each bowl, sprinkle with Parmesan, and serve.

Summer Corn Soup

Why toss your corn cobs when they add an extra layer of sweet corn flavor to this brothy summer soup? I like to make it nice and rich with a final addition of half-and-half, but that's purely optional—even without it, it's a lovely, light soup. Crab, lobster, and shrimp are all delicious additions.

SERVES 6

$10.50/ $1.75

MAKE THE BROTH. Heat the olive oil in a large soup pot over medium-high heat. Add the onion, carrot, and corn kernels, and cook, stirring often, until the onion is soft, about 10 minutes. Stir in the garlic and cook until fragrant, about 30 seconds. Pour in the broth and add the corn cobs. Bring to a boil, reduce the heat to low, and let simmer, covered, for 30 minutes.

REMOVE AND DISCARD THE CORN COBS and add the potatoes, zucchini, tarragon, sugar, salt, and pepper. Bring to a boil. Reduce the heat to low, cover, and simmer until the vegetables are tender, about 20 minutes. Add the half-and-half (if using) and serve.

D2D

Eat fresh, quick-to-fade items such as fresh corn, basil, lettuces, and asparagus early in the week and save hardier veggies such as broccoli, potatoes, and green beans for later in the week.

2 tablespoons olive oil

1 yellow onion, finely chopped

1 carrot, finely chopped

6 ears corn on the cob, husked, kernels removed, and the cobs reserved (about 4½ cups corn kernels) or 4½ cups frozen corn

3 garlic cloves, finely minced or pressed through a garlic press

6 cups chicken or vegetable broth, homemade (page 36) or store-bought

2 medium potatoes, peeled and finely chopped

2 medium zucchini, quartered lengthwise and finely chopped

2 teaspoons fresh or 1 teaspoon dried tarragon

1 tablespoon sugar

1 teaspoon salt

½ teaspoon freshly ground black pepper

1 cup half-and-half (optional)

COOK SMART

Even though this soup tastes so good made with fresh, farmstand corn, it's so tasty that I make it in the winter with frozen corn.

Grow Your Own

One of the most satisfying ways to save money in the kitchen is to grow your own vegetables. There are more seed types now than ever, with classic, international, and heirloom varieties hitting the market every season. Here is a step-by-step action plan for getting your plot growing.

1. Stake your space, assess your dirt.

If this is your first time planting a vegetable garden, start small (considering it a test-run year). After weeding the area and removing debris, test your soil's pH and moisture levels using a pH test (readily available at your hardware store or gardening center). The results will indicate if you need to correct the acidity levels by adding bonemeal, fertilizer, lime, or sulfur (again, the folks at your garden center will be able to guide you here). To test the moisture level, simply dig a hole and squeeze some of the dirt in your hand. It should be like pie dough that holds together, yet breaks apart easily. If it's too dry, add water; if it's too wet, wait a few days for it to dry out a bit before tilling.

2. Prepare the bed.

Before planting vegetables, you need to give your plot a facial. Add a few inches of rich compost (preferably organic) and till it in. If you need to correct your soil's pH, now is the time to add in the soil boosters mentioned above.

3. Plot your garden: seeds or seedlings?

Besides offering a wider variety of varietals, starting from seeds is much less expensive than using seedlings (you can buy seed packets for an average $2 to $3 per pack versus seedlings for $3 to $4 per plant). That said, many plants, such as tomatoes, eggplants, and parsley, can be tricky to start from seed, so you may be better off buying seedlings. When you buy your seeds, be sure to check how quickly they germinate—if it's already August and you want a Cinderella garden of pumpkins, you might be out of luck, as they take several months to germinate. On the other hand, vegetables such as zucchini, peas, and green beans are quick to germinate. In addition, you may want to plant extra crops of lettuces and carrots throughout the season so you get several harvests.

4. Choose your source.

You have many options when it comes to finding the best place to buy your plants. I've purchased plants and seeds from 4-H clubs, school fund-raisers, hardware stores, supermarkets, garden centers, warehouse stores, local businesses, botanical gardens, and even online. Do your research and check prices to see who has the best deal.

5. Watch your garden grow—then eat it!

THE FRESHMAN GARDENER The 5 easiest veggies and herbs to grow

Summer squash (yellow and/or zucchini)	Herbs (basil, chives, mint, parsley, rosemary, sage, tarragon, and thyme)	Eggplant
		Tomatoes
		Bell peppers

SENIOR ELECTIVES The next tier of vegetables for your garden

Green beans	Radishes	Lettuce
Cucumbers	Peas	

GRAD STUDIES For advanced green thumbs

Carrots	Cauliflower	Cabbage
Potatoes	Brussels sprouts	Winter squash (acorn, butternut, pumpkin)
Onions	Artichokes	
Broccoli	Corn	

breakfast for dinner

There's a reason so many restaurants proudly announce "Breakfast Served All Day"—it's everyone's favorite meal. But if your family is like mine, mornings tend to feel more like rush hour at Grand Central Station than a time to sit down to a leisurely meal together. On top of that, I'm often out of the house starting breakfast service at the Rock before anyone is even awake! So while the notion of gathering around the table to have breakfast together is a nice one, it rarely happens. Then one day I had a brainstorm: How about breakfast for dinner? It was an instant hit, and now we make it a weekly event.

Eating pancakes, French toast, or huevos rancheros for dinner is just plain fun; it shakes up our routine—and it doesn't hurt that breakfast is one of the least-expensive meals to cook up, either. One of our favorite go-to recipes is a quick egg and crispy tortilla scramble—it's unbelievably tasty with some salsa and soft tortillas on the side. If I have a little more time in the kitchen, I'll make my Jack-and-bacon quiche—it's like eggs, bacon, and toast in fancy dress. Sometimes nothing is more comforting for dinner than griddlecakes—I'll whip up a stack when we need a little pick-me-up. Whether your breakfast tastes lean to the sweet or the savory, you'll find plenty of choices here to end your day just right.

Top 5 for Breakfast

1. Stock up on breakfast sausage and bacon when they're on sale and keep them in the freezer for quick breakfast side dishes that are always on hand.

2. Skip the expensive equipment. Nothing's better than a cast-iron skillet for making eggs, hotcakes, or sausage.

3. Instead of buying boxed products, premix your own pancake ingredients and store in a large, airtight container.

4. Leftovers, such as roasted or sautéed vegetables, roasted chicken, and even the last few slices of deli meat or cheese, can be turned into delicious fillings for an omelet, crêpe, or quiche.

5. Keep powdered buttermilk on hand for pancakes or biscuits so you can mix up just as much as you need when you need it.

Tried & True Griddlecakes

SERVES 4

$1.80/
$.45

Ordering pancakes in a restaurant has always been one of my pet peeves. Why pay 10 times what it costs to make them at home when I know mine will be better anyway? I've been making these pancakes from my great-grandmother's recipe for as long as I can remember, and I even cook them up in the same 14" cast-iron skillet she used. This recipe is the starting point for a whole menu's worth of breakfast dishes, including crepes, beignets, and my Dipped French Toast (page 214), but they're great just as is, too. Sometimes I like to stir bananas, blueberries, or strawberries into the batter for fruity griddlecakes, or chocolate chips or dried fruit and nuts if I'm in the mood for double-sweet griddlecakes. For a savory approach, I'll toss herbs such as thyme or sage into the batter and serve the hotcakes up with a side of pan-seared ham steak.

MAKE THE BATTER. Heat the oven to 250°F and place a baking sheet on the middle shelf. Whisk together the flour, baking powder, sugar, and salt in a large bowl. Whisk the eggs in a small bowl and then pour in the milk and 10 tablespoons of the butter, whisking to combine. Stir the milk mixture into the dry ingredients, mixing until just a few lumps remain.

COOK THE GRIDDLECAKES. Heat a large cast-iron or nonstick skillet or a griddle over medium-high heat. Set the remaining 2 tablespoons of melted butter next to your stovetop. Add some melted butter to the pan and pour in the batter, using about ½ cup per pancake. You should be able to fit 2 or 3, depending on

(continues...)

3   cups all-purpose flour

1   tablespoon + 1 teaspoon baking powder

⅓   cup sugar

1½ teaspoons salt

3   large eggs

3   cups low-fat or whole milk

¾   cup (1½ sticks) unsalted butter, melted

    Room-temperature butter and maple syrup, for serving

MAKE IT A MEAL
+ Bacon

D2D

Don't turn your nose up at dried milk powder. It's often $1 less than fresh milk per gallon and stores indefinitely in your pantry. I sneak it in by adding 2 cups of reconstituted dried milk to a regular gallon jug of milk once we've used about half of the regular milk. Give the jug a shake and no one will ever know the difference.

how large your skillet is, leaving enough space between the pancakes so they can be easily flipped. Once bubbles form across the top of the cakes and the edges look dry, use a spatula to flip the pancakes. Cook the other side until golden brown, 2 to 3 minutes. Transfer the pancakes to the baking sheet in the oven to keep warm while you cook the remaining batter, adding more melted butter to the pan as necessary. Serve the pancakes warm with butter and maple syrup.

COOK SMART

Cook a double batch of griddlecakes and wrap each one individually in plastic wrap. Freeze them in a gallon-size resealable freezer bag for up to 3 months. Microwave a few at a time for a meal or a snack.

Better Than Boxed

For your own homemade pancake mix, triple or quadruple the dry ingredients above, whisk together, and store in a resealable gallon-size bag or in an airtight container. Whenever you want to make a batch of pancakes, simply measure out 3½ cups of dry mix, then proceed with the recipe as instructed. It makes a great gift when presented in a nice gift bag or tin with the recipe attached. Seal the deal with a pretty bottle of maple syrup or fun mix-ins such as pecans or chocolate chips.

Waffles with Chicken & Gravy

This is a deliciously savory meal that I like to make when I have leftover chicken or turkey in the fridge. If you don't have leftover roasted meat, just make the straight-up sausage gravy from page 221. You don't need a pricey Belgian waffle iron to make great waffles, either; there are lots of models out there for less than $30, and they do the job just fine.

SERVES 8

$10.00/
$1.25

MAKE THE GRAVY. Heat the oven to 250°F and place a baking sheet on the middle shelf. Stir the chicken into the skillet of warm gravy and cook over low heat, stirring often, until the chicken is warmed through.

COOK THE WAFFLES. Melt the butter in the microwave or a small saucepan and set aside. Preheat a waffle iron according to the manufacturer's instructions. Brush the waffle iron with melted butter and pour in enough batter to fill the waffle mold but not overflow once the lid is closed (this amount varies depending on your waffle maker). Cook the waffle until the steam stops streaming out of the sides and the waffle is golden. Transfer it to the oven to keep warm while you cook the rest. Serve a ladleful of chicken gravy over each waffle with a few shakes of hot sauce if you like it spicy.

1½–2 cups (about ½ chicken) shredded rotisserie chicken or leftover roasted chicken (page 3)

1 recipe Mushroom-Sausage Gravy (page 221; made without the sausage)

2 tablespoons unsalted butter

½ recipe griddlecake batter (page 209)

Hot-pepper sauce (optional)

COOK SMART

Follow the freezing instructions for the griddlecakes on page 210 to freeze leftover waffles. Reheat in the toaster.

D2D

If you live in a somewhat urban area, chances are you have access to an online grocery service. Depending on your lifestyle, shopping online can be a great money saver— you're less likely to veer off your list, you save time, and you save gas money, too.

Turkey, Swiss & Asparagus Crêpes

Crêpes seem a bit intimidating to make, but if you can make pancakes, you can make these because the batter is essentially the same. Stuff them with just about anything, from a slice of Black Forest ham and jalapeño-Jack cheese, to leftover roasted vegetables and fontina, or even last night's roasted chicken with a quick mushroom sauce (see the biscuits and gravy recipe on page 221). Of course you can easily turn them into a sweet dish, too, just by adding a swipe of chocolate spread or a sprinkle of granulated sugar before rolling. There you go—breakfast-for-dinner and dessert in one fell swoop.

SERVES 6

☺

---➡

$12.00/
$2.00

16 (1½ pounds) asparagus spears, ends snapped off

Salt

1 cup + 2 tablespoons Griddle-cake dry mix (see "Better Than Boxed," page 210)

½ teaspoon herbes de Provence or ¼ teaspoon French Rub (page 118)

3 large eggs

1 cup low-fat or whole milk

½ cup water

1½ tablespoons unsalted butter, melted

12 slices Swiss cheese

12 slices deli turkey

STEAM THE ASPARAGUS. Bring a large pot with 1½" of water to a simmer. Add a steamer insert and the asparagus spears, cover, reduce the heat to low, and steam the asparagus until just tender, about 2 to 3 minutes. (If you don't have a steamer, bring ½ cup of water to a simmer in a large skillet; add the asparagus, cover, reduce the heat to low, and steam until tender. Lift the asparagus from the pan, leaving any extra water behind. You can also steam the asparagus in the microwave.) Sprinkle the asparagus with a little salt and set aside.

MAKE THE CRÊPE BATTER. In a large bowl, whisk together the dry mix and herbs, and set aside. Whisk the eggs together in a small bowl and then whisk in the milk, water, and half of the butter. Slowly pour the milk mixture into the dry ingredients, mixing until just a few lumps remain.

COOK THE CRÊPES. Place a baking sheet or ovenproof platter in the oven and heat the oven to 200°F. Place a medium skillet over high heat. Add ½ teaspoon of the remaining butter to the pan, tilt the pan toward you, and pour ¼ cup of batter into the upper part of the pan. Swirl and rotate the pan until the batter completely covers the pan bottom. When the crêpe is browned, about 2 minutes, flip it and reduce the heat to medium-low. Immediately top with 1 slice of cheese, 1 slice of turkey, and 2 asparagus spears. Cover the pan and cook until the underside of the crêpe is lightly browned, 1 to 2 minutes, then fold the ends of the crêpe over the filling to make a tidy package. Turn the crêpe out onto a plate, seam-side down, and serve immediately, or transfer the crêpe to the baking sheet or platter in the oven to stay warm while you make the remaining crêpes.

COOK SMART

You can whip up the crêpe batter a few nights ahead and store it covered in the refrigerator. It will keep for up to 3 days.

Dipped French Toast

SERVES 6

$4.80/
$.80

Like our neighbors in Texas, I think bigger is better, which is why I use thick slices of Texas toast for my French toast. Instead of dunking the thick slices in plain old eggs and milk, though, I use griddlecake batter as the coating. It yields a heartier version of this classic, with a rich, eggy crust that nicely holds up against powdered sugar *and* maple syrup. If you like your French toast made with buttery bread such as brioche or eggy challah, slice it just between ½" and ¾" thick for the best consistency.

½ cup milk

1 teaspoon vanilla extract

½ recipe griddlecake batter, (page 209)

1 tablespoon unsalted butter

12 slices Texas toast or other thickly sliced white bread

Confectioners' sugar, unsalted butter, and maple syrup, for serving

MAKE IT A MEAL

+ Yogurt or bacon

D2D

If you see whole loaves of bread on sale, buy one! Slice the loaf when you get home and freeze for French toast (or whatever) whenever the craving calls.

PREPARE THE BREAD AND BATTER. Heat the oven to 250°F and place a baking sheet on the middle shelf. Add the milk and vanilla to the griddlecake batter and then pour it into a 13" x 9" baking dish.

COOK THE FRENCH TOAST. Melt the butter in a large skillet over medium-high heat. Place a few slices of bread in the batter just long enough for the bread to be semisoaked on one side but not falling apart, 15 to 20 seconds. Gently turn the slices over and soak the other side for 5 to 10 seconds, then transfer to the hot pan. Cook until golden brown, 2 to 3 minutes, then flip and brown the other side. Transfer the French toast to the oven to keep warm while you cook the remaining pieces. Slice each piece in half on a diagonal and place 4 slices on a plate. Sprinkle with some confectioners' sugar and serve with butter and maple syrup.

COOK SMART

Maple syrup is delicious but can be quite pricey, so if I have some fresh fruit around, I make my own quick fruit syrup to serve instead. Place equal parts sugar (use brown for a more molasses-y flavor) and water in a small saucepan and bring to a simmer. Toss in a handful of fresh fruit (whatever you have on hand or in the freezer is fine), reduce the heat a bit, and cook until the fruit softens and "melts" into the liquid. Add a pinch of salt and a little vanilla extract if you like, and there you have it!

Grits with Eggs, Cheddar & Chives

People get so bent out of shape about poaching eggs—all you're doing is cracking an egg into a saucepan of hot water. Serve them soft-cooked over cheesy, creamy, hearty grits (and at 10 cents per serving, why not?), and no one will notice if the eggs aren't pretty and perfect. Even if you don't love poached eggs, you can still have your grits and eat them, too—just cook the eggs over easy or sunny-side-up.

4½   cups water

1½   teaspoons salt + extra for serving

1   cup quick-cooking grits

1   cup grated white Cheddar cheese

½   lemon

4   large eggs

½   teaspoon freshly ground black pepper

2   tablespoons chopped chives

FOR THE GRITS. Bring the water and salt to a boil in a medium saucepan over high heat. Stir in the grits, bring back to a boil, then reduce the heat to medium-low and cover. Cook until thick and creamy, stirring occasionally, 10 to 12 minutes. Stir in the cheese.

POACH THE EGGS. While the grits cook, fill a large skillet with 1½" of water and bring to a boil over high heat. Squeeze the juice from the lemon half into the boiling water. Reduce the heat to a gentle simmer. One at a time, crack the eggs into a small bowl and carefully slide them into the simmering water. Adjust the heat so the water is at a medium simmer, cover the pan, and cook until the yolks have an opaque film over them and the white is opaque throughout, 2 to 3 minutes. (The eggs can be poached up to 1 hour ahead; use a slotted spoon to transfer them to a bowl of tepid water until you're ready for them.)

ASSEMBLE AND SERVE. Divide the grits among 4 bowls. Use a slotted spoon to transfer one egg to each bowl. Sprinkle with salt, pepper, and chives, and serve.

 COOK SMART
Be patient with grits. They only take 10 minutes to make. Just hold tight and let the grits do their thing. Stir a few times, cover the pot, turn the heat to low, and forget them. You can get all fancy with them, but my favorite is just the grits, some Cheddar, eggs, a sprinkle of chives, and some cracked pepper. Perfection.

Leek & Mushroom Crustless Quiche

This has all the appeal of the Bacon and Cheddar-Jack Quiche (page 218) with half of the work, since it has no crust. Called a *clafoutis* in France, where it's often made with sour cherries or apricots, I think it's just as good made with savory ingredients. (Note: Add this filling to a crust for a traditional quiche.)

$14.70/
$2.45

COOK THE VEGETABLES. Heat the oven to 350°F. Grease a 9" pie plate with the tablespoon of softened butter and set aside. Melt the remaining butter in a large skillet over medium heat. Add the leeks and cook until they are wilted and just starting to color around the edges, 3 to 4 minutes, stirring often. Add the mushrooms, ½ teaspoon of the salt, and the pepper, and cook until the mushrooms release their liquid, 5 to 7 minutes, stirring occasionally. Mix in the garlic and cook until fragrant, about 1 minute. Transfer the mixture to a bowl and set aside.

BAKE THE QUICHE. Whisk together the eggs, sour cream, and the remaining ¼ teaspoon of salt in a large bowl. Add the cheese and stir to combine. Place the leeks and mushrooms in the buttered baking dish and cover with the egg mixture. Bake until the center of the quiche is golden brown and is set, yet still gives to slight pressure, about 45 minutes. Remove from the oven and cool for at least 30 minutes before serving, or cool completely and serve at room temperature.

- 2 tablespoons unsalted butter + 1 tablespoon at room temperature
- 2 leeks, white stalks only, trimmed, cleaned, halved lengthwise, and thinly sliced
- 10 ounces white button mushrooms, stemmed and thinly sliced
- ¾ teaspoon salt
- ½ teaspoon freshly ground black pepper
- 2 garlic cloves, finely minced or pressed through a garlic press
- 4 large eggs
- 2 cups sour cream
- 2½ cups shredded Gruyère or other Swiss-style cheese

MAKE IT A MEAL
+ French Onion Soup (page 200)

D2D
Leftover cheese ends and bits are great for making fondue, macaroni and cheese, or grilled cheese sandwiches. Grate them up, then store them in a resealable freezer bag until you have enough to make your favorite recipe.

Bacon & Cheddar-Jack Quiche in a Pepper Crust

SERVES 6

$10.80/
$1.80

My family does the happy dance when I make this quiche! I never even really understood how great a quiche could be before I traveled to Eureka Springs in Arkansas. Squeezed into the heart of the Ozarks, this little town is nicknamed "little Switzerland" due to its mountainous location and the quaint Victorian homes that are snuggled into the twisty streets. I tasted my favorite-ever quiche at a little inn I stayed at one weekend and now make my own take on it. I like to serve it with strawberry soup just like they did (see page 241 for the recipe), and I can't tell you how many tough biker-type guys come in to the Rock and just about die when they find out I have quiche and strawberry soup on the menu! If strawberries aren't your thing, it's just as nice with a good green salad on the side.

PEPPER CRUST

- ½ cup (1 stick) unsalted butter, at room temperature
- 1 large egg yolk
- 1½ teaspoons sugar
- 2 teaspoons finely ground fresh black pepper
- ½ teaspoon salt
- 1½ cups all-purpose flour + extra as needed

MAKE IT A MEAL
+ Stawberry Dessert Soup (page 241)

D2D
Store sour cream upside-down. It lasts longer that way!

MAKE THE CRUST. Place the oven rack in the lowest position and heat the oven to 375°F. Stir the butter in a large bowl until it is smooth. Add the egg yolk, sugar, pepper, and salt, and stir until combined. Add the flour, working it into the butter mixture by smearing it against the sides of the bowl. Once the dough comes together in large, rough-looking clumps, turn it out onto a lightly floured work surface, press it into a disk, and knead it just until it comes together. (If it doesn't come together easily, add up to 2 tablespoons of water, 1 tablespoon at a time, until it comes together.) Press the dough into a flat disk and transfer it to a 9" pie plate. Press the dough evenly into the bottom and up the sides of the plate. Run a knife around the rim of the pie plate to make a nice, clean edge, then press the tines of a fork into the edge to make a pattern. Freeze the pie shell for 30 minutes.

MAKE THE FILLING. While the crust chills, make the quiche filling. Heat a large skillet over medium heat for 2 minutes. Add the bacon strips and cook until browned and crisp, 7 to 9 minutes. Transfer the bacon to a paper towel–lined plate. Once cooled, crumble the bacon into small bits. Discard all but about 1 teaspoon of the bacon fat from the pan. Add the butter and melt over medium heat. Add the onion and cook, stirring often, until it's wilted and just beginning to color around the edges, 2 to 3 minutes. Stir in the green pepper and cook until it softens, about 2 minutes, and then add the mushrooms and ½ teaspoon of the salt. Cook until the mushrooms release their liquid, 3 to 4 minutes, stirring often. Add the garlic and cook until fragrant, about 1 minute. Transfer the vegetables to a medium bowl and set aside. Whisk together the eggs, sour cream, hot sauce (if using), and remaining ¼ teaspoon of salt in a large bowl. Add the cheeses and stir to combine.

BAKE THE QUICHE. Place the frozen pie shell on a rimmed baking sheet. Arrange the mushroom mixture in the pie crust in an even layer, sprinkle with the reserved bacon, then pour in the egg mixture. Set the quiche on the oven rack and bake for 15 minutes. Reduce the oven temperature to 350°F and bake until the edges of the crust are deep golden brown and the center of the quiche is set, yet still gives to slight pressure, 20 to 25 minutes. Remove from the oven and cool for at least 30 minutes before slicing and serving, or cool completely and serve at room temperature.

QUICHE FILLING

6	slices bacon
1½	tablespoons unsalted butter
½	small onion, finely chopped
½	green bell pepper, finely chopped
8	white button mushrooms, stemmed and finely chopped
¾	teaspoon salt
2	garlic cloves, finely minced or pressed through a garlic press
3	large eggs
1½	cups sour cream
	Dash of hot sauce (optional)
1½	cups shredded Cheddar cheese
1	cup shredded Monterey Jack cheese

 COOK SMART

My theory with quiche is if I'm going to make one, why not make two? If I don't feel like baking them both the same day, I'll just make a double crust recipe and leave one unbaked shell in the fridge (or freeze it) for a couple of days.

Unbaked shells are easy to freeze and cut half the time from making the quiche at a later date (I like to freeze crusts in a metal pie plate instead of glass). You can also freeze the filled and baked quiche: Let the quiche cool completely, then cover it tightly with a few layers of plastic wrap (or a few sheets of heavy-duty aluminum foil) and freeze for up to 3 months. Let it defrost in the fridge overnight, and warm it through in a 325°F oven before serving.

Country Omelet with Feta, Thyme & Spinach

Omelets are nothing more than 70 cents worth of eggs folded around $2 worth of filling, but they seem a lot fancier, don't they? In a way, they're kind of like a sandwich—a perfect vehicle for all your odds and ends in the fridge. If you like your omelets completely cooked through and folded in half diner-style, like I do, add the vegetables when the top of the omelet still glistens but doesn't have any pools of runny eggs. If you're a fan of softer rolled omelets, then you want to cook the omelet a little less, add the feta when the top of the omelet still looks pretty wet, and roll it up starting at the bottom and working your way up the pan.

3   tablespoons unsalted butter

½   small yellow onion, finely chopped

4   teaspoons finely chopped fresh thyme

½   teaspoon salt

¼   teaspoon freshly ground black pepper

2   garlic cloves, finely minced or pressed through a garlic press

½   cup finely chopped fresh spinach

4   large eggs

2   tablespoons half-and-half, whole milk, or low-fat milk

¼   cup crumbled feta cheese

COOK SMART

Omelets and frittatas are a great way to get rid of leftovers—anything from sautéed shrimp and roast chicken to those few florets of broccoli from last night's dinner.

SAUTÉ THE ONIONS. Heat the oven to 250°F. Melt 1 tablespoon of butter in a medium nonstick skillet over medium-high heat. Add the onion, thyme, ¼ teaspoon of the salt, and the pepper, and cook until the onion just starts to brown, about 4 minutes, stirring often. Mix in the garlic and cook until fragrant, about 1 minute. Stir in the spinach and set aside while you prepare the eggs.

WHISK THE EGGS. Whisk the eggs with the half-and-half or milk and the remaining salt in a bowl. Stir in the cooled onion-spinach mixture. Wipe the skillet out with a paper towel and set it back on the stove top.

MAKE THE OMELETS. Melt 1 tablespoon of butter in the skillet over medium-high heat. Add half of the egg mixture and reduce the heat to medium. Stir the eggs around in the pan just until the edges start to set, then stop stirring. Cover the pan and let the omelet cook until its surface is semidry, 1 to 2 minutes. Sprinkle half of the feta over half of the omelet and fold it over. Cook, uncovered, until the feta just starts to soften, about 30 seconds. Slide onto a plate and place in the oven to keep warm. Make the second omelet and serve.

Sage Biscuits & Mushroom-Sausage Gravy

Honest gravy was the first recipe that my mom ever taught me, and I make it the same way to this day (goes to show that some traditions shouldn't be fussed with). Gravy is born from humble stock, and I just love the fact that you can turn ordinary ingredients such as butter, flour, and milk into a classic sauce. For a vegetarian version, just kill the sausage.

SERVES 8

☺

$8.00/
$1.00

MAKE THE BISCUITS. Heat the oven to 450°F. Whisk the flour, baking powder, baking soda, salt, and sage together in a large bowl. Whisk the buttermilk and butter together in another bowl and then slowly pour the mixture into the dry ingredients while stirring until all the liquid is added and no dry spots remain. Using a large spoon, scoop a heaping ¼ cup of the biscuit dough and onto a rimmed baking sheet. Repeat with the remaining dough. You should make about 8 biscuits. Bake the biscuits until they've risen and are golden, 10 to 12 minutes. Remove from the baking sheet and place them on a cooling rack until the gravy is ready.

MAKE THE GRAVY. While the biscuits are in the oven, start the gravy. Heat the oil in a large skillet over medium-high heat. Add the sausage and cook, stirring often, until it is just starting to brown, about 2 minutes. Stir in the mushrooms and cook until they release their liquid and start to brown, stirring often, 4 to 6 minutes. Begin adding the flour, 1 tablespoon at a time, stirring each tablespoon into the sausage mixture and browning it well before adding the next tablespoon of flour. Once all of the flour is added, add the milk, drizzling it in slowly and stirring constantly so you don't get any lumps. Cook and stir until the gravy is lightly thickened, about 8 minutes, then add the salt.

SERVE. Split a hot biscuit in half and place on a plate. Cover with gravy.

BISCUITS

- 2 cups all-purpose flour
- 2 teaspoons baking powder
- ¼ teaspoon baking soda
- 1 teaspoon kosher salt
- 1 tablespoon chopped fresh sage or 1½ teaspoons dried sage, crumbled
- 1 cup buttermilk
- ½ cup (1 stick) unsalted butter, melted

GRAVY

- 1 teaspoon canola or vegetable oil
- 8 ounces bulk breakfast sausage (if all you can find are links, just squeeze the meat out of the casings)
- 8 ounces button mushrooms, wiped clean, stemmed, and thinly sliced
- 4 tablespoons all-purpose flour
- 4 cups 2% or whole milk
- 1½ teaspoons salt

Ham, Egg & Cheese Breakfast Biscuits

If you don't have the time or inclination to whip up half a batch of biscuits, no problem. These breakfast sandwiches are just as nice on a toasted bagel or English muffin.

SERVES 4

$6.20/
$1.55

½ recipe biscuit dough (page 221)

2 tablespoons unsalted butter + 2 tablespoons unsalted butter, melted

4 slices Canadian bacon (leftover baked ham works well, too)

4 large eggs

Salt

Freshly ground black pepper

4 slices Cheddar or Swiss cheese

 D2D

Eggs are a quick and inexpensive protein. Fry them in toasted sesame oil for fried rice (push around in a hot skillet with a wooden spoon for that restaurant-shredded look), poach for a salad, or place an over-easy egg over pasta with butter and Parmesan cheese.

MAKE THE BISCUITS. Follow the recipe on page 221 to make half a batch of biscuits, or make a full batch and freeze half of them for later (you may want to pull these biscuits out at around the 8-minute mark, when they're just starting to color). When you remove the biscuits from the oven, adjust an oven rack to the upper position and heat the broiler to high.

BROWN THE HAM AND COOK THE EGGS. Melt 1 tablespoon of butter in a large skillet over medium-high heat and cook the ham until browned on both sides, 3 to 4 minutes total. Transfer the ham to a paper towel–lined plate and add another tablespoon of butter to the skillet. When it melts, crack the eggs into the pan, sprinkle with salt and pepper, and cook until set to your liking (2 to 3 minutes for a runny yolk; 3 to 4 minutes for a firmer yolk).

TOAST THE BISCUITS. While the eggs cook, split the biscuits. Brush each cut half with some melted butter. Place the halves buttered-side up on a sheet pan. Cover the bottom halves with a slice of ham and then with a slice of cheese. Broil the covered and uncovered biscuits on a sheet pan until the cheese is soft and wilts over the ham. Remove from the oven and top with an egg, followed by the other biscuit half.

Huevos Rancheros

My huevos rancheros is a pretty classic version made from very common ingredients and just happens to taste like a million bucks. For a leaner version, char the tortilla over an open flame of a gas burner (or you can warm it between sheets of damp paper towels in the microwave) and then fill it with the browned vegetables, tomatoes, and scrambled eggs instead of fried. Whatever you do, don't forget the salsa or hot sauce, depending on what squeals your wheels.

☺ **$6.80/ $1.70**

FRY THE TORTILLAS. Heat the oven to 250°F. Warm 3 tablespoons of oil in a large skillet over medium-high heat. Add a tortilla and fry until crispy and brown on each side. Transfer it to a paper towel–lined plate (an opened-up brown paper bag works too) to drain, and then put it on a rimmed baking sheet and place in the oven to stay warm. Repeat with the remaining tortillas, reducing the heat and adding more oil if necessary.

COOK THE VEGETABLES. Add the onion, bell pepper, garlic, salt, and black pepper to the same skillet you used for the tortillas, cooking them until the onion and pepper soften and the garlic is fragrant, 6 to 8 minutes. Stir in the tomatoes, cilantro, chili powder, and cumin, bring to a strong simmer, reduce the heat to medium-low, and cook until the tomatoes begin to break up, about 5 minutes.

FRY THE EGGS AND ASSEMBLE. Melt 1 tablespoon of the butter in a nonstick skillet over medium-high heat. Crack 4 eggs into the pan, sprinkle with salt and pepper, cover the pan, and fry until the white is opaque, about 3 minutes. Place the tortillas on 4 plates. Slide 2 eggs onto 2 of the tortillas and top each of the 2 plates with a quarter of the tomato mixture and some cheese. Serve the first 2 portions immediately while you fry up the second batch of eggs.

3–4 tablespoons canola or vegetable oil

4 corn tortillas (4"–6")

1 medium yellow onion, finely chopped

1 large red or green bell pepper, seeded, ribbed, and thinly sliced

2 garlic cloves, finely minced or pressed through a garlic press

½ teaspoon salt

Freshly ground black pepper

1 can (14.5 ounces) diced tomatoes with juices

2 tablespoons finely chopped fresh cilantro

2 teaspoons chili powder

¼ teaspoon ground cumin

2 tablespoons unsalted butter

8 large eggs

1 cup grated Mexican Blend cheese

Hot sauce or salsa for serving

Tortilla Scramble

This has a lot of the same flavors as Huevos Rancheros (page 225), but instead of frying your own tortillas, you use crumbled tortilla chips instead. It's delicious served with warmed corn tortillas on the side.

8 large eggs

2 tablespoons finely chopped fresh cilantro

2 teaspoons chili powder

¼ teaspoon ground cumin

¼ teaspoon salt

¼ teaspoon freshly ground black pepper

2 tablespoons unsalted butter

3 scallions, white parts only, finely chopped

1½ cups coarsely crushed yellow corn tortilla chips

8 corn tortillas (4" to 6") (optional)

Red or green salsa or the tomato-pepper sauce from the Huevos Rancheros on page 225 for serving

MAKE THE SCRAMBLE. Whisk the eggs, cilantro, chili powder, cumin, salt, and pepper together in a bowl. Melt the butter in a large nonstick skillet, add the scallions, and cook until soft, 1 to 2 minutes, stirring often. Add the chips in an even layer and pour the egg mixture over the top. Cook the eggs to your liking, stirring often.

WARM THE TORTILLAS AND SERVE. If you're using them, wrap the tortillas in a paper towel and microwave for 20 to 30 seconds until warm. Serve the scramble with red or green salsa or the tomato-pepper sauce from the Huevos Rancheros recipe and the tortillas on the side.

 D2D

Making your own tortilla chips is a snap and saves you money, too. See page 37 for a traditional fried method and a lighter baked version.

 MAKE IT A MEAL

+ Ranch-Style Beans (page 159)

Shakshouka Eggs, Tomatoes & Peppers

Though the name shakshouka (shock-SHOE-ka) sounds exotic, this quick, one-pan Middle Eastern–style dish is nothing more than eggs simmered in a sauté of fresh tomatoes, peppers, and onions. It's beautiful served up in a cast-iron skillet. Just bring the whole pan to the table (tell everyone to mind their fingers as the pan will be hot!) and serve it family-style, straight from the skillet. Warm pita bread for dipping is a must.

$8.70/
$1.45

SAUTÉ THE VEGETABLES. Heat the oven to 300°F. Heat the olive oil in a large skillet (preferably cast-iron) over medium-high heat. Add the onion and cook, stirring often, until it begins to soften, 2 to 3 minutes. Add the bell peppers and cook until they begin to soften, an additional 2 to 3 minutes. Stir in the garlic, cumin, oregano, red-pepper flakes, ¾ teaspoon of the salt, and a few grinds of pepper, and cook until the garlic is fragrant, 1 to 1½ minutes. Add the tomatoes (if your tomatoes don't look juicy, add ¼ cup of water to the skillet along with them), reduce the heat to medium, and cook until the tomatoes break down and are saucy, 4 to 5 minutes. (If your pan looks dry, add ¼ to ½ cup of water to the skillet and let it cook in for a minute or two before adding the eggs.)

COOK THE EGGS AND SERVE. Crack the eggs over the tomatoes and sprinkle with the remaining ¼ teaspoon of salt. Reduce the heat to medium-low and cook, covered (any lid that is larger than the circumference of the pan will work—it doesn't have to be a perfect fit or match), until the whites are set and the yolks are still soft, 4 to 6 minutes. While the eggs cook, place the pita bread in the oven to warm. Divide the shakshouka among 6 bowls, making sure each gets an egg on top. Serve with the pita bread for dipping.

3   tablespoons olive oil

1   large yellow onion, halved and thinly sliced

1   small red bell pepper, ribbed, seeded, and thinly sliced

1   small green bell pepper, ribbed, seeded, and thinly sliced

1   garlic clove, finely minced or pressed through a garlic press

½   teaspoon ground cumin

½   teaspoon dried oregano

¼   teaspoon red-pepper flakes

1   teaspoon salt

    Freshly ground black pepper

3   large tomatoes, cored and sliced into ½"-thick wedges

6   large eggs

    Pita bread, for serving

 COOK SMART

This is a special treat made with ripe and juicy tomatoes, but in the winter, when tomatoes lose their appeal and prices skyrocket, I'll use canned tomatoes in juice instead.

sweet!

I'm not the kind of person to skip dessert—no way, no how! But we don't have many bakeries in my small town, so when a sweet craving strikes, I take out a mixing bowl and get baking. Sure, I could go buy a boxed mix and go through the dump-stir-bake motions, but have you checked the ingredient labels on those mixes? Wow. They are just loaded with multisyllable words that I can't even pronounce, much less understand what they're doing in a cake mix. I'd much rather keep my sweets clean, simple, and delicious, and I'm guessing you feel the same way, given the choice. And really, why buy dessert when it's so inexpensive and easy to make yourself? With butter, sugar, eggs, and some extras, you can make just about anything to satisfy your sweet tooth.

Take bread pudding: In a restaurant, you might pay anywhere from $5 to $9 for a serving. Why dish out that kind of cash when you can make a whole pan for $3? No thanks—I'd rather keep the bread in my wallet rather than spend it on something I know I can make for less. Now you know, too—it simply costs too much *not* to make dessert.

Favorite Sweets for Giving

Double Ginger Bundt Cake with Marmalade and Orange Icing (page 256)

Cookie Assortment (pages 248 to 252)

Favorite Sweets for Celebrating

Pink Lemonade Ice Cream Cake (page 254)

Chocolate Peanut Butter Pie (page 246)

Favorite Post-Brunch Sweets

Dollars to Glazed Donuts (page 231)

Mocha-Streusel-Drizzle-Swirl Cake (page 258)

Favorite Crowd Pleasers

Peach Crisp (page 236)

Bread Pudding with Hot Buttered Rum Sauce (page 253)

Dollars to Glazed Donuts

I ask you, what could possibly be better than just-made donuts, still hot and delectably glazed? These donut holes are just the thing to impress people, yet they could hardly be any easier to make. You can even opt out of the glazes and simply roll the donuts in confectioners' sugar or cinnamon-sugar.

MAKE THE DOUGH. Whisk together the buttermilk, egg, and vanilla in a medium bowl and set aside. Place the flour, sugar, butter, baking powder, baking soda, nutmeg, and salt into the bowl of a stand mixer (or in a large bowl if using a hand mixer). Beat on medium-low speed until the mixture looks sandy, about 30 seconds. Add the buttermilk mixture and continue to blend until the dough comes together (it will be a little wet), about 20 seconds, stopping to scrape the bottom of the bowl if necessary.

CUT OUT THE DONUTS. Generously flour your work surface and turn the dough onto it. Pat the dough into a circle about ½" thick. Using a 1" round biscuit cutter, stamp out as many donuts as you can, stamping the circles out as close together as possible. Gather the dough scraps into a ball, press into a ½"-thick circle, and stamp out the remaining donuts (discard any remaining scraps).

FRY THE DONUTS. Heat the oil in a large pot or Dutch oven until it registers between 350°F and 375°F on an instant-read thermometer. Fry the donuts in small batches for 6 to 8 minutes, using a slotted spoon or frying spider to turn the donuts so all sides become golden brown. Transfer to a paper towel–lined baking sheet and repeat until all of the donuts are fried. Let the donuts cool for 10 minutes before glazing.

(continues...)

DONUTS

- ½ cup buttermilk
- 1 large egg, lightly beaten
- 1 teaspoon vanilla extract
- 2 cups all-purpose flour + more for rolling
- ½ cup sugar
- 4 tablespoons unsalted butter, at room temperature
- 2 teaspoons baking powder
- ¼ teaspoon baking soda
- ¼ teaspoon nutmeg
- ½ teaspoon salt
- 4 cups canola oil

GLAZE

- 1 cup confectioners' sugar
- 6 tablespoons whole milk

($) D2D
I keep a container of dried, cultured buttermilk in the fridge. Just mix some with water and it's instant buttermilk. It's easy and 75 cents less per quart than fresh buttermilk.

MAKE THE GLAZE AND FINISH THE DONUTS. While the donuts cool, whisk together the confectioners' sugar and the milk in a medium bowl until no lumps remain. Dunk the donuts into the glaze and use a fork to roll them around to evenly coat. Transfer to a cooling rack set over a rimmed baking sheet (line it with parchment or plastic wrap to make cleanup a snap) until the glaze is set. The donuts are best when eaten within a few hours of making.

Chocolate-Glazed Donuts

Place ¼ cup of milk in a small saucepan over medium heat until it begins to steam. Add 1 cup of chocolate chips (6 ounces) and stir until they melt, then dip the donuts in the chocolate glaze and place on a cooling rack to set up.

Coconut Macaroon Donuts

After glazing the donuts, roll them in ½ cup sweetened, shredded coconut.

Nut Crunch Donuts

After glazing the donuts, roll them in ½ cup of finely chopped roasted almonds or peanuts.

D2D

If you have brown paper bags cluttering up a closet, by all means rip them up and use them instead of paper towels for draining fried food. They magically wick away excess oil, and they're free.

COOK SMART

Don't stress it if you don't have buttermilk. Just add a teaspoon of fresh lemon juice (or vinegar in a pinch) to a cup of regular milk, and it will supply a similar tang.

D2D

If you're looking to curb your kid's sweet tooth, try this rule: They can have whatever they want, they just have to pay for it out of their allowance. Once they see how much chips, candy bars, and soda pop cost, they'll quickly change their tune. You'll save money on the grocery bill and have a healthier household.

Easiest Beignets

MAKES 42

$6.30/
$.15

When I was in Breaux Bridge, Louisiana, I fell in love with a homey little restaurant that made the most delicious fried beignets, kind of in between a fritter and a donut. I asked a waitress if she knew how they made them, and she actually spilled the secret—they used pancake mix! Of course, I absolutely had to try this out when I got back to the Rock, only I didn't use boxed mix, I used my homemade pancake mix (page 209). I toyed with the recipe a bit, and now it's one of my faves, especially piled high with powdered sugar and drizzled with melted chocolate!

2¼   cups all-purpose flour + extra for dusting

2   tablespoons sugar

4   teaspoons baking powder

¼   teaspoon salt

1½   cups millk

2   tablespoons (¼ stick) unsalted butter, melted

6   cups canola oil

2   cups confectioners' sugar

MAKE THE DOUGH. Whisk the flour, sugar, baking powder, and salt together in a large mixing bowl. Whisk the milk and butter together, then slowly add it to the dry ingredients, stirring as you pour it in, and mixing just until all of the dry ingredients are incorporated. A few lumps are okay; don't overmix, or the beignets will be tough. If the dough is too loose and soft to hold its shape, stir in additional flour 1 tablespoon at a time until it's tacky and workable.

HEAT THE OIL. Line a baking sheet with paper towels and place it next to your stove top. Pour the canola oil into a large pot (the depth of oil should be 1½" to 2" deep). Heat over medium-high heat until it reaches between 350°F and 375°F on an instant-read thermometer.

CUT AND FRY THE BEIGNETS. Meanwhile, dust your work surface with some flour. Turn the beignet dough onto your work surface and sprinkle the top of the dough with some flour. Gently press it into a ½"-thick oval shape. Using a knife or pizza wheel, cut the dough into 1" squares. Drop some squares into the hot oil (don't add too many at once or the temperature of the oil will drop and the beignets will be greasy—the oil temperature should stay between 350°F and 370°F) and fry them, turning often, until both sides are browned, about 2 minutes. Use a slotted spoon to transfer the beignets to the paper towel–lined baking sheet to drain and cool. Fry the remaining beignets. Transfer them to a plate, sift lots of confectioners' sugar over the top, and serve warm.

 D2D
Store-bought chocolate sauce is expensive, especially when you can make it yourself so easily. Just pop some chocolate chips in the microwave and, once melted, stir in a tablespoon or 2 of heavy cream.

My Two Cents on Keeping Fit

There is nothing I don't eat, desserts included. People sometimes ask me how I keep so trim, and I tell them it's because I keep moving. Between the restaurant and my 2 kids, I'm always running off to do something. While I do my fair share of driving, I always try to walk wherever I can, whenever I can. Walking is free, and whether I need to run down a few blocks to the bank or get to the kids' school for a track meet, getting some gentle exercise time in helps me feel healthy. It also allows me to indulge in something I crave even more than dessert—quiet time to think.

Peach Crisp

SERVES 8

$4.40/
$.55

I used to sell peach crisp for $1 a serving at the Cafe—and I still made money on it! This is really a big-bang dessert. It tastes fabulous, couldn't be simpler, and hardly costs anything (especially if you befriend someone with a peach tree!). I usually make it with canned peaches, but sometimes use frozen peaches, and always use fresh and juicy peaches when they're ripe and in season (if using fresh or frozen peaches, add a few tablespoons of sugar to make up for the lack of syrup).

1 cup all-purpose flour

1¼ cups sugar

Pinch of salt

6 tablespoons (¾ stick) unsalted butter, melted

2 cans (16 ounces each) sliced peaches in light syrup

Vanilla ice cream (optional)

 D2D

Frozen fruit is often a great bargain, especially when the fresh fruit you want to buy is out of season and being shipped in from the other end of the world (and at super-high markups). Use frozen fruit to make a dessert sauce, to blend with yogurt for a smoothie, or to add flavor and texture to a crisp or cobbler. And don't forget to freeze your own fruit if you end up with too much or have an overproductive tree or bush in the yard. See page 241 for more information.

MAKE THE TOPPING. Heat the oven to 350°F. Whisk the flour, sugar, and salt together in a medium bowl. Drizzle in the melted butter, using a fork to toss the streusel together until there aren't any bits larger than the size of a small pea.

BAKE THE CRISP. Strain the peaches, saving 3 tablespoons of juice. Place the peaches and reserved juice in a 9" pie dish. Evenly sprinkle the sugar mixture over the peaches and bake until the topping is golden brown and the peaches are juicy and bubbling, about 30 to 40 minutes. Cool slightly before serving warm or at room temperature with vanilla ice cream, if desired.

Fresh Peach Crisp

When tree-ripened peaches are in season, you better believe I'm using them in this crisp! Bring a large pot of water to a boil. Use a paring knife to make an "X" in the bottom of 4 large or 5 medium ripe peaches. Place the peaches in the water and boil for 1 minute. Remove and plunge into ice water to cool, then peel away the skin, halve, pit, and cut the peaches into ½"-thick slices and place them in a 9" pie dish. Toss the peaches with ¼ cup of sugar, make the crisp topping, and bake as instructed.

Apple Oat Crisp

SERVES 8

$2.80/
$.35

Crisps will quickly become your best friend when it comes to making a speedy dessert on short notice. They taste more or less like a pie, minus all the hassle of rolling out pie crust. I make this with apples or pears in the fall (I might toss in a handful of fresh cranberries and an extra few tablespoons of sugar around the holidays), with strawberries and rhubarb in the spring, and with plums, berries, and nectarines in the summer.

¾ cup dark brown sugar

¾ cup all-purpose flour

¾ cup quick-cooking oats

Pinch of salt

½ cup (1 stick) unsalted butter, melted + 1 tablespoon unsalted butter, at room temperature

3 large Granny Smith apples, peeled, cored, halved, and sliced ¼" thick

3 large McIntosh apples, peeled, cored, halved, and sliced ¼" thick

⅓ cup granulated sugar

Vanilla ice cream (optional)

MAKE THE TOPPING. Heat the oven to 350°F. Combine the brown sugar, flour, oats, and salt in a medium bowl and whisk together until blended. Drizzle in the melted butter, using a fork to toss the streusel together until there are no bits larger than a small pea.

BAKE THE CRISP. Grease a 13" x 9" baking dish with the remaining 1 tablespoon of butter. Place the apple slices in a large bowl, toss with the sugar, and then turn them out into an even layer in the baking dish. Cover with the streusel topping and bake until the juices are bubbling and the topping is golden brown, 30 to 35 minutes. Cool slightly before serving warm or at room temperature with vanilla ice cream, if desired.

 D2D

Big-box warehouse stores are great for deals on fresh fruit. Sometimes you can find a whole flat of blueberries or mangoes for just a few dollars. Instead of feeling pressure to use all of the fruit in a few days, use some now and freeze the rest (see page 241 for information on freezing fresh fruit).

Three-Banana Bread

We always have bananas in the house, and probably just like you, we usually let 1 or 2 go uneaten. Instead of tossing them, I let them get nice and dark. Even though the skins aren't so pretty to look at, believe me, what's inside is worth its weight in gold: insanely sticky-sweet bananas. If I can't make banana bread right away, I place the bananas (peels and all) in the freezer. When I'm ready to make banana bread, I'll thaw them in a bowl and then peel. I'll often make a double or triple batch of banana bread—the loaves freeze really well and come in handy when people drop by for morning coffee.

1 LOAF

$4.00/ $.50

PREP THE PAN. Heat the oven to 325°F. Grease a 9" x 5" loaf pan with ½ tablespoon of butter and dust with 1 tablespoon of flour, tapping out the excess.

MAKE THE BATTER. Whisk the remaining 2 cups of flour, the baking soda, and salt together in a large bowl. Using a stand mixer or a hand mixer, cream the remaining ½ cup of butter with the sugar until it is light, about 1½ minutes. Add the eggs, one at a time, beating for 1 minute between additions. Add the bananas and vanilla, beating until combined, and then add half of the dry ingredients. Combine on low speed until mostly incorporated. Scrape down the sides of the bowl and add the rest of the flour mixture and the nuts and/or chocolate chips (if using). Mix until incorporated, scraping the bottom and sides of the bowl to make sure there aren't any dry patches of flour. Scrape the batter into the prepared loaf pan, spreading it into an even layer and smoothing its surface.

BAKE THE BREAD. Bake the loaf until it's golden brown, the center resists light pressure, and a cake tester inserted into the center comes out clean, about 65 to 75 minutes. Remove it from the oven and cool the loaf for 20 minutes before turning it out onto a cooling rack and allowing it to cool completely. Slice and serve, or wrap in plastic wrap for up to 3 days.

- ½ cup (1 stick) + ½ tablespoon unsalted butter, at room temperature
- 2 cups + 1 tablespoon all-purpose flour
- 1 teaspoon baking soda
- ½ teaspoon salt
- 1 cup sugar
- 2 large eggs
- 3 very ripe bananas, peeled and lightly mashed
- 1 teaspoon vanilla extract
- 1 cup toasted and chopped pecans or walnuts (optional)
- 1 cup (6 ounces) semisweet chocolate chips (optional)

D2D

Many grocery stores prebag bananas and grapes as a "service," and then sell them to you by the pound. Don't be afraid to break open the bag or break apart the bunch and buy only what you need.

Strawberry Dessert Soup

Strawberry soup is a light, refreshing dessert that also makes a nice accompaniment to fruit platters, quiche (page 218), or spinach salad. It's often on the menu at the Rock, and you'd be surprised to see who orders it—tough guys and bikers just eat it up. I don't blame them; it's that good!

SERVES 6

$6.90/
$1.15

HALVE THE STRAWBERRIES while still partially frozen and place them in a large bowl. Add the sour cream and gently mix together with the strawberries, using a rubber spatula, until well combined. Stir in the sugar, grenadine, and vanilla, then add the ¼ cup half-and-half and stir to blend. Chill for at least 1 hour or up to 4 hours in a plastic container with a tight-fitting lid. Shake vigorously before dividing among 6 bowls. Drizzle a little of the remaining 2 tablespoons half-and-half over each bowl, swirl it in, and serve.

1 bag (1 pound) frozen and partially thawed strawberries, with juices

2 cups sour cream

¾ cup confectioners' sugar

1 tablespoon grenadine syrup

1 tablespoon vanilla extract

¼ cup half-and-half + 2 tablespoons, for serving

The Fruit Deep Freeze

The worst part about buying fruit out of season—worse than the outrageously high prices, the possibility of pesticides and other imported contaminants, and the excess energy used to transport it—is that it usually just doesn't taste very good. For that reason, I tend to rely on frozen fruit during those times of the year when I can't get fresh seasonal fruit. Whenever I can, I freeze fruit myself. It's really easy to do, especially if you have an extra freezer. Frozen fruit keeps beautifully for 8 to 12 months.

1. Place the unwashed fruit (peeled, seeded, and chopped, if necessary) in a single layer on a rimmed baking sheet.

2. Freeze on a level surface until the fruit is hard, 1 to 2 hours.

3. Transfer the semifrozen fruit to gallon-size resealable freezer bags, making sure to remove any air before sealing the bag.

4. Use a permanent marker to write the date on the bag. If you open the bag to remove a handful of fruit occasionally, try to use it up within 8 months; a never-opened bag of frozen fruit may last up to 12 months.

"Key" Lime Pie with Graham Crust

Key limes are ping pong ball–size sweet limes that can cost a pretty penny, so I make my "key" lime pie with regular limes. Using the food coloring isn't a must—even without it, the pie will be a very pretty pale yellow color with specs of green from the pistachios.

CRUST

- 1 cup graham cracker crumbs (from about 7 whole graham crackers)
- 3 tablespoons sugar
- 4 tablespoons (½ stick) butter, unsalted melted and cooled slightly

FILLING

- 1 envelope unflavored gelatin
- 1 cup sugar
- ¼ teaspoon salt
- 4 large eggs, separated
- ½ cup fresh lime juice (from about 6 limes)
- 1 teaspoon lime zest (from limes used for fresh lime juice)
- 4 drops green food coloring (optional)
- 1 cup heavy cream
- ½ cup finely chopped pistachios (optional)

MAKE THE CRUST. Heat the oven to 350°F. Stir the graham cracker crumbs and the sugar together in a medium bowl. Drizzle with the butter and stir with a fork until the crumbs are evenly moistened. Transfer the crumb mixture to a 9" glass pie plate and, using the flat bottom and side of a measuring cup or drinking glass, press the crust evenly into the bottom and up the sides of the pie plate. Bake the crust until it's fragrant and browned, 10 to 12 minutes, and then let it cool on a wire rack.

COOK THE LIME CUSTARD. Whisk the gelatin, ½ cup of the sugar, and the salt together in a saucepan. Beat the egg yolks with the lime juice and ¼ cup of water in a bowl, then pour the mixture into the saucepan with the gelatin. Warm the mixture over medium-low heat just until it coats the back of a spoon and begins to steam (about 150°F on an instant-read thermometer). Stir in the lime zest and food coloring, if using (if the mixture gets lumpy, strain it through a fine-mesh sieve). Scrape the mixture into a large bowl and refrigerate, stirring often, until it is thick and sets up in a creamy mound when dropped from a spoon, about 45 minutes.

ASSEMBLE THE PIE. While the custard chills, beat the egg whites using a stand mixer (or in a large bowl if

 D2D
To get the most juice from citrus fruit, microwave it for 20 seconds and then roll it on your work surface while applying gentle yet firm pressure to get the juices flowing.

using a hand mixer) on medium-high speed until they become foamy. Slowly begin sprinkling in the remaining ½ cup sugar, continuing to beat the egg whites on medium-high speed until they form stiff peaks. Gently transfer the egg whites to a large bowl and pour the heavy cream into the mixing bowl. Beat the cream on high speed until it forms medium-stiff peaks. Use a whisk to whip a quarter of the whipped cream into the lime mixture, and then gently fold in the rest. Scrape the filling into the cooled graham crust. Sprinkle with pistachios (if using) and chill for at least 2 hours (or up to 3 days) before serving.

D2D
Your juiced lemon and lime halves can do double duty as household cleaners. To get your coffeepot extra clean, scrub it with a juiced lemon or lime half and coarse kosher salt, and to freshen your garbage disposal, grind up a few juiced halves.

COOK SMART
After I've squeezed the juice from a lemon or lime half, I toss the rind into a resealable freezer bag and pop it in the freezer. Rinds are great to have handy, especially for recipes where you want the flavor of the lemon, not necessarily fresh juice.

Chocolate-Chip Oatmeal Pie with Press-In Butter Crust

SERVES 8

$6.80/ $.85

This pie is essentially a thrifty pecan pie that uses oatmeal in place of nuts. I've been making it at home and at the Cafe ever since a waitress at the Rock shared the recipe with me. It's unbelievably delicious.

CRUST

- ½ cup (1 stick) unsalted butter, at room temperature
- 1 large egg yolk
- 2 tablespoons heavy cream or whole milk
- 2 tablespoons granulated sugar
- ½ teaspoon salt
- 1½ cups all-purpose flour + extra as needed

FILLING

- 3 large eggs + 1 large egg yolk, lightly beaten
- 1 cup corn syrup
- 1 cup granulated sugar
- 3 tablespoons dark brown sugar
- 1 teaspoon vanilla extract
- Pinch of salt
- 1¾ cups quick-cooking oats
- 1 cup (6 ounces) semisweet chocolate chips

MAKE THE CRUST. Place the oven rack in the lowest position and heat the oven to 350°F. Stir the butter in a large bowl until it is smooth. Add the egg yolk, 1 tablespoon of cream or milk, the sugar, and the salt and stir until combined, then add the flour, working it into the butter mixture by smearing it against the sides of the bowl. Once the dough forms large, rough clumps (if it is too crumbly and dry, add the remaining 1 tablespoon of cream or milk), turn it out onto a lightly floured work surface, form and chill the crust, and knead it just until it comes together.

Press the dough into a flat disk and transfer it to a 9" pie plate. Press the dough evenly into the bottom and up the sides of the pan, using the bottom of a measuring cup dipped in some flour (to prevent sticking) to press and smooth it out. Run a knife around the rim of the pie plate to make a nice, clean edge, and then press the tines of a fork into the edge to make a pattern. Freeze the pie shell for 30 minutes.

FILL AND BAKE THE PIE. While the crust chills, make the pie filling. Whisk together the eggs and additional egg yolk, corn syrup, sugars, vanilla, and salt in a large bowl, and then use a wooden spoon to stir in the oats and chocolate chips. Pour the mixture into the pie shell and bake until the crust is set and starting to color, about 20 minutes. Reduce the oven temperature to 325°F and continue to bake until the crust is golden brown and the filling is set around the edges, but the center still jiggles a little when the side of the pie plate is tapped, another 30 to 40 minutes (if the edges begin to get too brown, loosely cover the top of the pie with a piece of aluminum foil). Cool to room temperature before slicing and serving.

D2D

When recipes call for just egg yolks, save the whites to make fluffy egg-white omelets on the weekend. They'll keep in the fridge for up to 5 days, or in the freezer for up to 2 months (defrost overnight in the refrigerator).

Homemade Instant Oatmeal

My kids absolutely love those sugared-up instant oatmeal packets loaded with goodies such as dried apples and chocolate chips, but if you check out the price per ounce, you'll see that you're paying for the convenience of single-serving packaging. Make your own instead by pouring a container of quick-cooking oats into an airtight container or resealable plastic bag and adding whatever mix-ins suit your fancy. To serve, just pour 1 cup of boiling milk or water over ½ cup of the oat mix or add the water and heat in the microwave for about 1½ minutes. Portion it up in small plastic storage containers so they're ready to grab and go—no bowl or measuring needed—for breakfast or a snack. Here are some of our favorite blends:

+ Chocolate chips and dried cherries

+ Dehydrated apples and cinnamon-sugar

+ Slivered almonds, crumbled brown sugar, and finely chopped candied ginger

Chocolate Peanut Butter Pie

SERVES 8

$9.60/ $1.20

As in most homes, peanut butter is an absolute staple in my house for PB&J sandwiches or a quick snack spread onto multigrain crackers. Since we always have it around, I've incorporated it into a few desserts, such as the No-Bake Oat-Peanut-Chocolate Chews on page 252, and this totally decadent peanut butter pie that tastes like a cross between a peanut butter cup and a cheesecake. Chocolate wafers and even crumbled biscotti make a great crust for this special dessert.

CRUST

- 1 cup graham cracker crumbs (from about 7 whole graham crackers)
- 3 tablespoons granulated sugar
- 4 tablespoons (½ stick) unsalted butter, melted and cooled slightly

FILLING

- ¾ cup creamy peanut butter, at room temperature
- 6 ounces cream cheese, at room temperature
- 2 teaspoons vanilla extract
- ½ cup heavy cream
- ½ cup light brown sugar

TOPPING

- ⅔ cup heavy cream
- 2 tablespoons light corn syrup
- 4 ounces bittersweet chocolate, finely chopped
- ⅓ cup chopped, roasted, salted peanuts

MAKE THE CRUST. Heat the oven to 350°F. Stir the graham cracker crumbs and the sugar together in a bowl. Drizzle with the butter and stir with a fork until the crumbs are evenly moistened. Transfer the crumb mixture to a 9" glass pie plate and, using the flat bottom and side of a measuring cup or drinking glass, press the crust evenly into the bottom and up the sides of the pie plate. Bake the crust until fragrant and browned, 12 to 15 minutes, and then let it cool on a wire rack.

MAKE THE FILLING. Beat the peanut butter, cream cheese, and vanilla in the bowl of a stand mixer at medium-high speed until lightened in color and texture, about 3 minutes, scraping the sides and bottom of the bowl once or twice. Transfer the mixture to a large bowl. In the empty mixer bowl (no need to clean it), whip the heavy cream and brown sugar at medium speed until slightly thickened, about 1 minute. Increase the speed to high and continue to whip until it holds soft peaks, scraping the sides and bottom of the bowl once or twice, 2 to 3 minutes. Add about one-third of the whipped cream to the peanut butter mixture and fold until just combined. Add the remaining whipped cream and fold until incorporated. Transfer the filling to the cooled crumb crust and spread in a smooth, even layer. Press plastic wrap directly against the surface of the filling and refrigerate until firm and chilled, at least 2 hours.

MAKE THE TOPPING AND SERVE. Bring the heavy cream and corn syrup to a simmer in a small saucepan over medium heat, stirring occasionally. Add the chocolate to the saucepan, turn off the heat, cover, and let stand until the chocolate is melted, about 3 minutes. Whisk until smooth and then let the mixture cool until just barely warm. Pour the chocolate mixture over the chilled filling and spread evenly. Sprinkle with the peanuts and refrigerate the pie until the chocolate is slightly firm, about 1 hour, before slicing and serving (if the pie is refrigerated for longer than 2 hours before serving, let it stand at room temperature for about 30 minutes before slicing).

D2D

If your brown sugar has turned hard, it's an easy fix: Place it in a microwaveable bowl and sprinkle the top of the sugar with a few drops of water. Microwave on high for 15 to 20 seconds and stir. It should soften right up.

Soft & Chewy Chocolate Chip Cookies

MAKES 36

$8.28/
$.23

Honestly, I haven't needed to make chocolate chip cookies in years because my kids have taken over! They come home from school and whip a batch up in no time. Homemade cookies taste infinitely better than a bag of store-bought cookies. I consider making cookies a productive after-school activity, too, one we can all enjoy hot-from-the-oven together.

2 cups all-purpose flour

½ teaspoon baking soda

½ teaspoon salt

¾ cup (1½ sticks) unsalted butter, at room temperature

1 cup packed light brown sugar

½ cup granulated sugar

1 large egg

1 large egg yolk

1 tablespoon vanilla extract

2 cups (12 ounces) semisweet chocolate chips

PREHEAT THE OVEN. Line a baking sheet with parchment paper and set aside. Heat the oven to 400°F.

MAKE THE COOKIE DOUGH. Whisk together the flour, baking soda, and salt in a large bowl. Cream together the butter and sugars in another bowl, using a stand mixer or hand mixer, until light and creamy, about 2 minutes. Beat in the egg, egg yolk, and vanilla, scraping the bottom and sides of the bowl as necessary, and once well combined, add the chocolate chips. Add the flour mixture in 3 additions, mixing just until combined after each addition.

BAKE AND COOL. Drop heaping tablespoonfuls of dough onto the prepared baking sheet. Bake until golden and set around the edges, yet still soft in the center, 12 to 15 minutes. Remove from the oven and cool on the baking sheet for 5 minutes, then use a spatula to transfer them to a cooling rack. Eat warm or cool completely before storing in an airtight container.

 D2D

With a bag of cookie dough balls in the freezer, you have access to a fresh-baked cookie or 2 whenever the craving strikes. After making the dough, shape it into tablespoon-size balls. Freeze on a parchment paper–lined baking sheet until hard, about 1 hour, and then transfer to a gallon-size resealable freezer bag. They keep in the freezer for up to 3 months (not that they'll last that long!).

 D2D

Many discount stores often have great kitchen items for sale, as well. I've found beautiful wooden salad bowls, high-quality kitchen knives, and even enameled, cast iron Dutch ovens and casserole dishes, all at unbelievable markdowns.

Oatmeal-Cranberry Cookies

Follow the instructions for the Chocolate Chip Cookies above, substituting ½ cup of quick-cooking oats for ⅓ cup of the flour, and 1½ cups of dried cranberries for the chocolate chips. You can whisk ½ teaspoon of ground cinnamon into the flour mixture (before you add it to the wet ingredients) if you like.

Spiced Molasses Rollers

Follow the instructions for the Chocolate Chip Cookies on the opposite page. Increase the amount of flour to 2¼ cups and whisk 1 teaspoon of ground cinnamon, ½ teaspoon of ground cloves, ½ teaspoon of ground ginger, and ¼ teaspoon of freshly grated nutmeg into the dry ingredients. Reduce the amount of light brown sugar to ¾ cup and add ⅓ cup of molasses to the butter/sugar mixture after beating in the eggs. Leave out the chocolate chips. Roll the dough into smooth balls, and then roll each ball in a bowl of sugar before placing on the prepared baking sheet and baking. For chewy molasses rollers, reduce the baking time by 3 minutes.

Kitchen Sink Bars

Follow the instructions for the Chocolate Chip Cookies on the opposite page, eliminating the chocolate chips from the dough. Grease a 13" x 9" baking dish with 1 tablespoon of softened butter and then press the cookie dough into an even layer in the pan. Sprinkle the dough with ¾ cup of semisweet chocolate chips, ¾ cup of butterscotch chips, ½ cup of sweetened shredded coconut, and ½ cup of pecan pieces. Pour 1 can (12 ounces) of condensed milk over the top and bake until the center is golden brown, 28 to 32 minutes. Cool completely before cutting into squares.

 D2D
Flea markets, tag sales, junior league clubs, and churches are great sources for inexpensive regional and old-fashioned cookbooks. You'll find inspiration for dinner, probably laugh a bit, and support your community all at the same time.

No-Bake Oat-Peanut-Chocolate Chews

Kids who won't eat a bowl of oatmeal for breakfast change their tune when it comes to these no-bake oatey cookies, our version of homemade chewy granola bars. I can whip them together in less than 10 minutes for snacks after a track meet or basketball game. If you like, skip the chocolate and add toasted nuts and dried fruit to give them a healthier bent.

1	cup sugar
4	tablespoons unsalted butter
¼	cup smooth or crunchy peanut butter
1¾	cups instant oatmeal
¼	cup whole milk
1	cup (6 ounces) semisweet chocolate chips

MIX AND SHAPE THE COOKIES. Place the sugar, butter, and peanut butter in a small saucepan and melt over medium heat. Bring to a simmer and cook for 2 minutes, then pour the mixture into a large bowl. Stir in the oatmeal and milk and then stir in the chocolate chips. Drop by tablespoonfuls onto a parchment paper–lined baking sheet. Refrigerate until they're hard, about 30 minutes. Transfer to a sealed plastic container and store in the refrigerator until serving.

D2D

Kids are notorious binge shoppers, and you can save money at the grocery store big-time by leaving them at home. If you must do your marketing with the teeny-boppers in tow, then limit them to 1 special item per trip—let them pick out whatever they want, but reinforce that they only get to pick out 1 item.

D2D

Make your own granola with dried fruits (chopped if large), nuts, seeds, and rolled oats, and you'll save big time over store-bought versions. Mix it up in a large bowl and then stir in some honey or maple syrup, a little canola oil, and a pinch of salt. Toast on a baking sheet in the oven at 325°F until fragrant and golden, about 30 minutes.

Bread Pudding with Hot Buttered Rum Sauce

Bread pudding really highlights the idea of making something from nothing. I always have hot dog buns, rye, wheat, or sandwich bread on hand, so when I'm stuck on what to make for dessert, I cobble them all together and break out this recipe. Texas toast (thick-cut sandwich bread) is my favorite kind to use, but I like using bread heels (the two end slices of the loaf) because they don't absorb as much of the liquid, so the bread hangs on to a little more texture.

SERVES 8

$6.40/
$.80

SOAK THE BREAD. Grease an 8" baking dish with the softened butter and set aside. Heat the oven to 325°F. Whisk the milk and eggs in a large bowl until well combined, and then whisk in ¾ cup of the sugar. Pour in the melted butter and whisk to combine. Place the bread in the egg/milk mixture, using a rubber spatula to submerge it in the liquid. Soak the bread until evenly moistened, about 20 minutes, and then transfer it and any remaining liquid to the prepared baking dish.

BAKE THE PUDDING. Whisk the remaining ¼ cup of sugar with the cinnamon in a small bowl, and evenly sprinkle it over the top of the pudding. Bake until the pudding is set and a cake tester inserted into the center comes out clean, 35 to 40 minutes. Set aside to cool slightly.

MAKE THE RUM SAUCE. Whisk the evaporated milk, whole milk, sugar, and butter together in a medium saucepan over medium heat. Place the cornstarch in a small bowl and dissolve with 4 teaspoons of cold water. Once the milk mixture is hot, add the cornstarch slurry and then stir slowly and constantly until it reaches a thin, gravylike texture and a few bubbles rise to the surface. Turn off the heat, stir in the rum, and serve over the bread pudding.

BREAD PUDDING

- 1 tablespoon unsalted butter, at room temperature + 4 tablespoons unsalted butter, melted
- 1½ cups whole milk
- 3 large eggs
- 1 cup sugar
- 9 slices (½" to ¾" thick) sandwich bread, sliced or torn into 1" pieces
- 1½ teaspoons ground cinnamon

SAUCE

- 1 can (12 ounces) evaporated milk
- ¾ cup whole milk
- ⅔ cup sugar
- 3 tablespoons unsalted butter
- 2 tablespoons cornstarch
- 3–4 tablespoons rum of your choice

Pink Lemonade Ice Cream Cake

Angel food cake is one of the few cakes I'll actually buy at the supermarket bakery rather than make it myself. It's usually on special, and since it takes so many egg whites to make from scratch, it's a better value to buy it premade.

SERVES 12

$9.60/ $.80

- 2 pints vanilla bean ice cream
- 1 can (12 ounces) pink lemonade concentrate, partially thawed
- 1 store-bought angel food cake Confectioners' sugar
- 1 bag (16 ounces) frozen and defrosted strawberries with juices (optional)

 D2D

Who can resist a sundae? No one in my family! Trips to the ice cream shop add up, though, so we make our own sundae bar at home for about a quarter of the price. I set out all the fixings, such as sugar cones (they're awesome broken up and sprinkled over ice cream!), sprinkles, homemade whipped cream, chocolate chips, peanuts, maraschino cherries, and even quick chocolate sauce (see page 235).

SOFTEN THE ICE CREAM. Soften the ice cream for about 10 minutes before peeling away the cardboard carton and placing the ice cream in the bowl of a stand mixer fitted with the paddle attachment (or a large bowl if you're using a hand mixer). Add the lemonade concentrate and blend on low speed until partially combined, then increase the speed to medium until the mixture is completely combined (it will be a little slushy). Place a piece of plastic wrap flush against the ice cream and refrigerate for 1 hour or overnight (if refrigerating longer than 1 hour, you will probably need to let the ice cream sit out at room temperature for 10 to 15 minutes to soften before you spread it on the cake layers).

DIVIDE THE ANGEL FOOD CAKE. Meanwhile, using a bread knife, slice the angel food cake horizontally into thirds, separate each layer, and set aside.

ASSEMBLE THE CAKE. Place the bottom layer of the cake on a large plate. Spread with half of the ice cream mixture (it should be soft and spreadable, but not so soft that it is melting), and then cover with the second cake layer. Repeat with the remaining ice cream and top with the last cake layer. Wrap the cake tightly in plastic wrap and freeze until solid, at least 2 hours.

FINISH AND SERVE. Let the cake stand at room temperature for 10 to 20 minutes before dusting the top with confectioners' sugar and cutting into 12 slices. Serve with some strawberries and sauce on the side, if desired.

Double Ginger Bundt Cake with Marmalade & Orange Icing

SERVES 12

$9.00/
$.75

This Bundt cake tastes even better a few days after you make it. If you don't have a Bundt pan, you can make this cake in two 9" x 5" loaf pans instead. Bundt pans are a great tag-sale find—just remember to grease yours really well, as most vintage pans don't have any kind of nonstick coating. If slightly bitter orange marmalade isn't your thing, you can use raspberry or strawberry jam instead.

CAKE

- 1 cup (2 sticks) + 2 tablespoons unsalted butter, softened
- 2½ cups + 2 tablespoons unbleached all-purpose flour
- 1½ teaspoons baking powder
- ¼ teaspoon baking soda
- 1¾ cups sugar
- ¾ teaspoon salt
- 1 large egg yolk
- 4 large eggs
- 1 tablespoon vanilla extract
- ⅓ cup minced crystallized ginger
- 3 tablespoons grated fresh ginger
- ¾ cup buttermilk, at room temperature
- ⅓ cup orange marmalade

ICING

- 2½–4 tablespoons pulp-free orange juice
- 1½ cups confectioners' sugar

PREP THE BUNDT PAN. Heat the oven to 350°F. Grease a 12-cup Bundt pan with 2 tablespoons of butter and then dust the pan with 2 tablespoons of flour, knocking out the excess.

MAKE THE CAKE BATTER. Whisk the remaining 2½ cups of flour with the baking powder and baking soda in a bowl until combined. Cream the remaining 1 cup of butter, the sugar, and the salt in a stand mixer (or in a large bowl if using a hand mixer) at medium-high speed until light and fluffy, about 3 minutes, scraping the bottom and sides of the bowl once or twice. With the mixer running, add the egg yolk and beat until combined, then beat in the eggs one at a time, scraping down the bowl after each addition. Reduce the speed to low and add the vanilla, crystallized ginger, and fresh ginger, beating until just combined, about 30 seconds. Add the flour mixture in 3 additions alternately with the buttermilk in 2 additions, mixing just until combined after each addition. Give the batter a final stir with a rubber spatula to ensure that no pockets of flour remain.

BAKE THE CAKE. Spread half of the batter in the prepared pan. Spoon the marmalade over and in the center of the batter (try not to let the marmalade run to the pan sides). Cover with the remaining batter and smooth the surface. Bake the cake until deep golden brown and a wooden skewer inserted into the center comes out clean, 55 to 60 minutes. Set the cake aside for 10 minutes before inverting onto a greased wire rack and lifting off the Bundt pan. Let the cake cool to room temperature.

GLAZE THE CAKE AND SERVE. If using fresh-squeezed juice, strain it through a fine-mesh sieve to remove any pulp. Whisk the confectioners' sugar with 2½ table-spoons of the orange juice in a small bowl, until smooth. The glaze should be thick, yet thin enough to drizzle; whisk in additional juice as needed. Spoon the glaze over the cake and allow the glaze to drip down the sides. Let stand until the glaze dries and hardens slightly, about 30 minutes. Slice into wedges and serve.

 D2D

If you have an Asian market in your area, check out their prices on crystallized ginger— you'll be amazed! A tiny jar in your supermarket's spice aisle can cost $4 or more, while Asian shops offer half-pound packages of the same thing (though in large slices, not tidy cubes) for just a couple of dollars. Chop it yourself using a heavy, very sharp knife, and save a bundle.

Instant Cocoa

Hot cocoa mix is easy to make and less expensive than many store-bought brands. Plus you can personalize it by adding fun mix-ins such as semisweet chocolate chips or white chocolate chips, crushed candy canes, and mini marshmallows. Wrapped inside a mug, it makes a nice gift, too. Combine 2 cups of nonfat dry milk with 2 cups of sugar and 1 cup of unsweetened cocoa powder (preferably Dutch processed) in a food processor until well combined. Transfer to a quart-size resealable bag or airtight container. For each 8-ounce cup of hot water, add ½ cup of cocoa mix (this recipe makes 10 cups of hot cocoa).

Mocha-Streusel-Drizzle-Swirl Cake

This cake is for anyone who wants all the lusciousness of a chocolate layer cake in half the time and none of the fussy frosting and filling. I swirl some chocolate into the cake batter to create a marble effect, top the cake with streusel, and then finish it with a quick chocolate drizzle. It's delicious for after dinner or brunch and freezes beautifully, too.

CAKE

- 1 cup (2 sticks) + 1 tablespoon unsalted butter, at room temperature
- 2½ cups + 2 tablespoons all-purpose flour
- 2 teaspoons baking powder
- ½ teaspoon baking soda
- 1 teaspoon salt
- 1 cup granulated sugar
- 3 large eggs
- ½ cup sour cream
- 2 teaspoons vanilla extract
- 2 tablespoons instant coffee
- ¼ cup confectioners' sugar

 D2D

For special occasions, instead of blowing your budget on Champagne for a toast, buy cheaper prosecco (from Italy) or cava (from Spain) sparkling wine instead. Even better, turn straight sparkling wine into sparkling cocktails (just add fruit nectar) or punch to serve many people from a single bottle.

PREP THE CAKE PAN. Heat the oven to 350°F. Grease a 13" x 9" baking dish with 1 tablespoon of butter and then dust with 2 tablespoons of flour, tapping out the excess.

MAKE THE GLAZE. Warm the milk in a small saucepan over medium-high heat until it begins to steam. Add the chocolate chips and stir until they melt. Measure out ½ cup to use in the cake batter and set the rest aside.

MAKE THE STREUSEL. Blend the butter, brown sugar, and flour together on low speed in a stand mixer (or in a medium bowl if using a hand mixer), until the streusel looks like wet sand, about 30 seconds. Set aside.

MAKE THE CAKE BATTER. Place the remaining 1 cup of butter, the remaining 2½ cups of flour, the baking powder, baking soda, salt, and granulated sugar in the bowl of a stand mixer or in a large bowl if using a hand mixer. Mix on low, using the paddle, until no butter lumps remain and the mixture looks like cornmeal, about 3 minutes. Whisk the eggs, sour cream, vanilla, and instant coffee together in a medium bowl, add to the dry ingredients, and blend on medium-high speed until the batter is light and fluffy, about 30 seconds, scraping down the sides and bottom of the bowl as necessary.

MARBLE AND BAKE THE CAKE. Spread half of the cake batter into the greased and floured pan (it's okay if the layer is very shallow, or even if the batter doesn't cover the whole pan). Stir the reserved ½ cup chocolate glaze into the remaining batter (just enough to combine), scrape the chocolate batter over the plain batter in the pan, and then, starting at one corner, drag a knife back and forth through the batter to create a marbled effect. Sprinkle the streusel over the top of the cake and bake until a cake tester inserted into the center of the cake comes out clean, about 1 hour.

FINISH AND SERVE. Remove the cake from the oven and set aside until completely cooled, 1 to 2 hours. Sift the confectioners' sugar over the top and then drizzle with the remaining chocolate glaze (if the glaze has stiffened, zap it in 10-second increments in the microwave until it's fluid—but not hot). Cut into squares and serve.

GLAZE

- ½ cup whole milk
- 1½ cups (about 9 ounces) semisweet chocolate chips

STREUSEL

- ½ cup (1 stick) unsalted butter, at room temperature
- 1 cup packed light brown sugar
- 1¼ cups all-purpose flour

DIY Chai

A cup of steaming spiced tea can be just the thing to warm your insides on a raw day. Next time you're in need of some comfort from the inside out, skip the coffee shop and make your own chai instead.

To make 1 cup of chai, fill a tea ball with:

- 1 tablespoon loose black tea
- 2 whole cloves
- 2 black peppercorns
- 1 split cardamom pod (optional)
- ½ star anise

Drop the tea ball into a mug, add half of a cinnamon stick, and cover with boiling water. Steep for 4 minutes, remove the tea ball, and top off with some warm milk and sugar if you like. (If you're using a tea bag, steep the spices directly in the mug with the tea bag and remove them with a spoon before adding the milk and sugar.)

Chocolate Coconut Snowball Cake

SERVES 10

$19.00/
$1.90

In this celebration-worthy cake, I sandwich 2 fluffy coconut cake layers with a silky chocolate frosting that's somewhere between buttercream and ganache, and then cover it with lots of delicate shredded coconut flakes. It's totally decadent, delicious, and quite easy, since I'm not splitting each cake into layers but rather just placing one cake on top of the other.

CAKE

- ¾ cup (1½ sticks) + 1 table-spoon unsalted butter, at room temperature
- 2¼ cups cake flour
- 1 cup + 2 tablespoons coconut milk, stirred well
- 1 teaspoon vanilla extract
- 1½ teaspoons coconut extract
- 1 tablespoon baking powder
- 1⅔ cups sugar
- 1 teaspoon salt
- 6 large egg whites, lightly beaten, at room temperature

 SHOP SMART

Different brands of coconut milk vary in texture. After opening the can, pour it all into a small bowl and whisk it well to combine. If it seems thicker than heavy cream, thin it out with ¼ cup of water.

PREP THE PANS. Adjust the oven rack to the lower-middle position and heat the oven to 325°F. Using ½ tablespoon of butter for each pan, grease two 9" round cake pans, line the bottoms with parchment-paper rounds, butter the rounds, and then dust each pan with 2 tablespoons of flour, tapping out the excess.

MAKE THE CAKE BATTER. Whisk the coconut milk, vanilla, and coconut extract in a small bowl until combined. Set aside. Sift the remaining 2 cups of flour and the baking powder into a medium bowl. Cream the remaining ¾ cup of butter with the sugar and salt at medium-high speed in the bowl of a stand mixer (or a large bowl if using a hand mixer) until light and fluffy, about 3 minutes. With the mixer running on medium-low, add the egg whites in 3 additions, beating well and scraping the bottom and sides of the bowl after each addition. Add the flour mixture in 3 additions alternately with the coconut-milk mixture in 2 additions, mixing just until combined after each addition. Give the batter a final stir with a rubber spatula.

BAKE AND COOL THE CAKES. Divide the batter evenly among the prepared cake pans and smooth the surfaces. Bake until the cakes are golden brown and begin to pull away from the sides of the pan, and a cake tester inserted into the centers comes out clean, 25 to 30 minutes. Cool the cakes in the pans on a wire rack for 10 minutes before

(continues...)

FROSTING

- 2 cups (about 12 ounces) chopped bittersweet chocolate
- 1 cup heavy cream
- 2 tablespoons corn syrup
- Pinch of table salt
- ¾ cup confectioners' sugar, sifted
- 1 teaspoon vanilla extract
- ¾ cup (1½ sticks) unsalted butter, at room temperature
- 1½ cups sweetened shredded coconut

COOK SMART

The cakes should bake up perfectly level. If they don't, level off the domed tops using a serrated knife. Save the cake crumbs in the freezer for rum balls or to add to a layered pudding dessert or ice cream cake.

running a paring knife around the pan sides and inverting each cake onto a cooling rack. Turn the cakes right side up on the rack and cool to room temperature.

MAKE THE FROSTING. While the cakes cool, place the chopped chocolate in the bowl of the stand mixer (or a large bowl if using a hand mixer). Bring the cream, corn syrup, and salt to a boil in a small saucepan over medium heat, stirring occasionally. Pour the cream mixture over the chocolate and set aside until the chocolate is melted, 5 to 7 minutes. Beat the mixture on medium-low speed until smooth, about 1 minute, scraping the bottom and sides of the bowl with a rubber spatula as necessary. Add the confectioners' sugar and vanilla and continue to beat until incorporated and the mixture is slightly cooled, 2 to 4 minutes. With the mixer running on medium speed, add the butter, 1 tablespoon at a time, beating until the frosting is smooth and shiny, 3 to 5 minutes, scraping the bowl once or twice. If the frosting is too soft, place it in the refrigerator for 10 to 15 minutes or until it is spreadable (about the consistency of room-temperature peanut butter), stirring it occasionally.

FROST THE CAKE AND SERVE. Place a cooled cake layer on a cake plate or large, flat platter. Spread 1 to 1½ cups of chocolate frosting evenly over the top. Set the second cake layer on top. Frost the sides and the top of the cake. Sprinkle coconut on the top of the cake and gently press some onto the sides. Dust any excess coconut off of the cake plate. Let the frosted cake stand at room temperature for about 1 hour before serving to allow the frosting to set slightly and the layers to settle. Cut into wedges and serve. (If refrigerating before serving, then let the cake stand at room temperature for 20 minutes before slicing and serving.)

five ways (besides banana bread) to use overripe bananas

1. Banana Pancakes: Add mashed bananas to the batter on page 209.

2. Banana Fritters: Add mashed bananas to the beignet batter on page 234.

3. Peanut Butter and Banana Pie: Stir mashed bananas into the peanut butter pie filling on page 246.

4. Banana-Ginger Bundt Cake: Cream mashed bananas with the butter and sugar for the cake batter on page 256 (omit the marmalade filling).

5. Banana Smoothies: Blend frozen bananas with plain yogurt and honey for a healthy breakfast on the go.

weekly menu maker

Here are weekly meal plans based on a weekly budget of $100 or less for a family of 4.
Go to myd2d.com for more sample menu plans and recipes.

WEEK 1

MONDAY		TUESDAY		WEDNESDAY		THURSDAY	
Recipe	Price	Recipe	Price	Recipe	Price	Recipe	Price
Oven-Baked Crispy Chicken Parmesan	$8.40	Tortilla Scramble	$4.40	Sicilian Pasta with Tuna and Capers	$8.20	Bucket-Style Oven "Fried" Chicken	$10.80
Pasta	$1.30	Green Salad with Honey-Mustard Dressing	$2.00	Green Salad with Greek Vinaigrette	$2.00	Homestyle Smashed Potatoes with Dill	$2.00
Roasted Carrots	$1.00			Garlic Toast (from steamed mussels recipe)	$2.40		
TOTAL	$10.70		$6.40		$12.60		$12.80

WEEK 2

MONDAY		TUESDAY		WEDNESDAY		THURSDAY	
Recipe	Price	Recipe	Price	Recipe	Price	Recipe	Price
Pulled Pork Sandwiches with Barbecue Sauce	$7.10	One-Pot Chicken Paprikash and Noodles	$12.80	Roast Pork, Beans, and Bangers	$6.60	Turkey BLT Sliders	$7.80
Spoon-Tender Green Beans with Bacon	$2.80			Steamed Broccoli	$2.30	Spiced Sweet Potato Fries with Dijon Dip	$8.40
TOTAL	$9.90		$12.80		$8.90		$16.20

Note that the Monday and Wednesday Week 2 dinners call for using the leftovers from Week 1's Sunday Roast Pork, so the cost of

FRIDAY		SATURDAY		SUNDAY		WEEKLY TOTAL
Recipe	Price	Recipe	Price	Recipe	Price	
Salmon Teriyaki	$13.00	Caramelized Onion and Sausage Pizza	$11.00	Roast Pork Shoulder	$13.20	
Veggie-Loaded Fried Rice	$3.20	*No-Bake Oat-Peanut-Chocolate Chews	$3.85	Ranch-Style Beans	$4.50	
				Straight-Up Cornbread	$1.20	
				Apple Oat Crisp	$2.80	
	$16.20		$14.85		$21.70	$95.25

FRIDAY		SATURDAY		SUNDAY		WEEKLY TOTAL
Recipe	Price	Recipe	Price	Recipe	Price	
Turkey, Swiss, and Asparagus Crepes	$12.00	Crispy Salmon Cakes	$6.20	Fajitas on the Fly	$18.80	
Green Salad with Honey-Mustard Dressing	$2.00	Roasted Cauliflower	$6.00	Peach Crisp	$4.40	
	$14.00		$12.20		$23.20	$97.20

ose recipes reflects the use of "free" pork.

Weekly Shopping List for 2-Week Menu Maker

Here's your shopping list for the 2-week menu maker on pages 264–265. I've divvied up the list by what you'll probably need to shop for and what you probably already have in your pantry. Just remember to check your pantry before you head out to the store—while you may have eight eggs in the fridge, you'll need 18 for Week 1 alone, so you may have to beef up your supply!

Week 1

Bakery

1 baguette

Canned & Packaged

2 cans (14 ounces each) pinto beans
   (check your pantry first)

1 can (#10; 3 quarts) crushed tomatoes
   (or eight 14-ounce cans)

1 can (10 ounces) diced tomatoes
   with green chiles

1 bag (14 ounces) yellow-corn tortilla chips

1 bag (8 ounces) chocolate chips

Condiments &Sauces

Asian sauce (black bean, hoisin, or teriyaki)

sesame oil

Dairy

1 pound mozzarella cheese

1 quart orange juice

2 cups plain yogurt

Frozen

4 cups Asian-blend vegetables

Meat & Seafood

4 boneless, skinless chicken breasts
   (6 to 8 ounces each)

3 pounds bone-in chicken breasts or thighs

1 pork shoulder (5 to 6 pounds)

4 salmon fillets (4 to 6 ounces each)

½ pound Italian sausage

Pasta &Grrains

2 pounds spaghetti (check your pantry first)

Produce

3 large Granny Smith apples

3 large McIntosh apples

12 large or 16 small limes

2 lemons

1 bunch fresh basil

1 bunch fresh cilantro

1 bunch fresh dill

1 bunch fresh oregano

1 bunch flat-leaf parsley

3 heads garlic (check your pantry first)

fresh ginger (a 2" piece)

1 head lettuce

8 yellow onions

1 green bell pepper

5 Yukon Gold or Russet potatoes

1 bunch scallions

1 bag (16 ounces) carrots

Week 2

Bakery

4 kaiser buns

6 mini buns or dinner rolls

Canned & Packaged

3 cans (15 ounces each) beans (kidney, pinto, or cannellini)

2 cans (14.75 ounces each) salmon

2 cans (16 ounces each) sliced peaches in light syrup

Dairy

2 pints heavy cream or half-and-half

Deli

12 slices deli turkey

12 slices Swiss cheese

Meats & Seafood

½ pound bacon

1¾ pounds bone-in, skin-on chicken breasts/thighs

12 ounces sausage (chicken, andouille, or kielbasa)

1¼ pounds flank or skirt steak

1 pound ground turkey

Pasta & Grains

½ pound no-boil egg lasagna noodles

Produce

1 lemon

2 limes

1 orange

1½ pounds asparagus

1 head (2 pounds) cauliflower

1 pound green beans

1 head lettuce

1 head broccoli

½ pound button mushrooms

1 small and 1 large white onion

3 yellow onions

2 large green or red bell peppers

1 to 2 jalapeño peppers

1 bunch scallions

3 large sweet potatoes

2 tomatoes

Other

1 cup dry white wine

1 can cola

Pantry Essentials

What you probably already have in the house (check your pantry before heading out to the store to make sure you're not running low)

Beans, Breads, Grains & Pastas

bread crumbs

graham crackers

quick-cooking oats

panko bread crumbs

rice

tortillas (corn or flour)

Flours, Leaveners & Thickeners

all-purpose flour

baking powder

cornmeal

unflavored gelatin

yeast (dry-active or instant)

Dried Fruits, Nuts & Sweeteners

semisweet chocolate chips

dried fruits (apricots, cherries,
    cranberries, or raisins)

honey

dried nuts (almonds, pecans, pine nuts,
    or walnuts)

peanut butter (creamy or crunchy)

sugar (granulated, dark brown, light brown)

Herbs, Oils, Spices & Vinegars

herbs (dried basil, dried oregano)

spices (black peppercorns, cayenne,
    celery salt, chili powder, ground coriander,
    ground cumin, garlic powder, ground mustard,
    sweet paprika, red-pepper flakes, salt,
    ground turmeric)

oils (canola, extra-virgin olive)

Dairy

unsalted butter (1 pound plus 6 tablespoons)

cheese (shredded Cheddar or Monterey Jack,
    Parmesan)

large eggs (2 dozen plus 4)

mayonnaise

whole milk

Quick Flavor Add-Ins

capers

hot sauce

ketchup

liquid smoke (optional)

mustard (Dijon and yellow)

salsa

soy sauce

Worcestershire sauce

Canned Goods

low-sodium chicken broth

1 can (28 ounces) chopped tomatoes

2 cans olive oil–packed canned tuna

acknowledgments

I would like to acknowledge the people who made this book possible: Eileen Opatut and Melinda Fishman of Channeling Media, who created the concept of *Dollars to Donuts* and found a kindred spirit in Pam Krauss, the most talented editor in publishing. Pam recognized this philosophy and that my way of life was right for the times. I would especially like to thank Raquel Pelzel, who hand-crafted my stories and recipes into a legacy I will always treasure. And thanks to Joseph De Leo, Stephana Bottom, Shellee Graham, and the entire team who created such beautiful photographs for the book.

Writing *Dollars to Donuts* started before the fire that destroyed all but the four original rock walls of the cafe. The book was a welcome distraction while our home-away-from-home was rebuilt. There are so many people to thank by name, but it would take another 300 pages. Let's just say that it takes a village of family and friends to maintain our way of life here in Stroud. Over the 16 years I've owned the Rock, so many people have touched my life, and without them this book would have been impossible to write.

I would like to thank the following people by name: my children, Alexis and Paul, who always look at me as if I'm a superhero and whose support and desire to be an active part of this family make me proud to be their mother; my mom, Linda Longacre; my employee and BFF, Beverly Thomas, and her children, Jonathon, Mathew, and Garvis; historic preservationist David Burke, who restored the cafe and my faith that it was doable; and let's not forget Jerry Murfin, preacher, plumber, auto restorer, mayor, and my "pseudo-father"!

I thank all the Route 66'ers for their continued support, and especially Michael Wallis for recognizing the value of this old Mother Road. I put my life in your hands so many years ago when you told me to stay the course, that you wouldn't let the world forget I was here! Well, you came through on that promise times 1,000! And of course, to John Lasseter, for telling the story of Route 66 with memorable characters and emotion, embedding this tale into the minds of youth forever. The impact you had on Route 66 is all I hoped for and so much more.

Dawn Welch

Writing *Dollars to Donuts* taught me a lot—first and foremost that you don't need to be a coupon clipper to be a smart and conscientious cook (who happens to save a few bucks along the way). I can honestly say that from the first day of working on *D2D* I started making smarter choices when it comes to cooking and shopping, and for that I must thank Dawn Welch, Eileen Opatut, and Melinda Fishman; our conversations changed my whole approach. Dawn, your spirit is unflappable—no wonder you can do everything you do! Eileen and Melinda, this was most definitely an adventure. Thanks for believing in me and bringing me into the fold. A giant, ebullient thank-you to Dawn Yanagihara-Mitchell and Meg Suzuki for cooking up a storm (and at warp speed)—you ladies rock. Thanks to Pam Krauss at Rodale for connecting me to this great project, and of course to my friend and agent, Angela Miller.

To all my friends and family who generously offered their time and money-saving tricks and wisdom, you're part of *D2D,* too. To Billie and Jerry, and Lauren and Yosi, thanks for your help and support—as always, I couldn't do any of this without you. To Matt, Julian, and Rhys, you guys keep me smiling, laughing, and inspired, even when you do spend way (way) too much money on pork chops. I love you anyway.

Raquel Pelzel

Index

S